The Muslim Merchants of

In this major new history of Muslim merchants and their trade links with China, John W. Chaffee uncovers 700 years of history, from the eighth century, when Persian and Arab communities first established themselves in southeastern China, through the fourteenth century, when trade all but ceased. These were extraordinary and tumultuous times. Under the Song and the Mongols, the Muslim diaspora in China flourished as legal and economic ties were formalized. At other times the Muslim community suffered hostility and persecution. Chaffee shows how the policies of successive dynastic regimes in China combined with geopolitical developments across maritime Asia to affect the fortunes of Muslim communities. He explores social and cultural exchanges, and how connections were maintained through faith and a common acceptance of Muslim law. This groundbreaking contribution to the history of Asia, the early Islamic world and maritime history explores the networks that helped to shape the premodern world.

John W. Chaffee is Distinguished Service Professor in the Departments of History and Asian and Asian American Studies at Binghamton University. He also directs the Institute for Asia and Asian Diasporas. He co-edited with Professor Denis Twitchett Volume 5, Part 2 of The Cambridge History of China: *Sung China, 960–1279*.

New Approaches to Asian History

This dynamic new series publishes books on the milestones in Asian history, those that have come to define particular periods or to mark turning points in the political, cultural and social evolution of the region. The books in this series are intended as introductions for students, to be used in the classroom. They are written by scholars whose credentials are well established in their particular fields and who have, in many cases, taught the subject across a number of years.

Books in the Series

The Muslim Merchants of Premodern China

The History of a Maritime Asian Trade Diaspora, 750–1400

John W. Chaffee

Binghamton University

CAMBRIDGE
UNIVERSITY PRESS

CAMBRIDGE
UNIVERSITY PRESS

University Printing House, Cambridge CB2 8BS, United Kingdom

One Liberty Plaza, 20th Floor, New York, NY 10006, USA

477 Williamstown Road, Port Melbourne, VIC 3207, Australia

314–321, 3rd Floor, Plot 3, Splendor Forum, Jasola District Centre, New Delhi – 110025, India

79 Anson Road, #06–04/06, Singapore 079906

Cambridge University Press is part of the University of Cambridge.

It furthers the University's mission by disseminating knowledge in the pursuit of education, learning, and research at the highest international levels of excellence.

www.cambridge.org
Information on this title: www.cambridge.org/9781107012684
DOI: 10.1017/9780511998492

© John W. Chaffee 2018

First published 2018

Printed in the United States of America by Sheridan Books, Inc.

A catalogue record for this publication is available from the British Library.

Library of Congress Cataloging-in-Publication Data
Names: Chaffee, John W., author.
Title: The Muslim Merchants of Pre-Modern China : The History of a Maritime Asian Trade Diaspora, 750–1400 / John Chaffee.
Description: Cambridge ; New York : Cambridge University Press, 2019. | Series: New Approaches to Asian History | Includes bibliographical references and index.
Identifiers: LCCN 2017061450| ISBN 9781107012684 (hardback) | ISBN 9781107684041 (paperback)
Subjects: LCSH: Muslim merchants – China – History – To 1500. | China – Commerce – History – To 1500.
Classification: LCC HF3835 .C43 2019 | DDC 381.088/2970951–dc23
LC record available at https://lccn.loc.gov/2017061450

ISBN 978-1-107-01268-4 Hardback
ISBN 978-1-107-68404-1 Paperback

Contents

Figures

Maps

Acknowledgments

In many ways the origins of this book can be dated to 1997, when Angela Schottenhammer invited me to attend an international conference at Leiden University on maritime trade and the economic and social development of the Quanzhou region during the Song and Yuan dynasties. I was just finishing work on my history of the Song imperial clan, who during the Southern Song were concentrated in Quanzhou and, I had discovered, had been much involved in maritime trade. My findings with regard to that involvement were presented both in the conference volume, *The Emporium of the World*, and in my book on the imperial clan, but this exposure to maritime trade whet my appetite. I was particularly fascinated by the Muslim communities of the Song and Yuan periods, whose physical legacy is much in evidence in the mosques of Guangzhou and Quanzhou and in the cemetery and huge collection of tombstones in Quanzhou. Just who they were and how they evolved through the centuries are questions with which I have been engaged for many years. This volume represents an attempt to provide my answers to them. That these merchants were, with few exceptions, without names or individual identities – in the sources we have about them – has been a constant frustration. However, that has not dimmed my admiration for their fortitude or accomplishments in establishing themselves so far from their homelands.

The list is long of those who have aided me in my work, whether through their own writings, their responses to my writings and presentations, or through conversations and email exchanges. My greatest debt of gratitude is to Angela Schottenhammer, who through her friendship as well as the many conferences and publications she has organized and edited has provided me with opportunities to share my ideas and my research. In a similar vein I am thankful to Elizabeth Lambourn, Kenneth Hall, Tansen Sen, and Robert Antony for their work and for the conferences that they have organized. I am grateful to John Guy, not only for his stimulating work on the material culture of this era but also for permission to use two of his photographs in the book. My work would not have been possible without the many important scholars in this field who have been kind enough to share ideas with me: Oded Abt, Michael Brose, Hugh Clark, the late Fu Zongwen, Derek Heng, Ralph Kauz, Hermann Kulke, Li Yukun, Liu Yingsheng, Ma Juan, Pierre Manguin, Mukai Masaki, Nakamura Tsubasa, Oka Motoshi, Hyunhee Park, Roderich Ptak, Morris Rossabi, Billy So, Nancy Steinhardt, Geoff Wade, Jon Whitmore, Yokkaichi Yasuhiro, and Wang Gungwu. In a more general vein, I have benefited from conversations and exchanges with Karen Barzman, Bettine Birge, Leonard Blussé, Patricia Ebrey, Valerie Hansen, Stephen Haw, Huang K'uan-chung, Liu Guanglin, Ma Guang, Gerald Kadish, David McMullen, Manel Ollé, Paul Smith, Barbara Seycock, Mathieu Torck, Nancy Um, and Zhang Qifan, and also from my students Hu Yongguang, Lee Changwook, Zhao Siyin, Travis Schutz, Eric Lee and Zou Jiajun. I would like to thank Bradley Hutchison for his assistance in standardizing my spellings of Arabic and Persian names and terms. And I am grateful to the editors at Cambridge University Press who aided me greatly throughout this process.

Finally, I would like to thank my wonderful sons Tim, Philip and Conrad, and Conrad's wife Luba, for the steadfast love and support that they have given me since the death of my wife, Barbara, five years ago. She would have been delighted to see this volume finally appear.

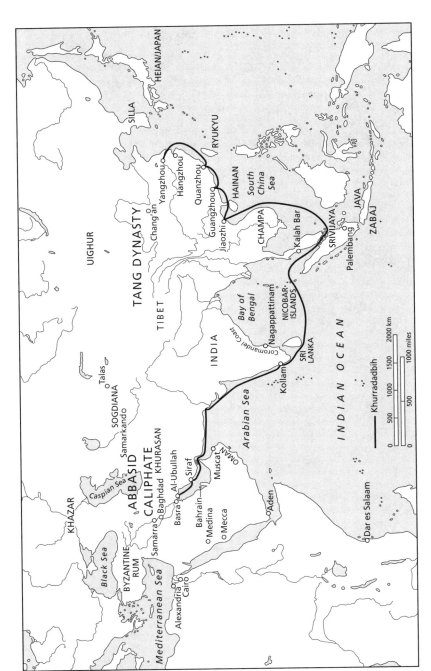

Map 1 Maritime Asia during the Tang

Map 2 China and southeast Asia in the ninth to tenth centuries

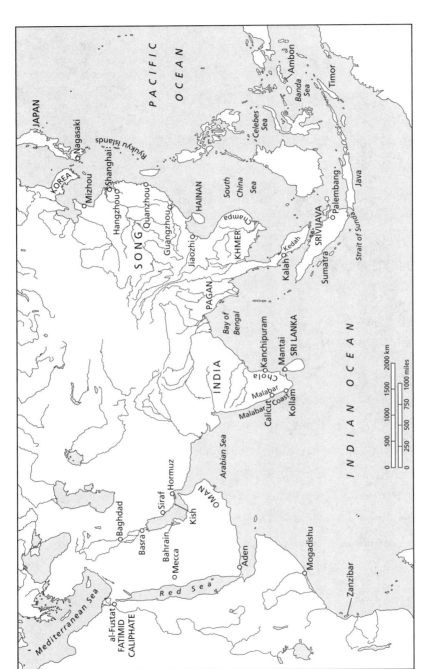

Map 3 Maritime Asia during the Song

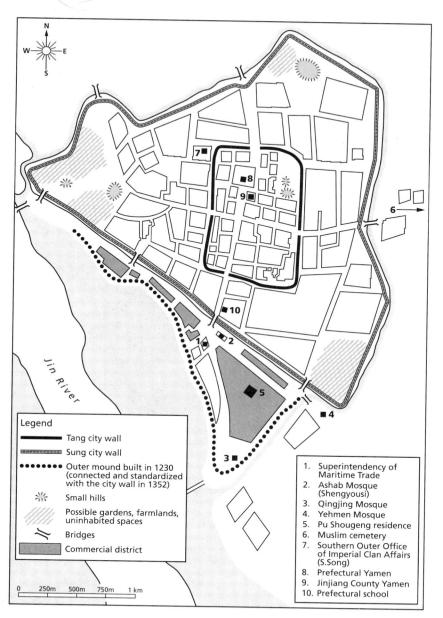

Legend

─────── Tang city wall

▦▦▦▦▦ Sung city wall

●●●●●● Outer mound built in 1230
(connected and standardized
with the city wall in 1352)

☼ Small hills

▨ Possible gardens, farmlands,
uninhabited spaces

⌇ Bridges

▨ Commercial district

0   250m   500m   750m   1 km

1. Superintendency of
   Maritime Trade
2. Ashab Mosque
   (Shengyousi)
3. Qingjing Mosque
4. Yehmen Mosque
5. Pu Shougeng residence
6. Muslim cemetery
7. Southern Outer Office
   of Imperial Clan Affairs
   (S.Song)
8. Prefectural Yamen
9. Jinjiang County Yamen
10. Prefectural school

Jin River

Map 4 Quanzhou city

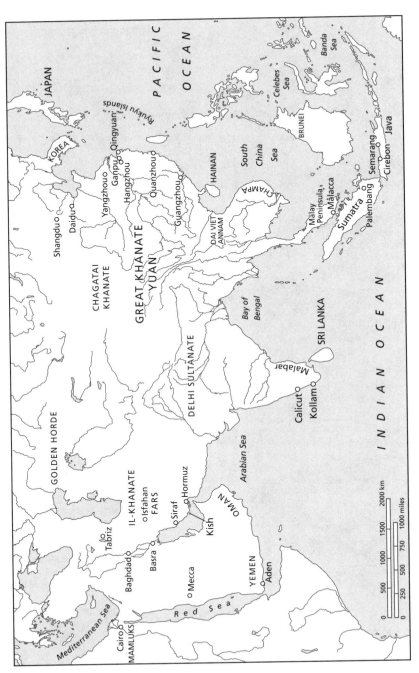

Map 5 Maritime Asia during the Yuan

Introduction

For over 600 years, from the mid-eighth to the late fourteenth century, ports of southeastern China were home to communities of Muslim maritime merchants living thousands of miles away from their predominantly western Asian places of origin. That they were in China at all was remarkable, given the length and danger of sea travel between the two ends of Asia; that they were there for centuries in numbers great enough to constitute sizeable multi-generational communities is important for our understanding of world history. The nature of the trade that was their lifeblood varied over time, as did their composition, their competitors, their places of settlement and their relationship to the authorities in China, and the records relating to these changes are frustrating in their scarcity. But collectively, the sources present a wealth of information concerning these Muslim merchant communities in China's port cities, their critical role in China's trade with maritime Asia and their evolution over time.

The existence of the Muslim merchant communities and most of the evidence relating to them have long been known to historians. They are commonly mentioned in works on Chinese overseas trade, maritime commerce and world history. But they have almost always been treated either as brief points of reference or, in the more detailed studies, in the context of single dynasties, and seldom have they examined the ways in which the communities were embedded in commercial networks that spanned maritime Asia. Thus their remarkable longevity and the long-term arc of their history have been largely unexamined. Indeed, the references typically present the communities with fixed characteristics – for example, a foreign quarter with foreign headmen, mosques and cemeteries – that seemingly stand outside of time.

It is the goal of this book to recover their history, and there is an eventful and often dramatic story to be told. But before turning to that story we must acknowledge the commercial order spanning maritime Asia that supported the Muslim communities in China for centuries. The waters of Asia witnessed the movement of ships, goods and people from at least antiquity, as evidenced by the Roman trading port of Muziris (among others) on the southwestern coast of India. As we will see, the flourishing Abbasid–Tang trade of the eighth and ninth centuries CE peopled by Persian and, increasingly, Arab merchants produced the first truly trans-continental commercial system and the beginnings of the Muslim community in Guangzhou. However, it was a conjunction of factors in the tenth and eleventh centuries that led to the emergence of what Janet Abu-Lughod has described as a world system.[1] These included the rise of the Fatimid and then Mamluk regimes in Cairo – offsetting the decline of Baghdad during the late Abbasid and Buyyid – the assertive roles played by Chola, Java and Champa, and especially Srivijaya, and the appearance of new ports like Calicut, Palembang and Quanzhou. Most important was the great size and dynamism of the Song economy, with its policies that supported rather than restricted maritime trade. Demands for Chinese silks, copper and especially ceramics were reciprocated by the Chinese appetite for such luxuries as rhinoceros horn and pearls, but also spices and a wide variety of medicines, perfumes and incense. Over time, bulk commodities including grains and other foodstuffs and manufactured goods like iron implements entered this commercial world, especially between China and southeast Asia. These developments were accompanied by a diversification of traders, notably south Indians, Malays, Koreans, Japanese and, beginning in the Song, Chinese. But the role of Muslim merchants was particularly prominent, and while they were generally associated with Arabia (*Dashi* 大食) and Persia (*Bosi* 波斯) in Chinese sources, there is also evidence of their occupying prominent positions in southeast Asian states.

The Tang communities of Persian and Arab merchants located in the cities of Yangzhou and especially Guangzhou in the far south, where a kind of Wild West atmosphere seems to have prevailed, apparently lived in a state of tension with their Chinese hosts, if the massacres directed against them in both cities are any indication. This contrasts vividly with the well-integrated communities that were to be found in the twelfth century in Guangzhou, Quanzhou, Mingzhou and other coastal cities when the southeast was the economic and political center of the empire. Then in the late thirteenth century, a large influx of privileged Muslims and other foreigners under Mongol rule created profoundly different urban communities, stratified and complex in their internal organization, with many not involved in maritime commerce. As we shall see, these differences extended beyond the communities themselves, for their interactions with the Chinese economy, society and government

---

[1] Janet L. Abu-Lughod, *Before European Hegemony: The World System A.D. 1250–1350* (Oxford: Oxford University Press, 1989), chapter 1.

around them varied greatly over time, as did the cultural interchanges between them and the host Chinese.

Nor did their activities stop at the water's edge. I would argue that these trading communities, whose livelihood depended on the movement of goods across the waters of Asia, constituted the Chinese end of a far-flung trade diaspora, a geographically dispersed collection of communities sharing some common identity and interdependent through their commercial activities. In his discussion of modern "trading diasporas," Abner Cohen points to a host of characteristics, such as their structures of authority, means of communication, organization and the like, but he also notes that these are old phenomena, as seen in the medieval Jewish trading diaspora made famous in the work of S. D. Goitein.[2] Philip Curtin, in his influential *Cross-Cultural Trade in World History*, developed a model for trade diasporas, arguing that diasporic merchants in port cities served the particular function of acting as cultural middlemen between their fellow merchants and local authorities, a function that disappeared with the rise of the modern world system.[3] The concept of "trade diaspora" has had its critics. K. N. Chaudhuri has argued premodern traders almost all "conducted business through close-knit groups, irrespective of their location," thus obviating the need for a special category of traders. For him, all of the purported characteristics of trade diasporas – the attempt to monopolize the trade in particular commodities, the possession of informal social and political organization and the restriction of commercial information to their closed group – are "general characteristics of human behavior" and not unique to a spatially dispersed diaspora.[4] Sebouh David Aslanian, in his fine study of Armenian merchants, also takes issue with the concept of "trade diaspora," though for different reasons. While acknowledging that it has been useful as a descriptive tool in painting broad pictures of early modern merchant groups, he questions its analytic utility, and instead uses "trade networks" or "circulation societies," in the latter case focusing upon the networks of commercial communication, as found in business correspondence.[5]

---

[2] Cohen, Abner, "Cultural Strategies in the Organization of Trading Diasporas," in Claude Meillassoux, ed., *The Development of Indigenous Trade and Markets in West Africa: Studies Presented and Discussed at the Tenth International African Seminar at Fourah Bay College, Freetown, December 1969* (London: Oxford University Press, 1971), pp. 266–281.

[3] Philip D. Curtin, *Cross-Cultural Trade in World History* (Cambridge: Cambridge University Press, 1984).

[4] K. N. Chaudhuri, *Trade and Civilization in the Indian Ocean. An Economic History from the Rise of Islam to 1750* (Cambridge: Cambridge University Press, 1985), pp. 224–226.

[5] Sebouh David Aslanian, *From the Indian Ocean to the Mediterranean: The Global Trade Networks of Armenian Merchants from New Julfa* (Berkeley: University of California Press, 2011), pp. 232–233.

I largely agree with these critiques of "trade diaspora" as an analytic model, for it is true that many of the characteristics ascribed to it were shared by most premodern commercial networks. My use of "trade diaspora" in this study is, rather, descriptive and historical, focused upon the communities and networks of Muslim merchants operating outside the *Dar al Islam* (the realm of Muslim polities and law).[6] The problem with "trade networks" or "circulation societies" is that they are essentially static constructs, whereas "trade diaspora" – even as a descriptive category – provides a better sense of its members as being dispersed geographically and constituting a historical entity with its own history of development. Uncovering that history is a primary goal of this study.

It is important to note that the Muslim trade diaspora involved more than communities in western Asia and China. The issue of dispersion became increasingly complex as time went by, but its essential glue was Islam. At its heart were the innumerable ties generated through commercial transactions, political charges, legal obligations, religious beliefs, friendships, family alliances (sometimes operating over generations) and shared cuisines and customs, which together produced the network that gave the diaspora its coherence. Moreover, trade diasporas were by their very nature constantly in flux, not only because of the unstructured nature of many of these ties, but also in response to changes in political context (everything from the rise and fall of dynasties to changes in tax laws) and demography (including the maturation of diasporic communities).

The Muslim trade diaspora that established and maintained footholds in the ports of China extended into ports and polities across maritime Asia from quite early times. Well before the tenth century, we know that Muslims had established themselves in the Sind and were to be found in Sri Lanka, the Coromandel coast of India and in the major states of southeastern Asia.[7] And as we shall see, from the tenth century on Muslims – especially Muslim traders – were increasingly numerous and important throughout this vast region.

The Muslim trade diaspora was constantly evolving and at times segmenting into smaller diasporic networks, but it was continuously connected by personal ties and kinship, by language, and most importantly by faith: a common belief that they had to survive in the *Dar al harb* (the

---

[6] Andre Wink also uses a concept of "trade diaspora" – which he describes as open and historical rather than closed – in the sense of an essential alien element in their host societies. Ancre Wink, *Al-Hind. The Making of the Indo-Islamic World. Vol. I. Early Medieval India and the Expansion of Islam 7th to 11th Centuries* (3rd edition. Leiden, New York, Köln: E. J. Brill, 1996), p. 67.

[7] See Wink, *Al-Hind*, pp. 67–81 for a historical overview of the spread of Islam.

world outside of Islam) and a common acceptance of Muslim law, which governed such practices as partnerships and *commenda* contracts that were essential to their commercial livelihood. While we can often only infer what those networks were, they also underwent fundamental changes over the course of this seven-century history, and the discernment of those changes is yet another essential element in this process of historical recovery.

One challenge of this project concerns the scarcity of sources. Any records kept by the medieval Muslim merchants have long since disappeared, and China's Confucian elite evinced little interest in these foreigners, though we will make full use of the exceptional writers who paid them attention. Our information must therefore be culled from the writings of Arab geographers and travelers and Persian historians (for the thirteenth and fourteenth centuries); from a range of Chinese sources, including government records, histories, local gazetteers, geographies, genealogies and the writings of those exceptional individuals mentioned above; and finally from the buildings and cemeteries produced by these communities and the archaeological record, including stone funeral inscriptions and the excavations of shipwrecks. Amassing these has been a daunting task, especially for one who does not read Arabic or Persian. Fortunately, there is a vast literature of secondary studies and translations on which to draw, and while only a small portion of it deals specifically with the merchant communities themselves, such well-studied topics as historical geography, the spread of Islam, Chinese maritime administration and the history of trade throughout maritime Asia have made it possible to discern a composite picture of those groups and their history.

In this context, it is important to acknowledge some of the most important scholarship relating to the Muslim merchant communities in China, work that has been crucial for this study. Kuwabara Jitsuzō's 桑原騭藏 study of the Sino-Muslim official and merchant Pu Shougeng 蒲壽庚 (d. 1296) marks the beginning of modern studies of the communities, for Kuwabara, in the course of demonstrating the important role played by Pu in the Song–Yuan transition, identified a remarkable array of sources treating the Muslim merchants in China.[8] In recent years,

---

[8] Kuwabara Jitsuzō 桑原騭藏, "On P'u Shou-keng, a Man of the Western Regions, Who Was the Superintendent of the Trading Ships' Office in Ch'üan-chou towards the End of the Sung Dynasty, Together with a General Sketch of Trade of the Arabs in China during the T'ang and Sung Eras, Part 1," *Memoirs of the Research Department of the Tōyō Bunko* 2 (1928), pp. 1–79; "On P'u Shou-keng, Part 2," *Memoirs of the Research Department of the Tōyō Bunko* 7 (1935), pp. 1–104. See also his *Ho Jukō no jiseki* 蒲壽庚 no 事蹟 (Tokyo: Kazama shobō, 1935), translated into Chinese by Chen Yujing 陳裕菁 as *Pu Shougeng* 蒲壽庚 (Beijing: Zhonghua shuju, 1954).

Hugh Clark and Billy So have been instrumental in delineating the role maritime commerce and foreign merchants in Song Fujian.[9,10] This is important, not only because the Fujian port of Quanzhou was the center of foreign merchant activity from the late eleventh century on, but also because of the Song and Yuan mosque and cemetery remains and the hundreds of Muslim stone inscriptions that have been discovered there. In that regard, special mention should be made of Wu Wenliang 吳文良, a Quanzhou teacher who in the 1930s began collecting inscribed stones that were being ignored by the authorities (often being used for construction purposes),[11] and Chen Dasheng 陳達生, whose lifelong work organizing, transcribing and translating those stones has contributed enormously to what we know about the Quanzhou Muslims.[12]

It is important to point out topics that will not be covered in this book. Because the geographical scope of Muslim merchant activity was overwhelmingly from the southeastern coast of China south into southeastern Asia and west across the Indian Ocean, we will not consider the flourishing trade of eastern Asia, particularly with Korea, Japan and the Ryukyu Islands. Muslim merchants were known to make their way to those countries on occasion, but not enough to make that historically consequential.[13] We will also have little to say about Buddhism, that Indian religion that had an enormous impact on China and that came by sea as well as land. As important as that transmission was, especially during the sixth through tenth centuries when Buddhist-related Sino-Indian maritime trade and communication were especially active, there

---

[9] Hugh Clark, *Community, Trade, and Networks. Southern Fujian Province from the Third to the Thirteenth Centuries* (Cambridge: Cambridge University Press, 1991); "Moslems and Hindus in the Economy and Culture of Song Quanzhou," *Abstracts of the 1993 Annual Meeting*, 4 (Ann Arbor: Association for Asian Studies, 1993); "Muslims and Hindus in the Culture and Morphology of Quanzhou from the Tenth to the Thirteenth Century," *Journal of World History* 6.1 (spring 1995), pp. 49–74.

[10] Billy Kee Long [Su Jilang 蘇基朗], *Prosperity, Region, and Institutions in Maritime China. The South Fukien Pattern, 946–1368* (Cambridge, MA: Harvard University Asia Center, 2000); *Tang Song shidai Minnan Quanzhou shidi lungao* 唐宋時代閩南泉州駛抵論稿 (Taipei: Shangwu yinshuguan, 1991).

[11] Wu Wenliang 吳文良, ed., *Quanzhou zongjiao shike* 泉州宗教石刻, edited and expanded by Wu Youxiong 吳幼雄 (Beijing: Kexue, 2005). For a description of Wu's lonely early efforts, see Nancy Shatzman Steinhardt, *China's Early Mosques*. Edinburgh Studies in Islamic Art (Edinburgh: Edinburgh University Press, 2016), p. 38.

[12] Chen Dasheng 陳達生, *Quanzhou Yisilan jiao shike* 泉州伊斯兰教石刻 (Fu-chou: Ningxia renmin chubanshe, Fujian renmin chubanshe, 1984); with Ludvik Kalus, *Corpus d'Inscriptions Arabes et Persanes en Chine, Vol. 1, Province de Fu-jian* (Paris: Librairie Orientaliste Paul Geuthner, 1991). Today most of those stones are in the collection of the Quanzhou Maritime Museum.

[13] For the evidence concerning Muslim merchants in Korea, see Hee-Soo Lee, *The Advent of Islam in Korea: A Historical Account* (Istanbul: Research Centre for Islamic History, Art and Culture, 1997).

is little to suggest that Muslim merchants were involved in it.[14] Finally, my attention here is on groups and their economic, social and political roles. Their religions and beliefs and practices and their cultural influence – topics of great importance – are treated only in passing and must await another study.

We must also be mindful of the very concrete realities of travel across Asian seas. Until the eleventh century, long-distance shipping was dominated by the Arab dhow or its close cousin, the southeast Asian Kunlun ship, both of which were characterized by planking sewn together by coconut fiber rope. The Belitung wreck, discovered off of the coast of Sumatra and dated to the early ninth century, provides important evidence for the use of dhows in long-distance trade (see Map 2). With a keel 15.3 meters (49.7 feet) in length, the ship carried a cargo of 60,000 objects, the great majority of which were ceramics from China. The Arabic representation of a dhow at sea (see Figure 1.1 on p. 16) dates towards the end of our period, but illustrates the relationship between the sailors and merchants, with the former busy above deck while the merchants peered out of the portholes. This painting also underrepresents the size of the ships. We have no way of telling the size of its crew, but literary evidence suggests that dhows could carry very large complements. Buzurg ibn Shahriyar (c. 900–953) described the loss of three ships en route from Siraf to Saba in 918, on board of which were "1,200 persons, merchants, shipowners, sailors, traders, and others."[15] By the eleventh century, the dhow began to be supplanted by the Chinese junk, a ship characterized by iron-nailed planks and bulkhead compartments that made the ships more seaworthy and allowed them to be built bigger. Marco Polo has a detailed account of a junk – on which he traveled on his return to Europe – describing 13 watertight bulkhead compartments, 60 cabins for merchants and their merchandise and a crew of 150 to 300.[16] Writing a half-century later, Ibn Battuta described even larger Chinese ships that carried complements of a thousand men.[17] The nautical sophistication evident in these descriptions bears witness

---

[14] See Tansen Sen, *Buddhism, Diplomacy, and Trade: The Realignment of Sino-Indian Relations, 600–1400* (Honolulu: University of Hawaii Press, 2003), and "Buddhism and the Maritime Crossings" in Dorothy Wong and Gustav Heldt, eds., *China and Beyond in the Mediaeval Period: Cultural Crossings and Inter-Regional Connections* (Amherst and Delhi: Cambria Press and Manohar Publishers, 2014), pp. 39–61.

[15] Buzurg ibn Shahriyar (c. 900–953), *The Book of the Wonders of India, Mainland, Sea, and Islands (Kitab 'Aja'ib al-Hind)*, G. S. P. Freeman-Grenville, translator (London and The Hague: East-West Publications, 1981), p. 97 (CXIV).

[16] Marco Polo, *The Travels of Marco Polo*, translated and with an introduction by Ronald Latham (London: Penguin Books, 1958), pp. 241–242.

[17] Ibn Battuta, *The Travels of Ibn Battuta, A.D. 1325–1354*, translated with revisions and notes from the Arabic text edited by C. Defrémery and B. R. Sanguinetti, edited by

to the flourishing nature of maritime trade, but it should not blind us to the fact that seagoing was hazardous, involving high rates of mortality, whether from storms, shoals, pirates or hostile governments. Describing a Captain Abhara, who had made multiple trips to China, Buzurg exclaims:

> Only adventurous men had made this voyage before. No one had done it without an accident. If a man reached China without dying on the way, it was already a miracle. Returning safe and sound was unheard of. I have never heard tell of anyone, except him, who had made the two voyages there and back without mishap.[18]

Although clearly hyperbolic, since we know that many Arabs and Persians made the trip to China, Buzurg's statement illustrates the reputation that the China trade had as a dangerous venture, and makes even more understandable the tendency of Muslim merchants to seek the company and support of their co-religionists when far from their home.

The approach of this book is historical, with each of its five chapters describing a discrete phase in the history of the Muslim merchant communities. The first chapter begins with the great age of Tang–Abbasid trade (c. 700–879), a trade in luxury goods focused largely upon China and the Persian Gulf region. The early eighth century was a remarkable period in Eurasian history, with two great and vigorous empires in frequent contact with each other, both through embassies (sent by land) and as military rivals in central Asia. From the ports of the Abbasid Caliphate ventured merchants, with Arabs joining the Persians, who had for at least a couple of centuries been active throughout maritime Asia. The settlements they developed in China, anchoring the eastern terminus of their trade, were located primarily in the cities of Guangzhou, a distant outpost of the Tang empire, and Yangzhou, at the juncture of the Grand Canal and the Yangzi River, but also included an intriguing settlement in southern Hainan. They were not alone: traders from south and southeast Asia also flocked to the ports of China. But the Persians and Arabs dominated the flourishing and lucrative luxury trade with western Asia, with the Tang imperial court the principal consumer of the incense, rare woods, rhinoceros horn, pearls and other exotic goods that they brought. Thanks to the writings of Arab travelers and geographers, we know quite a bit about the sea route that connected the two ends of Asia and we have

---

H. A. R. Gibb, and annotated by C. F. Beckingham, 5 vols. (London: The Hakluyt Society, 1994), vol. 4, p. 813. Its explanation of the thousand men is worth quoting: "... six hundred of whom are sailors and four hundred men-at-arms, including archers, men with shields and arbalists, that is men who throw naphtha." Perhaps shipping in the Indian Ocean world was not as peaceful as it is often portrayed.

[18] Buzurg, *The Book of Wonders*, p. 50 (XLVI).

access to perceptive accounts of Chinese life and customs. The chapter also considers the introduction of Islam into China, which occurred at this time. While there were Muslims in the capital of Chang'an who had come by land, Islamic traditions regarding the religion's introduction into the south include a legend that Muslim missionaries arrived within a generation of the death of Muhammad. Whether or not there is any truth to this, the story's very existence points to a religious dimension of the Muslim communities that was always there. As to their relationship to the Han Chinese with whom they interacted, Edward Schafer has noted that the seafaring merchants, though able to garner great wealth, were "often badly mistreated by the masters of the Chinese realm,"[19] and in fact, as we shall see, relations between the merchants and the Tang authorities were at times marked by hostility: the reported plundering of Guangzhou by Persians and Arabs in 758, a massacre of the same in Yangzhou in 760 and a major massacre of Christians, Jews, Muslims and Mazdeans in 879. This last was of particular importance, for it resulted in the foreign merchants abandoning the port of Guangzhou and centering their operations in southeast Asia, thus effectively bringing to an end the first phase of the foreign coastal communities.

The short but crucial second chapter deals with a fundamental reorientation of trade that began in the aftermath of the 879 massacre. According to Arab sources, that massacre caused a flight of the merchant community from Guangzhou into southeast Asia, most particularly to Kalah on the Malay peninsula, which for decades served as the primary base of their east Asian commercial activities. These flourished, thanks in good part to the continued economic vitality of the Abbasid Caliphate and the prosperity of Chola in south Asia and the southeast Asian states of Srivijaya, Champa and Java, but the attractions of China soon reasserted themselves. With the disintegration of the Tang empire, the southeastern Chinese states of Southern Han and Min welcomed the Muslims and other foreign merchants, and for the first time in Chinese history treated employed taxation from maritime imports as a centerpiece of their state revenue systems, and set the stage for several centuries of uninterrupted commercial prosperity. The chapter concludes with a treatment of the first 60 years of the Song dynasty (960–1279), when the Chinese tried to use a Tang-style tributary system to channel the large and growing volume of maritime trade.

The third chapter of the book explores the varied aspects of the Muslim merchant communities from the 1020s to the end of the Song in 1279, an

---

[19] Edward Schafer, *The Vermilion Bird: T'ang Images of the South* (Berkeley: University of California Press, 1967), p. 76.

era of free trade that was taxed by the government. At the center of this approach were the offices and superintendencies of maritime trade, which assumed general oversight and welfare functions for the foreign merchant communities in addition to taxation, and which were located in nine cities at one time or another, the most important being Guangzhou and Quanzhou. Under the paternalistic gaze of the superintendencies, the Muslim communities flourished, aided by the continuous growth of maritime commerce (through at least the end of the twelfth century) and tolerant policies on the part of Song officials, which resulted in a merchant elite that was remarkably well assimilated into the urban societies of the port cities. These activities were influenced by two important geopolitical developments. The Song loss of northern China in the 1120s made the resulting Southern Song (1127–1279) more dependent on revenues from maritime commerce, while the eleventh-century collapse of the Abbasid Caliphate attenuated the home-country anchor of the Muslim trade diaspora – or diasporas, for they had increased in complexity. As a result, the communities in China assumed even greater importance for the trade diasporas across the oceans of Asia.

The fourth chapter begins with the Mongol conquest, which, despite taking most of the thirteenth century, impacted maritime Asia only from the 1270s, and it continued to the end of the Yuan in 1368. In a Eurasian world that they had militarily reconfigured, the Mongols were enthusiastic supporters of maritime trade, albeit in ways that primarily benefited their favored merchants, while at the same time they militarized the maritime world through invasions of Japan, Vietnam and Java. Because of internecine Mongol conflicts on the continent in the late thirteenth century, the sea route to western Asia gained strategic as well as economic importance, since it connected Khubilai to his allies in the Persian Il-Khanate. Thus the tie with western Asia was refashioned more strongly than ever before, particularly since the Mongols also brought large numbers of foreigners to China, most notably Muslims from Persia and central Asia. The impact on the Chinese Muslim communities was profound, for they became larger than ever before, privileged and politically powerful, yet also more separated from their Han Chinese peers than they had been from their Song predecessors. As a result of these developments, the Muslim trade diaspora was once again anchored in its western Asian homelands and was dominated at its higher levels by politically powerful merchants in the Persian Gulf and India as well as in China. Whether the growing complexity of commerce throughout the maritime Asian world also resulted in the development of a less-visible Sino-Muslim trade diaspora active in southeast Asia is an issue that will be explored.

The fifth and final chapter deals with the demise of the Muslim merchant communities in the early Ming. With the collapse of Mongol rule, the Muslims went from being a privileged group to one regarded as alien and untrustworthy. Zhu Yuanzhang 朱元璋, the Ming founder, sharply curtailed foreign trade, forbidding merchants in China from venturing abroad and restricting trade with specific countries to specific ports, and he mandated that all *semu* 色目 people (foreigners, including Muslims, who assisted Mongol rule during the Yuan) adopt Chinese dress and names and marry only with Chinese. Although the seven famed naval expeditions led by the Muslim admiral Zheng He 鄭和 under the Yongle Emperor in the early fifteenth century marked China's most extensive interaction with the Asian maritime world, they proved to be short lived – they did not long outlast the admiral and emperor, and the Ming again turned its back on the sea.

As to the Muslim merchant communities that had thrived for centuries in China, the early Ming marked their end. In the worst case, an anti-Muslim massacre in Quanzhou during the dynastic interregnum led to the killing and mutilation of untold numbers of foreigners. A number of families that we know of fled the cities for the countryside, where they took up a new existence as farming families. A number stayed in the cities but took up other occupations, since the overseas trade was no longer an option. Others left China, making their way to southeast Asia, where they continued their merchant activities and as Sino-Muslims became one of the sources of the Islamization of that region. For those who remained in China, I argue that their identity made a fundamental shift from being part of a trade diaspora active across the maritime world to becoming an ethnic minority, a status that their descendants maintain to this day.

Looking more broadly, the role of the maritime Muslim communities in introducing Islam to China has given them a prominent place in the historical narrative of Islam in China. In recent times, the Chinese authorities have embraced their legacy as evidence of China's Maritime Silk Road, as have many of the Arab governments of the Middle East. But for our purposes, it is their role in global history, their centuries of connecting to the interconnectedness of maritime Asia, that most concerns us in this study.

1   Merchants of an Imperial Trade

One day in late September of 758, Persians and Arabs raided the frontier port city of Guangzhou (Canton). According to two sources, they plundered the city and burned its warehouses and storehouses before departing by sea.[1] Another source describes them as troops from the countries of Arabia (Dashi 大食) and Persia (Bosi 波斯) and recounts that they captured the city after the prefect, Wei Lijian 韋利見, abandoned the city and went into hiding.[2] Who were these men who – thousands of miles from their homes in west Asia – were able to seize one of the major cities of the Tang, if only briefly? Speculative answers have included seeing them as a reflection of the newly established Abbasid Caliphate, as disgruntled troops sent by the Caliph to quell a rebellion in central Asia (who somehow made their way to the coast of China), or as followers of the Hainanese warlord Feng Ruofang 馮若芳, who specialized in capturing and enslaving Persian sailors, about whom we will have more to say. They might also have been traders enraged by grievances against local officials or some other trade issue (thus the burning of the warehouses). We will be returning to this question; here it is enough to note that this incident marks the first mention of Arabs in Tang documentary sources – a signpost, as it were, for the early stages of the first great age of Asian maritime commerce.

This age was a period quite distinct from those that followed. At its height, it involved a flourishing and lucrative trade in luxuries between the two great Asian empires of the day: the Abbasid Caliphate (750–1258) in the west and the Tang Empire (618–907) in the east. It was also a period of significant change at both ends of the continent. The Abbasids continued the process of the Islamicization of much of southwestern and central Asia, which the Umayyad Caliphate (661–750) had initiated, but

---

[1] Liu Xu 劉昫, *Jiu Tangshu* 舊唐書 (Beijing: Zhonghua shuju, 1987), 15b, p. 5313, and Ouyang Xiu 歐陽修, *Xin Tangshu* 新唐書 (Beijing: Zhonghua shuju, 1975), 221B, p. 6259. These works will hereafter be cited respectively as JTS and XTS.
[2] JTS, 10, p. 253. A fourth account, the least informative, simply states that Arabs and Persians plundered Guangzhou. XTS, 6, p. 161.

also took to the sea, adding an Arab overlay to the Persian seafarers who until then had dominated long-distance trade (in ways that often make it difficult to distinguish between the two), and by the tenth century had accumulated a large body of information concerning China and routes to it. For their part, the Tang's greatest engagement in the maritime trade corresponded with a weakened dynasty facing great internal challenges, notably the rebellions of An Lushan 安祿山 (755–763) and Huang Chao 黃巢 (874–884), and in fact events associated with the latter resulted in a lengthy hiatus in Chinese involvement in that trade.

Against this backdrop we can discern the emergence of China's first Muslim merchant communities in a number of southeastern cities, most particularly Guangzhou 廣州 or Canton, known to the Arabs as Khanfu. To understand these communities, this chapter will explore the historical context of their development, the nature of the trade and the associated challenges of travel, the communities themselves and, finally, the break in the 870s that resulted in that hiatus.

Persians, Arabs and Muslims

China's maritime contact with western Asia – the Western Regions (*xiyu* 西域), as they are often referred to in Chinese sources – long predated the coming of the Muslim merchants. Textual and archaeological evidence points to the existence of maritime trade ties connecting China with southeast Asia, southern India and Rome in the west as early as the first century C.E., a commerce in which Chinese silks, Roman glass, wine and specie, and pearls, ivory and peppers from various parts of maritime Asia were actively traded.[3] In the period following the early third-century fall of the Han empire, and especially during the fourth through sixth centuries when China was divided into northern and southern dynasties, Chinese ports hosted merchants from Kunlun 崑崙 (in Malaya) and southern India as well as Buddhist monks who had made their way from

---

[3] Kenneth R. Hall, *Maritime Trade and State Development in Early Southeast Asia* (Honolulu: University of Hawaii Press, 1985), pp. 29–38. In its discussion of Han relations with the west, the *Song shu* (c. 500 CE) depicts the travel of Chinese across envoys across the seas: "As regards the Roman Orient (Daqin 大秦) and India, far out on the Western Ocean (*da ming* 大溟), though the envoys of the two Han dynasties have experienced the special difficulties of this route, yet trade has been carried on, and goods have been sent out to the foreign tribes, the force of the wind driving them far across the waves of the sea." Cited in Frederick Hirth and W. W. Rockhill, translators, *Chau Ju-kua: His Work on the Chinese and Arab Trade in the Twelfth and Thirteenth Centuries, Entitled* Chu-fan-chi (St. Petersburg: Imperial Academy of Sciences, 1911; reprint, Taipei: Ch'eng-wen Publishing Company, 1971), p. 7. On the early usages of "Kunlun," a term that has evoked considerable disagreement among scholars, see Don J. Wyatt, *The Blacks of Premodern China* (Philadelphia: University of Pennsylvania Press, 2009), pp. 19–20.

India.[4] Trade with the distant west, however, was the domain of Persian traders from the Sassanid empire, which ruled a vast swathe of western Asia from 224 to 651, and over the course of that period they extended their activities from the Indian Ocean east into China (Figure 1.1).

Sailing across the Indian Ocean. From Harīrī's *Maqamat*.

Figure 1.1 Arab merchants sailing to India
(from Hariri's Maqamat. Bibliothèque Nationale, Paris Ms. Arabe
5847)

---

[4] Tansen Sen, *Buddhism, Diplomacy, and Trade*, pp. 163–164.

It is impossible to date the arrival of Persian merchants in China with any precision. The dynastic histories describe tribute envoys arriving from Persia in 455, 530, 533 and 535, but they almost certainly traveled by land.[5] Only in 671, half a century into the Tang, do we have definitive evidence of Persian seafarers in China, in the form of a travel account by the Chinese Buddhist pilgrim Yijing 義淨:

In the beginning of autumn [of 671, in Chang'an] I met unexpectedly an imperial envoy, Feng Xiaoquan of Kongzho; by the help of him I came to the town of Guangdong, where I fixed the date of meeting with the owner of a Persian ship to embark for the south... At last I embarked from the coast of Guangzhou (Canton), in the eleventh month in the second year of the Xianfeng period (671 A.D.) and sailed for the Southern Sea.[6]

From a half-century later (717), we learn of an Indian Buddhist who sailed in a convoy of 35 Persian ships from Ceylon to Palembang (Srivijaya), eventually arriving in Guangzhou in 720, quite possibly being met my merchants such as those in Figure 1.2.[7] A Chinese account by a Chinese monk from 727 of Persian commercial activities asserts that they

... are accustomed to sail into the Western Sea, and they enter the Southern Sea making for Ceylon to obtain all kinds of precious objects. Moreover they head for the K'un-lun [Kunlun] Country (Malaya) to get gold. Furthermore, they set sail for the Land of Han, going directly to Canton, where they obtain various kinds of silk gauze and wadding.[8]

The Chinese monk Ganjin (Jian Zhen 堅真) describes in his travel diary being shipwrecked in southern Hainan in 748, where he encountered a local warlord who reportedly captured "two or three Persian ships" each year and enslaved their crews, a topic to which we will return.[9]

---

[5] Edward H. Schafer, "Iranian Merchants in T'ang Dynasty Tales," in *Semitic and Oriental Studies: A Volume Presented to William Popper* University of California Publications in Semitic Philology, vol. XI. Berkeley, CA: University of California Press, 1951), p. 403, and Gungwu Wang, "The Nan-hai Trade. A Study of the Early History of Chinese Trade in the South China Sea," *Journal of the Malayan Branch of the Royal Asiatic Society*, 31(2) (1958), p. 60, 124–127.

[6] Hadi Hasan, *A History of Persian Navigation* (London: Methuen & Co., 1928), p. 97, citing J. Takakusu, *A Record of the Buddhist Religion* (Oxford: Oxford University Press, 1896), p. 211. I have taken the liberty of changing the romanization in the quotation from Wade–Giles to Pinyin. See also G. F. Hourani, *Arab Seafaring in the Indian Ocean in Ancient and Early Medieval Times* (Princeton, NJ: Princeton University Press, 1951), p. 62.

[7] Hasan, *A History of Persian Navigation*, p. 79; Hourani, *Arab Seafaring*, p. 62.

[8] Schafer, "Iranian Merchants in Tang Dynasty Tales," p. 406; Hourani, *Arab Seafaring*, p. 62.

[9] J. Takakusu, "Aomi-no Mabito Genkai (779), *Le voyage de Kanshin en Orient* (742–754)," *Bulletin de l'Ecole Française d'Extrême Orient*, vol. 28 (1928), p. 462.

Figure 1.2 Tang merchant figures
(Macao Museum)

These references to Persian maritime engagement in the China market are fully consonant with Edward Schafer's portrait of Iranian merchants in Tang dynasty tales, in which he argues that the Persian merchant had become a common cultural figure in Tang China, stereotypically regarded as wealthy, generous and at times something of a magician, though Schafer also makes the point that many of these merchants are described as living in the north and presumably came to China by land.[10] Less clear, however, is how the Persian presence in Tang China relates to the Muslim Umayyad's conquest of the Sassanid empire in 651 and the subsequent arrival in China of Arabs and Islam.

One cannot overstate the transformative impact that the founding of Islam by Muhammad (traditionally dated 622) and the subsequent rise of

---

[10] Schafer, "Iranian Merchants in Tang Dynasty Tales," pp. 403–422, especially 414–415. "Iranian" must be broadly construed here, for many of the Persian peoples active in Tang China were in fact Sogdians from Transoxia, and not from the Sasanian empire. For the Sogdians, see Étienne de la Vaissière, *Sogdian Traders: A History*, translated by James Ward (Leiden: Brill, 2005).

the Umayyad Caliphate (661–750) had upon western Asia, indeed upon the Eurasian and north African world. Their reverberations were certainly felt in China. In the 660s the Tang court entertained two embassies from Firuz (Pilusi 卑路斯), the son of the last Sasanian ruler Yezdegerd III, who had fled to Tokharestan (Tuhuoluo 土火羅) and was soliciting Chinese help in reviving the Sasanian cause. In the early 670s Firuz came to Chang'an himself and sought Chinese help in restoring his empire, and in response Emperor Gaozong sent him (or his son Narses; the sources differ on this) with a Chinese force that was already being sent to the west, but in fact the Chinese force never went beyond the Tarim Basin.[11] More important than this interesting sideshow was the steady stream of Umayyad envoys who came to Chang'an, beginning in 651 and continuing to 750.[12] Although many of these were traditional tribute missions, several in the early eighth century came demanding Tang submission, for the Muslim armies were engaged at this time in their dramatic expansion through central Asia.[13] Subsequent Umayyad weakness together with the expansive foreign policy of Emperor Xuanzong (r. 712–756) allowed for a return of Tang power in central Asia, but that ended abruptly in 751 when a Tang army under the Korean general Gao Xianzhi 高仙芝 was defeated at the Battle of Talas (near modern Tashkent) by an Arab army of the newly established Abbasid caliphate (750–1258).[14] The Abbasid caliphs sent no fewer than twenty embassies to the Tang between 751 and 798, while a recently discovered tomb stele indicates that the Tang sent at least one mission to the Abbasids.[15] We also have the revealing account by one Du Huan 杜環, a member of Gao

[11] F. S. Drake, "Mohammedanism in the T'ang Dynasty," *Monumenta Serica* 7 (1943), pp. 6–7, citing JTS, 198, pp. 5212–5213 (Beijing: Zhonghua shuju, 1975), and XTS, 221b, pp. 6258–6259. According to the *Old Tang History*, after parting with the Chinese troops Pirooz spent 20 years in Tokharestan, and after that returned to China, where he was given a military title and subsequently died. In the *New Tang History*, Firuz died in China in the 670s and it was his son Narses who traveled west and returned 20 years later.

[12] Donald Leslie, *Islam in Traditional China* (Canberra: Canberra College of Advanced Education, 1986), p. 31, lists over 20 Arab embassies in the century 651 to 750. Most of these were from the eighth century.

[13] Drake, "Mohammedanism in the T'ang Dynasty," pp. 7–9. The greatest Umayyad gains occurred between 705 and 712 under the Arab general Qutaiba ibn Muslim. These campaigns came to an end after Qutaiba's execution, for political reasons, in 715.

[14] Drake, "Mohammedanism in the T'ang Dynasty," p. 9. See Denis Twitchett, "Hsüan-tsung," in Denis Twitchett, ed., *The Cambridge History of China, Volume 3, Sui and T'ang China, 589–906, Part 1* (Cambridge: Cambridge University Press, 1979), pp. 443–444, on the significance on the loss at Talas for the Tang.

[15] The stele is of one Yang Liangyao 楊良瑤 (736–806), which describes his being sent by, by sea, by the emperor Dezong 德宗 in 785 to establish an alliance with the Abbasids, Indians, the kingdom of Nanzhao and the Uighurs against the Tibetans. Angel Schottenhammer, "Guangzhou as China's Gate to the Indian Ocean: The Importance of Iranian and Arab Merchant Networks for Long-Distance Maritime Trade during the Tang-Song Transition (c. 750–1050), Part 1: 750–c. 900)," *Harvard Journal of Asiatic Studies* 76 (2016), pp. 155, 172.

Xianzhi's army who was captured by the Arabs at Talas and returned to China on a merchant ship to Guangzhou in 761. In his account of Kufa (the initial capital of the Abbasids) and Abbasid society he describes Chinese painters, silk weavers and gold and silver craftsmen living and working there.[16]

The presence of Arab merchants and Muslims in Tang China is more difficult to document, even though there is no doubt that both were there. If one excludes Arabs in non-Chinese armies and, of course, those associated with the Abbasids, Tang references to Arabs are scarce.[17] There are a couple of mentions of Arab merchants from Tang stories, such as one where a young man sells a fabulous pearl to an Arab in the Persian Bazaar of Guangzhou, and another in which "A party of noble Arabs purchase a supposedly valueless gem from a Chinese temple. Their king had offered an emirate to its finder, for it had formerly belonged to the Arabs, who used it to bring forth water in the desert."[18] The Tang histories have only two sets of references (in each case, from both the *New* and *Old Tang Histories*), albeit very important ones, to Arabs in southeastern China. The first documents the 758 raid and brief seizure of the city of Guangzhou by Arabs and Persians that was described at the beginning of this chapter.[19] The second recounts the massacre of "several thousand" Arab and Persian merchants in Yangzhou in 760 by rampaging government troops that had occupied and looted the city.[20]

We will revisit these important incidents below; here, I would note the coupling of Persians and Arabs by the Chinese authors. This may reflect some understandable confusion by Chinese writers as to who these foreigners were, for "*bosi*" and "*dashi*" were first and foremost the names that were given to distant countries and not the terms that they commonly applied to the foreigners living among them. In fact, the most common terms used to describe foreign merchants in Tang China were "*hu*" 胡, a term most commonly applied to Persians but also to Tibetans, Turks and other pastoral nomads, and "*fan*" 番 (alternately, 蕃 or 藩), typically

---

[16] Hyunhee Park, *Mapping the Chinese and Islamic Worlds: Cross-Cultural Exchange in Premodern Asia* (Cambridge: Cambridge University Press, 2012), pp. 24–26. Du Huan's account is from Du You 杜佑, *Tong dian* 通典, 193, p. 1044.

[17] According to Hasan, *A History of Persian Navigation*, p. 79, the very name that Chinese used for the Arabs reflects prior Persian influence: "The Chinese know the Arabs under the name *Ta-shi* which is nothing more than the Persian *Tazi* or *Tajik*; it was therefore the Persians who made the Arabs known in China under the same name by which in earlier times they had called the Arabs themselves."

[18] Schafer, "Iranian Merchants in Tang Dynasty Tales," p. 418. These tales are from sections on "treasures" and "supernatural beings" in the *Taiping guangji* 太平廣記.

[19] JTS 10, p. 253 and 15b, p. 5313, and XTS 6, p. 161 and 221B, p. 6259.

[20] JTS 110, p. 3313 and 124, p. 3533, and XTS 141, p. 4655 and 144, p. 4702.

used for foreigners or aliens and often found in port cities, and combinations such as "*fan*-guests" (*fanke* 番客) and "*hu*-merchants" (*hushang* 胡商).[21] Without a doubt these terms or ethnonyms all involved degrees of ethnic stereotyping, a subject to which we will return, but the point to be made here is that these were the terms used for most of the evidence relating to the west Asian merchants in the ports of China.[22]

There is also reason to believe that Persians and Arabs made common cause in China. During the century following the Abbasid defeat of the Sasanians, a process of conversion was underway that resulted in the vast majority of Persians converting to Islam by the middle of the ninth century.[23] We also know that the Muslim Persian Samanid empire (819–999), a vassal state of the Abbasids in eastern Iran, was actively engaged in maritime commerce.[24] Even at the beginning of the Abbasid period, we have evidence from Du Huan about the commingling of Arabs and Persians. He writes that, in Dashi (the Abbasid caliphate), "Arabs and Persians are mixed and live together" (*dashi bosi canza juzhi* 大食波斯參雜居止).[25] So it is reasonable to assume that as they began making their way to China by sea, Arab merchants accompanied their Persian counterparts and traveled on Persian ships. Thereafter, the number of Arabs undoubtedly increased, but, given the commingling of Persian and Arab merchants, it might be best to consider their presence in China as that of an Arab-Persian community.

If Tang references to Arabs are rare, those for Muslims are virtually nonexistent, even though there is no doubt about their having been present in Tang China. We must first dismiss the intriguing but legendary accounts of Sa'd ibn Abi Waqqas (Sahaba Saadi Gangesi 撒哈八撒阿的乾葛思), who, according to Ming and Qing accounts, made three trips to China, the first as an envoy from the Prophet in 629, and finally to Guangzhou where he built two mosques and was eventually buried. Although an important part of Chinese Muslim lore, there is no support for this story from Tang sources, and it is moreover highly implausible that an associate of Muhammad would have made his way to China that

---

[21] Schafer, "Iranian Merchants in Tang Dynasty Tales," p. 413, and Abramson, Marc S., *Ethnic Identity in Tang China* (Philadelphia, PA: University of Pennsylvania Press, 2008), *passim*, but especially pp. 18–19 and 130–131.

[22] Other ethnonyms that one finds applied to foreign merchants include "*man*" 蠻, which was often applied generically to non-Han peoples in southern China, and "*lao*" 獠, usually denoting non-Han peoples from southeast Asia.

[23] See Richard W. Bulliet, *Conversion to Islam in the Medieval Period: An Essay in Quantitative History* (Cambridge, MA and London: Harvard University Press, 1979), pp. 16–32, which describes a process that at times led to resistance and rebellion, but was nevertheless overwhelmingly successful.

[24] Schafer, "Iranian Merchants in Tang Dynasty Tales," pp. 404–405.

[25] Du You, *Tong dian*, zhuan 193, p. 1044.

early.[26] The first Chinese description of Islam of which I am aware comes from Du Huan, though it not named as a religion but rather presented as the religious practices of the Arabs:

The gentlemen and women of this place are tall and well-built. They wear fine and clean garments, and their manners are gentle and elegant. When women go outdoors, they must cover up their faces with veils. Five times a day all the people, whether humble or noble, pray to Heaven. They eat meat as a religious observance, and they consider the killing of animals merit-worthy. They wear silver belts decorated with silver knives. They prohibit wine and music. When they quarrel, they do not come to blows. There is also a prayer hall which holds tens of thousands. Every seven days the king attends the prayers, mounts a high seat and expounds the religious law to the people, saying: "Men's life is very hard; this is a way of Heaven that would not change. If you commit one of the following crimes – lewdness, kidnapping, robbery, mean actions, slander, self-gratification at the expense of others, cheating the poor and oppressing the humble – your sins are among the most heinous. Those who are killed in battle by the enemy will be reborn in Heaven; those who kill the enemy will enjoy unlimited good fortune (on Earth)."[27]

There are also claims, mainly in stelae dating from the fourteenth century and beyond, of Tang origins for China's most ancient mosques, namely those in Guangzhou, Hangzhou, Yangzhou, Quanzhou and Xi'an (Tang Chang'an), and also for the Lingshan Holy Tomb (Lingshan sheng mu 靈山聖墓) in Quanzhou. In none of these cases is there Tang evidence for these early dates, and the scholarly consensus is that none of them predates the Song.[28]

---

[26] Leslie, *Islam in Traditional China*, pp. 70–75; Drake, "Mohammedanism in the T'ang Dynasty," pp. 23–28.

[27] Hyunhee Park, *Mapping the Chinese and Islamic Worlds*, pp. 26–27, citing Du You, *Tong dian zhuan* 193, p. 1044. Du You, in his general treatment of Dashi, presents a truncated version of these practices as the "law of the Arabs" (Dashi fa 大食法). *Tong dian zhuan* 193, p. 1041.

[28] See Leslie, *Islam in Traditional China*, pp. 40–48; Drake, "Mohammedanism in the T'ang Dynasty," 28–33 (treating only Guangzhou, Hangzhou and Chang'an), and Lo Hsiang-lin, "Islam in Canton in the Sung Period: Some Fragmentary Records," in F. S. Drake, ed., *Symposium on Historical Archaeological and Linguistic Studies in Southeast Asia* (Hong Kong: Hong Kong University Press, 1967), p. 179. Yang Hongxun 楊鴻勛, "A Preliminary Discussion on the Building Year of Quanzhou Moslem Holy Tomb and the Authenticity of Its Legend," in *The Islamic Historic Relics in Quanzhou*, edited by the Committee for the Preservation of Quanzhou Islamic Sites and the Chinese Cultural Historical Sites Research Center (Fuzhou: Fujian People's Publishing House, 1985), makes the case for a Tang date for the Lingshan Holy Tomb, which according to tradition is that two of the companions of Saad Wakkas but he is persuasively refuted by Su Jilang 蘇基朗 [Billy K. L. So] in "Lingshan sheng mu niandai kaobian" 靈山聖墓年代考辨, in Su Jilang, *Tang Song Minnan Quanzhou shidi lungao* 唐宋時代閩南泉州史地論稿 (Taipei: Taiwan Shangwu yinshuguan, 1992), pp. 62–94. Su dates the tomb to the Southern Song or Yuan.

There are, finally, Persian and Arabic sources claiming a Muslim presence in Tang China, and here we are more fortunate. The Arab physician and geographer Sharaf al-Zaman al-Marzawi (d. 1120) described a group of Shi'a Muslims fleeing Sunni persecution in Khurasan during the late Umayyad (c. 740s) who came to China and settled on an island in a river across from a large port (a port that, Schafer speculates, was Guangzhou) and continued in existence there for some time.[29] While plausible – the Shi'ites in Khurasan suffered persecution by the Umayyads and could well have fled to China – the lack of any corroboration from Chinese sources leaves the story's veracity in doubt.

Very different is the account of Muslim merchants in Khanfu (Guangzhou) from the *Akhbar al-Sin wa-'l-Hind* (*Account of on China and India*). This work is actually a collection of three documents with separate authors that was compiled by Abu Zayd al-Sirafi in 916. The account comes from a section written in 851 by an anonymous merchant who had been to India and quotes a merchant named Sulayman about China:

Sulayman the merchant reported that, in Khānfū, the meeting place of the merchants, there was a Muslim man appointed by the ruler of China to settle cases arising between the Muslims who go to that region and that the Chinese King would not have it otherwise. At the time of the 'Ids, this man would lead the Muslims in prayer, deliver the sermon, and pray for the Sultan of the Muslims. The Iraki merchants, Sulayman added, never dispute any of the judgments issued by the holder of this office, and they all agree that he acts justly, in accordance with the Book of God, mighty and glorious is He, and with the laws of Islam.[30]

This quotation, which is found in a collection of observations about China, is very like descriptions of Muslim merchant communities elsewhere in Asia, and is widely accepted as authentic.[31] It is, to my

---

[29] Hourani, *Arab Seafaring*, p. 63. Schafer's speculation, based upon Hourani, is in Edward H. Schafer, *The Golden Peaches of Samarkand: A Study of T'ang Exotics* (Berkeley, CA: University of California Press, 1963), p. 15.

[30] Abu Zayd al-Sirafi, *Account of China and India*, edited and translated by Tim Mackintosh-Smith, in *Two Arabic Travel Books*, Philip F. Kennedy and Shawkat M. Toorawa, eds. (New York, NY: New York University Press, 2014), p. 31. See also S. Maqqbul Ahmad, *Arabic Classical Accounts of India and China* (Calcutta: Indian Institute of Advanced Study, 1989), No. 12, pp. 37–38, and *Akhbar al-Sin wa 'l-Hind. Relation de la Chine et de l'Inde, rédigée en 851*, Arabic text, French translation and notes by Jean Sauvaget (Paris: Belles Lettres, 1948), p. 7; and Park, *Mapping the Chinese and Islamic Worlds*, pp. 64–72. For an excellent discussion of the complex authorship of *Akhbar al-Sin wa 'l-Hind*, see also Drake, "Mohammedanism in the T'ang Dynasty," pp. 17–22. His translation of the passage quoted is given on pp. 19–20.

[31] See Elizabeth Lambourn, "India from Aden: *Khutba* and Muslim Urban Networks in Late Thirteenth-Century India," in Kenneth R. Hall, ed., *Secondary Cities and Urban Networking in the Indian Ocean Realm, c. 1400–1800* (Lanham, MD: Rowman & Littlefield Publishers, 2008), pp. 55–98.

knowledge, the first reliable description of the practice of Islam in China, but describes it as a practice limited to the foreign merchant community. As we shall see, that insularity of religious practice characterized Islam in the port cities of China throughout the period covered by the book.

Abu Zayd al-Sirafi is also responsible for our only account of an Arab in Tang China. Ibn Wahb al-Qurashi was a native of Basra and a member of the family of Muhammad who, after the sacking of Basra by the Zanj in 871, went to Siraf. There he came across a ship departing for China, and on a whim embarked. On arrival in Guangzhou or Khanfu, as it was known to the Arabs, he further decided to proceed to the capital in hope of an imperial audience. Arriving after a journey of two months, he submitted petitions announcing himself as a descendent of the "prophet of the Arabs." The emperor, in response to his petitions, ordered the governor of Khanfu "to make investigations and inquiries among the Arab merchants about Ibn Wahb's alleged kinship with the prophet of the Arabs." After receiving a positive report, the emperor granted an audience – described in detail and involving back-and-forth exchanges via the interpreter – which dealt with Islam and its prophets, the states of western Asia, the age of the world and Ibn Wahb's reasons for coming to China. The emperor then plied him with gifts, ordered the use of post horses for his return to Khanfu, and instructed the governor there to treat him with honor until his departure. Ibn Wahb further gave Abu Zayd a description of Chang'an that included such realistic details as the east/west division between official households and merchants and commoners.[32]

This is a curious story. That an elderly man – described as being of advanced years but with his senses intact – who was neither an emissary nor a merchant, but an individual whose claim to fame was his religious lineage, would travel to China and then succeed spectacularly is implausible, and there are elements of the story that particularly defy belief. Notably, it is unthinkable that the Tang emperor would say, as Ibn Wahb reports, that he esteems only five kings: first and foremost the king of Iraq, who is "at the center of the world," with "the other kings ... ranged about him."[33] However, other parts of the account have the ring of veracity,

---

[32] Abu Zayd al-Sirafi, *Account of China and India*, pp. 79–87. See also Sulayman al-Tajir, *Ancient Accounts of India and China, by Two Mohammedan Travellers: Who Went to Those Parts in the 9th Century; Translated from the Arabic, by the Late Learned Eusebius Renaudot: With Notes, Illustrations and Inquiries by the Same Hand* (London: printed for Sam. Harding at the Bible and Author on the Pavement in St. Martins-Lane, 1733), pp. 51–59, and M. Reinaud, *Relations des voyages faits par les Arabes et les Persans dans l'Inde et à la Chine au IXe siècle de l'ère Chrétienne*, Tome 1 (Paris, 1895), pp. 79–91.

[33] Abu Zayd al-Sirafi, *Account of China and India*, pp. 79–81. The translator Timothy Mackintosh-Smith also comments on the implausibility of this claim, suggesting that it

such as a remarkably accurate description of Chang'an, which Ibn Wahb provides to Sulayman.[34] I would accept the basic outline of the story, but with the understanding that it was creatively shaped for its Arab audience. But in terms of our concern about Arabs living in China, it is noteworthy that the merchants of Khanfu are represented as an established group who, when consulted about Ibn Wahb, are able to vouch for his identity.

The Way to China and Its Trade

It is remarkable that the Tang–Abbasid trade existed at all. The sea route from Basra to Guangzhou was over 6000 miles in length, complex and treacherous (see Map 1). That a direct link not only existed but flourished during the Abbasid period is attributable to three factors. The first was the existence of a ship that was capable of making the voyage on a regular basis, namely the Arab dhow – known in southeast Asia as the Kunlun ship – characterized by sewn rather than nailed planking and, until the eleventh century, the only sea ship capable of such journeys.[35] That such ships actually made their way to China has been demonstrated by two discoveries of shipwrecked dhows of likely west-Asian origin. The Belitung shipwreck, whose remarkable cargo of ceramics was described earlier, was discovered in 1998 off the coast of the island of Belitung, which lies between Sumatra and Borneo (see Map 2). It has been dated to after 826 and, given its overwhelmingly Chinese cargo, had clearly come from China.[36] Then, in 2013, a remarkably well-preserved dhow was discovered in the Thai province of Samut Sakhon at the northern edge of the Gulf of Thailand.[37] Known as the Phanom Surin shipwreck and preserved in a mangrove swamp that preserved timbers, ropes and

---

was the result of an overly diplomatic interpreter or that Ibn Wahb was using the opportunity to make a point about his own society (p. 11).

[34] Abu Zayd al-Sirafi, *Accounts of China and India*, pp. 85–87.

[35] Pierre-Yves Manguin, "Trading Ships of the South China Sea," *Journal of the Economic and Social History of the Orient* 36.3 (Aug. 1993), pp. 253–280.

[36] Michael Flecker, "A Ninth-Century Arab or Indian Shipwreck in Indonesian Waters," *International Journal of Nautical Archaeology* 29.2 (2000), pp. 199–217, and Flecker, "A Ninth Century Arab or Indian Shipwreck in Indonesia: First Evidence for Direct Trade with China," *World Archaeology* 32.3 (February 2001), pp. 335–354.

[37] John Guy, "The Phanom Surin Shipwreck, a Phalavi Inscription, and Their Significance for the History of Early Lower Central Thailand," *Journal of the Siam Society*, 105 (2017), pp. 179–196, reporting on the excavations of 2014 and 2015. See too, Abhirada Pook Komoot, "Recent Discovery of a Sewn Ship in Thailand: Challenges," Proceedings of the Underwater Archaeology in Vietnam Southeast Asia: Cooperation for Development, Quang Ngai, Vietnam, 2014; "Up from the Deep: The Discovery of a 1,000-Year-Old Arab-Style Ship in Samut Sakhon May Give a Clearer Picture of Life and Trade during the Dvaravati Period," *Bangkok Post*, March 6, 2014. www.bangkokpost.com/lifestyle/interview/413237/up-from-the-deep.

wadding materials, it has been dated to the late eighth century, and its cargo – while not large – was revealing. It included ceramics from Guangdong, the Mon-speaking areas of Thailand, and the Persian Gulf, and, most remarkably, an inscription on a Persian jar in the Persian Pahlavi script. The inscription, which reads "*Yazd-bozed*"– a proper name, presumably for the merchant aboard the ship or perhaps the producer of the jars – is the earliest Pahlavi inscription to be found in south, southeast or east Asia, and points to the role of Persian merchants in the trade between western Asia and China.[38] The two heads of west Asians – one incised onto a brick and the other terracotta – both discovered in Thailand and dating to the eighth century (Figures 1.3 and 1.4), provide yet further evidence for a Persian presence in southeast Asia.

The second factor was the Asian monsoon, an annual weather pattern that both facilitated and conditioned long-distance travel in Asian waters. Specifically, the prevalence of southwest-to-northeast winds in the summer months and northeast-to-southwest winds in the winter months did not simply facilitate west-to-east and east-to-west travel, respectively, but also made possible the traversal of vast stretches of sea in the Indian Ocean by significantly shortening travel times.[39] Third was the trade itself, which was based upon the demands by the rulers and ruling classes of two great and prosperous empires for precious goods from the other end of Asia. We shall return to this trade, which constituted the lifeblood of the maritime merchants. Suffice it to say that both textual and archaeological evidence bear witness to a vital and flourishing commerce.

It should be stressed that west Asian merchants were not alone in their commercial endeavors. From the Han into the early Tang, China's most important sea trade was with the states of southeast Asia, and in the port cities the Kunlun merchants of that region predominated. According to Wang Gungwu, by the mid-eighth century a transition was underway in which the Kunlun merchants were giving way to Persians and Arabs with their long-distance trade, a change that became fully apparent in the ninth century. It should be stressed, however, that there was always an active trade with southeast Asia, most particularly with Srivijaya, the maritime power centered in eastern Sumatra, either in the course of travel between China and west Asia, as in the case of the two shipwrecks, or exclusively between China and southeast Asia.[40]

---

[38] Guy, "The Phanom Surin Shipwreck," pp. 183–190.
[39] Abu-Lughod, *Before European*, pp. 253–259.
[40] Wang, "The Nanhai Trade," pp. 103–104. Srivijaya, the dominant southeast Asian power from the late seventh to early eleventh century, was also a favored trading partner of the Tang. See Kenneth Hall, *A History of Early Southeast Asia: Maritime Trade and*

Figure 1.3 Graffiti-caricature of a west Asian merchant on a brick, early
eighth century
(courtesy of Fine Arts Department and John Guy)

By the ninth century, the knowledge of how to accomplish this lengthy
voyage was sufficiently widespread to result in descriptions of the route in
both Chinese and Arabic. In his "Route to Foreign Countries across the
Sea from Guangzhou" (Guangzhou tong haiyi dao 廣州通海夷道) from

Societal Development, 100–1500 (Lanham, MD: Rowman and Littlefield Publishers,
2011), pp. 109–120.

Figure 1.4 West Asian merchant head, eighth century
(courtesy of Fine Arts Department and John Guy)

801, the statesman and geographer Jia Dan 賈耽 (729–805) provided
a highly accurate sailing itinerary from Guangzhou to Baghdad, not only
with the primary route past Sumatra and Ceylon and on to the Persian
Gulf, Basra and Baghdad, but also providing alternate routes through
southeast Asian waters, and a further route skirting the Arabian
Peninsula and going down to the northeastern coast of Africa.[41] This
itinerary, which was excerpted from his now-lost 40-chapter geography of
the world, was clearly based on the reports of mariners who had come to

[41] XTS 43B, pp. 1146, 1153–1155. Among the many treatments of this important docu-
ment, see Frederick Hirth and W. W. Rockhill, trans., *Chau Ju-kua*, pp. 9–15, Wang,
"The *Nanhai* Trade," pp. 104–105, and especially Park, *Mapping the Chinese and Islamic
Worlds*," pp. 29–34.

China, who had made their way to the capital, for Jia himself was not a traveler and had not even served in Guangzhou.[42]

As valuable as Jia Dan's itinerary is, the Arab accounts are more useful for our purposes, drawing directly as they do on the accumulated knowledge of the west Asian mariners. Both the anonymous traveler writing in 851 (in *An Account of China and India*), whose description of the Muslims in Guangzhou was cited above, and the slightly later *Book of Routes and Realms* (*Kitab al-Masalik wa-l-mamalik*) of Ibn Khurradadbih (d. 885) offer detailed descriptions of the route from the Persian Gulf to Khanfu (Guangzhou).[43] The geographical information offered by the two is similar, and while *The Book of Routes and Realms* is more scholarly and authoritative, we will use the *Account of India and China*, since, as an example of *rihla* or travelogue literature, it is more likely to reflect the information actually used by Arab and Persian mariners.[44] After describing the primary western terminus Siraf (where goods from al-Basra and al-Ubullah were transshipped) and the sometimes-dangerous journey (owing to pirates and reefs) through the Persian Gulf, the ships cut across the ocean to the port of Kollam Malay on the southwestern coast of India,[45] where large China-bound ships were assessed a toll of 1000 *dirhams* (in contrast to other ships, which were assessed only 10 or 20 *dirhams*) (see Map 1). From there, the China-bound ship skirted the southern coast of Ceylon, made for the Nicobar Islands in the Bay of Bengal to replenish food and water, stopped at Kalah Bar in Malaya, passed through the Malacca Straits, made additional stops at the island of Tiyumah, Sanf in Champa and the nearby island of Sanf Fulau, and finally headed to Khanfu. The account further notes that the south China coast had a reputation for dangerous reefs and storms. The author provided a general timetable for the whole trip: roughly a lunar month (29–30 days) for each of the four legs of the trip, marked by Kollam Malay, Kalah Bar, Sanf and Khanfu. With stops, the whole trip would take around six months.[46] The most striking feature of this account

---

[42] See Jia's biography in XTS 166, pp. 5083–5085.

[43] Park, "The Delineation of a Coastline," pp. 83–86 on *The Book of Routes and Realms* and pp. 87–88 on *An Account of China and India*. Both are translated in Ahmad, *Arabic Classical Accounts*, while the latter has been newly translated in Abū Zayd al-Sīrafī, *Accounts of China and India*.

[44] See Raphael Israeli's discussion of the differences between the *rihla* accounts and the formal geographical works, such as *The Book of Routes and Realms*, which were organized according to *iqlims* (formal geographic units), in "Medieval Muslim Travelers to China," *Journal of Muslim Minority Affairs*, 20.2 (2000), pp. 315–317.

[45] The port of Quilon in modern Kerala, according to Ahmad, *Arabic Classical Accounts*, p. 38.

[46] Ahmad, *Arabic Classical Accounts*, Nos. 13–16, pp. 38–40; *Akhbar al-Ṣin wa-'l-Hind*, pp. 7–9; and Hourani, *Arab Seafaring*, pp. 69–75.

is how unremarkable it is. The route it describes was lengthy and complex but also well known and frequently traveled.

Khanfu was not the end of the road for many of the Arab and Persian merchants who made their way to China. In its account of the route to China, *The Book of Routes and Realms* has merchants stopping first at Luqin (Annan or Hanoi), then at Khanfu, then Khanju (Quanzhou), and then Qantu (Yangzhou) at the beginning of the Grand Canal.[47] Yangzhou was a major emporium for inter-Asian trade, with substantial populations of Arabs and Persians, which will be discussed later. There is evidence, moreover, that Persian merchants were active not only in the ports but in many Tang cities,[48] this in marked contrast to the Song period, when foreign merchants were restricted to designated port cities.

It was, of course, the wealth of exotic and much sought-after goods that caused this travel. Consider Ibn Khurradadbih's catalog of the goods to be had from across maritime Asia in *The Book of Routes and Realms*:

As for what can be exported from the Eastern Sea, from China we obtain white silk (*harīr*), coloured silk (*firand*) and damasked silk (*kīmkhāw*), musk, aloes-wood, saddles, marten fur (*sammūr*), porcelain, *sīlbanj* [a narcotic drug], cinnamon and galangal [*khūlanjān*, a spice and medicament]. From Wāqwāq we get gold and ebony; from India, various kinds of aloes-wood, sandalwood, camphor and camphor-water, nutmeg, cloves, cardamom, cubebs, coconuts, cloth made with grass, cloth made with cotton velvet, elephants. From Sarandīb all sorts of rubies and similar stones, diamonds, pearls, crystal and emery used in polishing metals; from Malay and Sindān, pepper; from Killah, the tin called *qala'y*; from the Southern regions, sappan-wood for tanning and dyeing, and *dādhī* [hypericum, used for making wine stronger and more aromatic]; from Sind, *qust* [an aromatic plant], rotang and bamboo.[49]

Among this plethora of goods, two stand out. Ever since Roman times, silks from China had been highly sought after throughout the Eurasian world, and the fact that Ibn Khurradadbih begins his list with three varieties of Chinese silk bears witness to the demand for it in Abbasid society. Second is porcelain, which was described by the author of *Account on India and China*: "They have excellent cohesive green clay, out of which they manufacture goblets as thin as flasks, through which sparkle one sees the sparkle of water can be seen."[50] However, if

---

[47] Park, *Mapping the Chinese and Islamic Worlds*, pp. 61–62.

[48] Schafer, "Iranian Merchants," p. 408.

[49] Pier Giovanni Donini, *Arab Travelers and Geographers* (London: Immel Publishing, 1991), p. 53, citing p. 51 of M. J. De Goeje's translation of *Kitab al-Masalik wa-l-mamalik*.

[50] Ahmad, *Arabic Classical Accounts*, No. 34, p. 46; *Akhbar al-Ṣin wa-'l-Hind, Relation de la Chine et de l'Inde, rédigée en 851*, p. 16. In a note, Sauvaget cites the claim by Paul Pelliot that this is the first description of porcelain in the west.

the Belitung shipwreck is any guide, porcelain constituted only a small portion of the ceramic goods that made their way west. Among the 60,000 artifacts excavated from this shipwreck, 400 were porcelain, which Regina Krahl identifies as referring to the translucent Xing ware from Hebei,[51] but there were also green-splashed wares from Henan, celadon from Zhejiang, and, most importantly, stoneware from Changsha in Hunan, of which there were 57,500 objects, many of these clearly intended for west Asian consumption.[52] These include white ware cups and saucers of a style widely imitated in west Asia; blue-and-white wares from the Gongxian kilns in Henan, whose cobalt-blue was produced using cobalt presumably imported by Arab or Persian merchants; and Guangdong jars (Dusun jars) – large vessels in which were stored smaller ceramic pieces, lead ingots and fruit star anise – which have been found across maritime Asia, including one excavated from the floor of the Friday Mosque in Siraf and dating to 841 CE.[53] Some of the bowls from Changsha also have what appears to be roughly copied Arabic script. According to Chen Dasheng 陳達生, Tang kilns in the Hunanese city of Changsha were using imported Muslim ceramics as prototypes for the mass production of ceramics, including some with Arabic inscriptions, "expressly for export to foreign Muslim markets through the port of Yangzhou."[54]

---

[51] Regina Krahl, "Chinese Ceramics in the Late Tang Dynasty," in Regina Krahl et al., *Shipwrecked: Tang Treasures and Monsoon Winds* (Washington, DC: Smithsonian Institution, 2010), p. 49.

[52] John Guy, "Rare and Strange Goods: International Trade in Ninth Century Asia," in Regina Krahl et al., *Shipwrecked: Tang Treasures and Monsoon Winds* (Washington, DC: Smithsonian Institution, 2010), p. 20. The preliminary details of the Samut Sakhon shipwreck are intriguing, for its cargo included earthenware and stoneware from both China and Thailand, some shaped much like Middle Eastern amphorae, and at least one pot containing betel nuts ("Up from the Deep").

[53] John Guy, "Early Ninth Century Chinese Export Ceramics and the Persian Gulf Connection: The Belitung Shipwreck Evidence," *China-Mediterranean Sea Routes and Exchange of Ceramics prior to 16th century/Chine-Méditerranée Routes et échanges de la céramique avant le XVIe siècle* (Suilly-la-Tour: Éditions Findakly, 2006), pp. 14–18; Rosemarie Scott, "A Remarkable Tang Dynasty Cargo," *Transactions of the Oriental Ceramics Society* 67 (2002–2003), pp. 13–26; David Whitehouse, "Chinese Stoneware from Siraf: The Earliest Finds," in Norman Hammond, ed., *South Asian Anthropology: Papers from the First International Conference of South Asian Archaeologists Held in the University of Cambridge* (Park Ridge, NJ: Noyes Press, 1973), pp. 241–256. According to Whitehouse, large numbers of Chinese ceramics were found at the Sīrāf site dating from the early ninth century on.

[54] Chen Dasheng, "Chinese Islamic Influence on Archaeological Finds in South Asia," in *South East Asia & China: Art, Interaction & Commerce*, eds. by Rosemary Scott and John Guy, *Colloquies on Art & Archaeology in Asia*, No. 17 (London: University of London Percival David Foundation of Chinese Art, 1995), pp. 59–60. As Chen notes elsewhere in the article, many examples of these Tang-era Changsha-produced Muslim

As for imports into China, Han Yu 韓愈 (768–824) is evocative: "The commodities of the outer nations arrive daily: pearls and aromatics, rhinoceros and elephant [horn and ivory], tortoise shells and curious objects – these overflow in the Middle Kingdom beyond the possibility of use."[55] We must note that while demand was great for certain commodities such as frankincense and myrrh, which came exclusively from western Asia, the majority of those luxury goods for which the demand was seemingly insatiable had a variety of sources across the Southern Seas and occasionally in China as well.[56] These included rhinoceros horn, ivory, kingfisher feathers and, in fact, many of the goods that Ibn Khurradadbih attributes to India and southeast Asia. Yet increasingly during the Tang it was the Arab and Persian merchants who arrived with them at Chinese ports.

Special mention should be made of pearls, for which there was a ready market in both east and west. Since pearl beds were to found throughout Asian waters, no region had a monopoly on them. However, given the great esteem in which pearls – especially large and lustrous pearls – had across Asia, and their portability, it is not surprising that they played a significant role in international commerce. Indeed, as Edward Schafer has shown, Persian merchants in Tang China were typically regarded as very wealthy and bearers of (or seekers after) valuable pearls, not infrequently pearls with magical qualities ascribed to them.[57]

We have no way of even estimating the quantity or value of the trade that flowed between Chinese ports and the Persian Gulf during the Tang. During his tenure as prefect of Guangzhou, which began in 769, the refusal by Li Mian 李勉 (715–786) to extort bribes was credited with increasing the number of ships arriving from the Western Regions from four to five per year to over forty.[58] This development occurred when Guangzhou was still suffering from the aftereffects of the Arab-Persia raid of 758. But the corruption to which it alludes was ongoing; Jitsuzō Kuwabara has amply documented the reputation of a posting in Guangzhou for allowing the accumulation of fabulous wealth, and that might be seen as another measure of the great value of the trade.[59]

From the west Asian side, we can also cite the *Kitab 'Aja'ib al-Hind* ("Book of the Wonders of India," c. 950), a travel book by the sea captain

ceramics have been unearthed at archaeological sites in northern Thailand (pp. 55–58). See also Rosemarie Scott, "A Remarkable Tang Dynasty Cargo," p. 18.
[55] Schafer, *The Vermilion Bird*, p. 77, citing Han Yu, *Han Changli quan ji* 韓昌黎全集.
[56] Schafer, *The Golden Peaches*, pp. 170–171.
[57] Schafer, "Iranian Merchants in Tang Dynasty Tales," p. 415.
[58] JTS, 81, p. 3635; XTS, 81, pp. 4507–4508.
[59] Kuwabara Jitsuzō 桑原騭藏, "On P'u Shou-keng, Part 2," *Memoirs of the Research Department of the Tōyō Bunko* 7 (1935), pp. 48–55.

(*nakhuda*) Buzurg ibn Shariyar (c. 952) that tells of Ishaq bin Yahuda, a Jewish merchant from Siraf (Oman) who visited China between 882 and 912, and who upon his return had transformed his initial capital of 200 dinars into "a shipload of musk, silk, porcelain, jewels and other precious-stones and other wonderful Chinese merchandise. The musk, silk and porcelain alone were reported to have been worth 3 million dinars."[60] Buzurg also relates an account of an audience that Ishaq had with the ruler of Lubin (a Chinese province), at which the ruler asked him if he had seen such wealth as was evident in his court and also addressed Ishaq as *ya 'arabi* (Arab).[61] Apart from the evidence that Ishaq's story offers for the involvement of Jewish merchants in the China trade – something confirmed by accounts of a massacre in 879 that will be discussed later – a story like this, with its aura of wealth in both China and Siraf, surely helped establish the promise of the China market as a place where fabulous profits could be gained.

Tang Supervision of Maritime Trade

Throughout the medieval maritime world, local rulers and governments had a natural interest in the merchant ships that arrived on their shores, and their policies included patronage of the traders, taxation, forced purchase and free trade. In many cases the foreign communities themselves acted on behalf of the local rulers. Although he is writing about a later period, André Wink's analysis is pertinent: "More often than not typical diaspora communities like the Badija Naidus, the Sayyids of Golconda or the Mappillas of Malabar appear to have been rooted in the revenue collection and even to have been

---

[60] Buzurg, *The Book of the Wonders*, pp. 62–64. See also, Moira Tampoe, *Maritime Trade between China and the West: An Archaeological Study of the Ceramics from Siraf (Persian Gulf), 8th to 15th centuries A.D.* (BAR International Series 555, 1989), p. 124. This was not the end of the story of Ishaq. After Ishaq's arrival in Sohar, Caliph al-Muqtadir, the overlord of Oman, attempted to have him imprisoned and his goods seized. In response, Ahmad, the governor of Oman, mobilized the merchants of the port, who closed the markets and announced that ships would cease stopping at Sohar if Ishaq was arrested and taken to the Caliph, "for Oman (Sohar) is a town where many important and rich merchants of all countries are to be found, and they have no other guarantee of security than the justice ... and protection of the Caliph and his governors." In response, the Caliph relented and Ishaq was freed, though the caliph's eunuch seized some of his money and he had to reward Ahmad (Tampoe, *Maritime Trade*, p. 129). Ishaq subsequently left on another voyage to China, but his ship was seized in Sumatra and he was killed there. See also Denis Lombard, "Introduction," in Denys Lombard and Jean Aubin, eds., *Asian Merchants and Businessmen in the Indian Ocean and the China Sea* (New Delhi: Oxford University Press, 2000), pp. 1–2.

[61] S. D. Goitein and Mordechai Akiva Friedman, *India Traders of the Middle Ages: Documents from the Cairo Geniza ("India Book")* (Leiden: Brill, 2008), p. 124.

able to obtain access to court politics."[62] Even in western Asia, with its highly developed political institutions, governmental interest in maritime trade was confined primarily to a concern for revenue and the demand for specific goods, and was little involved in the encouragement of trade.[63]

In Tang China, by contrast, the role of the government was far more central. According to Wang Zhenping, the Tang central government was theoretically not involved in foreign trade. Rather, trade was overseen by the governors of Guangzhou (for the south seas trade; trade with Korea and Japan was largely channeled through Yangzhou), and on a more ad hoc basis by "commissioners for trading with foreign ships" (*shibo shi* 市舶使), who were typically eunuchs.[64] The latter represented the compelling interests of the imperial palace and imperial family in the luxuries provided by the maritime trade, and, as Edward Schafer has noted, these eunuch officials were notorious for their exactions and corruption.[65] Indeed, so prominent was the role that they played that the author of the *Account of India and China*, writing in 851, described eunuchs governing Guangzhou alongside the civil governors.[66]

That said, to foreign eyes the Chinese approach to imports seemed highly organized and even generous, as can be seen in the description of the Chinese procedures in *Account of India and China*:

As soon as the sea merchants put in to harbor, the Chinese take charge of their goods and transport them to warehouses, guaranteeing indemnity for up to six months, that is, until the last of the sea merchants arrives. Then three-tenths of the goods are taken in kind, as duty, and the remainder is returned to the merchants. Any goods that the ruler needs he also takes, but he gives the very highest price for them and pays immediately, so he does no harm to the merchants. Among the goods he buys is camphor, paying fifty *fakkūjs* for a maund, the *fakkūj* being a thousand copper coins. The same camphor, if

---

[62] André Wink, *Al-Hind. The Making of the Indo-Islamic World*, p. 67.

[63] Goitein, S. D., 1967. *A Mediterranean Society: The Jewish Communities of the Arab World as Portrayed in the Documents of the Cairo Geniza*, vol. 1 (Berkeley, CA: University of California Press, 1967), p. 269.

[64] Wang Zhenping, "T'ang Maritime Trade Administration," *Asia Major* 4.1 (1991): pp. 25–37; and Schottenhammer, "Guangzhou as China's Gate to the Indian Ocean," pp. 153–154. Many historians have argued that these "commissioners" were in fact the heads of formal superintendencies of maritime trade (*shibosi* 市舶司) such as those that existed in the Song. I am persuaded by Wang Zhenping that the *shibo shi* were officials sent by the court irregularly for special purchases of foreign goods, and that the superintendency as an institution did not exist in Guangzhou or elsewhere.

[65] *The Vermilion Bird: T'ang Images of the South* (Berkeley, CA: University of California Press, 1967), p. 77.

[66] Abu Zayd al-Sirafi, *Accounts of China and India*, p. 7. See also Ahmad, *Arabic Classical Accounts*, No. 37, p. 47; *Akhbar al-Ṣin wa-'l-Hind*, p. 17.

the ruler had not bought it, would be worth only half that price on the open market.[67]

Contemporary Chinese accounts are considerably more critical, with an emphasis on the abuses of local officials and eunuchs. To quote an imperial edict from 834, unusual in addressing the issue of maritime trade:

The foreign ships from the Southern Seas are come from distant countries, expecting the merciful treatment of our Kingdom. Therefore, the foreigners should of course be treated with kindness, so as to excite their gratitude. We hear, on the contrary, that of late years the local officers are apt to over-tax them, and the voice of resentment is said to have reached to the foreign countries. It is needless to say, we are striving to lead a life of frugality and abstinence. How should we desire the curious foreign things? We deeply feel sorry that those foreign peoples should be so uneasy, and even feel that the present mode of taxation is too heavy for them. We should allow them lenience, so as to invite the good-will of those peoples. To the foreigners living at Lingnan, Fujian, and Yangzhou, the viceroys of these provinces should offer consolations, and except for the already fixed anchorage-duties, the court-purchase and the regular presents, no additional taxes should be inflicted on them, allowing them to engage freely in their trade.[68]

Whether such imperial attitudes had much impact is questionable, for Chinese sources suggest that the actions of the early ninth-century prefect and Lingnan military governor Wang E 王鍔 were more representative:

On arrival of trade-ships from the western and southern seas, Wang E bought up all goods that were profitable, by means of which his family property exceeded that of the public treasury. He sent out every day more than ten boatfuls of horns, tusks, pearls and shells, which he had bought, under the name of common goods through all seasons without interruption.[69]

However different their perspectives, Arab and Chinese authors are agreed on the major role played by officials in the treatment of maritime trade, and that was a fact that stood in sharp contrast to other ports of Asia and informed the lives of the merchant communities residing in the ports of China.

---

[67] Abu Zayd al-Sirafi, *Accounts of China and India*, pp. 45–47. See also Ahmad, *Arabic Classical* Accounts, No. 34, pp. 46–7; *Akhbar al-Ṣin wa-'l-Hind, p. 16.*

[68] Kuwabara Jitsuzō, "On P'u Shou-keng, a Man of the Western Regions, Who was the Superintendent of the Trading Ships' Office in Ch'üan-chou towards the End of the Sung Dynasty, Together with a General Sketch of Trade of the Arabs in China during the T'ang and Sung Eras, Part 1," *Memoirs of the Research Department of the Tōyō Bunko* 2 (1928), p. 13, citing the *Quan Tang wen* 全唐文 75. I have converted the romanization to Pinyin.

[69] JTS 151, p. 4060. The translation follows that of Kuwabara, "P'u Shou-keng," Pt. 2, p. 55.

Merchant Life in China

As the edict of 834 clearly demonstrates, a number of cities served as the termini for ships arriving from the Nanhai (South Seas) and hosted foreign communities, though information about most of those communities is frustratingly sparse. We have already encountered Yangzhou, with its strategic location at the entrance to the Grand Canal, as the site of the 760 massacre of Persians and Arabs as well as the port from which Chinese-manufactured Muslim ceramics were exported. We also know that Jiaozhou (near modern Hanoi but then the southernmost port of the Tang empire) was an important port of call for Arab and Persian ships coming to China – Ibn Khurradadbih described Luqin, presumably Jiaozhou or its port, as having "Chinese stones, Chinese silk, Chinese porcelains of good quality, and rice"[70] and also that it prospered in the years following the Persian and Arab raid of Guangzhou in 758.[71]

For a glimpse of what life was like for the maritime merchants in China, we must turn to the emporium of Khanfu (Guangzhou). It was, in the words of Wang Gungwu, a large trading settlement or frontier settlement, inhabited by merchant-adventurers, foreign traders, and non-Han peoples of Guangdong, a city in which Han Chinese were a distinct minority.[72] Writing in the tenth century, al-Mas'udi described the remarkable geographical spread of the merchant community in Khanfu in the mid-ninth century. Within the city "there were buildings [with occupants] from Basra, Siraf, Oman, the cities of India, the islands of Zabedj (Java) and Sinf (?), and other realms, and they were stocked with their merchandise and cargoes."[73] The city was substantial enough to impress the Chinese monk Ganjin (Jianzhen 鑒真), who visited Guangzhou in 750 and marveled at the "enormous variety of races" there and offered this description: "The city has triple fortifications. The governor general commands six banners, each constituting an army, and their dignity is no different than that of the Son of Heaven [i.e., the emperor]. The city is filled with purple and crimson and it is surrounded by the press of the suburbs."[74] Such a respectful impression of this frontier outpost might well not have been shared by Chinese officials coming from the great cities of the north, but from the perspective

---

[70] Park, *Mapping the Chinese and Islamic Worlds*, p. 61, citing the *Book of Routes and Realms*.
[71] Schafer, *The Golden Peaches*, p. 77.   [72] Wang, "The Nanhai Trade," p. 46.
[73] Abu al-Ḥasan ʿAli ben al-Ḥusain al-Masʿudi, *Muruj al-dhahab wa-maʾadin al-jawahir* (*Meadows of Gold and Mines of Gems*), in Barbier de Meynard und Pavet de Courteille, *Les Prairies d'Or. Texte et Traduction* (Paris: Imprimé par autorisation de l'Empereur à l'Imprimerie Impériale, 1861), tome I, p. 303.
[74] J. Takakusu, "Aomi-no Mabito Genkai (779), *Le voyage de Kanshin en Orient* (742–754)," *Bulletin de l'École Française d'Extrême Orient*, Vol. 28 (1928), 466–467.

of Heian cities or the port cities across the expanse of maritime Asia, Guangzhou could well have looked magisterial.

Within Guangzhou, the foreigners – and the west Asians particularly – resided primarily in the "foreign quarter" (*fanfang* 蕃坊), under the authority of a foreign headman. Discrete residential quarters for foreign merchants were a common feature of ports across maritime Asia, so Arab readers would not have been surprised by Sulayman's description of Khanfu's Muslim community with its judge that was cited earlier. Chinese sources provide confirmation of this. Li Zhao, writing in the early ninth century, mentions a foreign headman (*fanzhang* 蕃長) who presided over the foreign traders and cooperated with the authorities in drawing up the manifests for the arriving ships.[75] Liu Xun 劉恂 of the late Tang described this encounter with the Guangzhou headman: "At the house of the *Fan-ch'iu* [*Fanqiu*] 番酋 (lit. foreign chief), I once ate the Persian dates brought over from his own country. The fruit had sugar-like colour, soft skin and flesh and tasted as if it was first baked and then boiled in water."[76] Since the Chinese sources almost always use the ambiguous "*fan*" for "foreigner," we generally cannot determine the ethnic identity of the headman, or even determine whether there was only one headman at a time, but in the case of Liu Xun's account the Persian dates strongly suggest that the "chief" was in fact west Asian.

The adjudicatory functions that Sulayman ascribed to the Muslim judge in Guangzhou are supported by an important Tang text. According to the sixth chapter of the *Tanglü shuyi* 唐律疏議 of 635,

As to the Hua-wai-jen [Huawairen] 化外人 (lit. men outside the Chinese influence = foreigners) living in China, all offences committed between persons of the same group shall be tried according to their customs and laws, but the offences committed between persons of different customs and laws shall be tried according to the Chinese laws.

The commentary elaborates:

By the Hua-wai-jen are meant those foreigners from countries (*guo* 國) with sovereigns. They each have different customs, and their laws are not the same. Therefore if the offenders be of one and the same group, they shall be judged according to their own laws and customs; on the other hand if the offenders be of different groups, for example a Kao-li [Gaoli] 高麗 man against a Pai-chi [Baiji] 白濟 man [both parts of Korea], they shall be judged according to Chinese laws.[77]

---

[75] Kuwabara, "On P'u Shou-keng," Part 1, p. 40, and Denis Twitchett and Janice Stargardt, "Chinese Silver Bullion in a Tenth-Century Indonesian Wreck," *Asia Major*, 3rd Series, 15.1 (2002), p. 63, both citing *Tang guoshi bu* 唐國史補 by Li Zhao 李肇, fl. 806–820.

[76] Kuwabara, "On P'u Shou-keng," Part 1, p. 40.

[77] Kuwabara, "On P'u Shou-keng," Part 1, pp. 45–46, citing *Tanglü shuyi* 唐律疏議, 6. The translation has been modified.

Whether such fine distinctions as those that were applied to Koreans in the Chinese application of extraterritoriality were also made of west Asians we cannot say for sure, but the evidence from Sulayman suggests that the Chinese authorities were content to recognize religious rather than geographic identity in their case.

That Guangzhou had a foreign quarter does not mean that foreigners – and their families – were content to live in it. In the biography of the infamous Wang E, whose commandeering of imported goods for his private gain was detailed above, the statement is made that "The Cantonese and foreigners (yi ren 夷人 or 'eastern barbarians') lived amongst each other [in the foreign quarter]. Because the land was undesirable, they sought to live in the river market [area]."[78] Far more informative is the remarkable account in the biography (or biographies; the versions in the *Old* and *New Tang Histories* vary slightly) of Lu Jun 盧鈞, who came to Guangzhou as prefect and military governor in 836, a generation after Wang E had been there. After describing how Lu had reversed the corrupt policies of his predecessors and governed honestly, thereby relieving the vexations of the foreign merchants, it describes his response to conditions in Guangzhou that he found unacceptable. Foreigners were living together and intermarrying with the Chinese, and many foreigners had bought rice fields and built houses. If the local authorities tried to interfere with them, they combined and rose in revolt. In response, Lu Jun enacted laws forcing the foreigners to live in a separate quarter (yi chu 異處) and forbade them from marrying with Chinese or acquiring land and houses.[79]

To some extent this account reflects the social fluidity of a frontier city, a fluidity that Lu Jun, good Confucian official that he was, was attempting to counter. In the same biography we are told that Guangzhou had become a place of exile where the children of disgraced officials who had been sent there found themselves stranded, unable to return even after pardons had been secured. Jun arranged for assistance for their medical and marital needs, in all helping several hundred families. After his three-year term, "several thousand Chinese and foreigners" requested that a shrine be built to honor Jun.[80] For our purposes, the critical

---

[78] JTS 151, p. 4060. XTS 170, 5169, in its biography of Wang, says much the same, but states that the Cantonese and Man 蠻 (southern barbarians) lived together. See also Kuwabara, "On P'u Shou-keng," Part 1, pp. 57–58.

[79] JTS 177, pp. 4591–4592 and XTS 182, p. 5367. The account draws from both versions of Lu's biography. It should be noted that there were no legal prohibitions to Chinese-foreign intermarriages. An edict from Zhenguan 2 (628) stated that all foreign envoys were permitted to marry Chinese (Han) women (Han funü 漢婦女), but they were prohibited from taking those wives with them back to their home countries. *Tang huiyao* 唐會要 (Taipei: Shijie shuju, 1968), 100, p. 1796.

[80] JTS 177, p. 4592 and XTS 182, p. 5367.

question is, who were the foreigners who were intermarrying and settling with the local population? Were they tribal peoples from Lingnan, merchants from southeast Asia or west Asians? The *Old Tang History* uses the term *man liao* 蠻獠 (both terms for southern peoples) to describe those who lived together with local inhabitants (*turen* 土人), and that could be taken to mean the local tribal peoples. However, it also talks about the Man ships (*manbo* 蠻舶) of the South Seas arriving in Guangzhou, while the *New Tang History* states that it was *fan liao* 蕃獠 who lived together with the Chinese (*Huaren* 華人), thus employing the character commonly used for west Asians.[81] From this evidence we can conclude that the maritime merchants were certainly among those who were intermixing with the local population in Guangzhou, and while we cannot say conclusively that these included Persians and Arabs, there is no reason why they should have been excluded. More broadly, the passage indicates that at least portions of the foreign merchant community had put down roots in Guangzhou and assumed settler rather than sojourner status. This was an important development, and foreshadowed the Muslim merchant communities of later centuries.

One limitation of the Tang–Abbasid sources for the merchant communities in China is that they give us no almost information about individual merchants or about their internal functioning. Apart from the invaluable account of the Guangzhou community with its Muslim judge in the *Account of China and India*, which has been discussed above, the remainder of the ninth-century portion of this work containing the accounts of Sulayman and other anonymous sources contains nothing about individual merchants or their lives. What is does present, however, is a wealth of descriptive material concerning China (and India, though only the Chinese parts concern us here). If we view this material as constituting the Muslim maritime community's collective knowledge of China, then an analysis of these texts can tell us a great deal about the community's social positioning and the kinds of information to which they had access.

The descriptions of China with which we are concerned come from the ninth-century portion of the *Account* (later in the work, Abu Zayd has some additional information from the tenth century) and cover a wide range of topics presented in 72 numbered items, most of which are short entries in *the Akhbar al-Sin wa-l-Hind* translation.[82] Some of the entries are devoted to maritime travel, Asian port cities and India, and some compare India

---

[81] The "several thousand Chinese and foreigners" who requested a shrine for Lu Jun were Hua 華 and Man 蠻.

[82] Ahmad,   *Arabic   Classical   Accounts*,   pp.   56–57;   *Akhbar   al-Sin wa-'l-Hind*, pp. 2–27. The only lengthy entry is number 72, which contains eleven brief

and China. However, most concern China, and among them certain subjects stand out by virtue of the frequency of their occurrence or the detail of their coverage.

The subject of commerce is an instance of the latter. Although treated in only three entries, these are among the longest entries in the work. They detail how officials processed and taxed the cargoes of arriving ships (#34, quoted earlier), the mechanisms for borrowing, lending and handling defaults (#44), and the serious consequences of bankruptcy (#45), all matters of the utmost importance for merchants. The credit practices, we might note, were based upon written agreements and were backed up by the force of the law for those who defaulted. Related tangentially to commerce are the accounts of Chinese buildings, which are described as having been built with wood (#60, 72) and therefore a cause of the fires common to Guangzhou. The result, we are told, was to increase the rarity of merchandise in the Sino-Arab trade, since it would burn in the warehouses.[83]

By far the two most frequently occurring subjects are government and the personal lives of the Chinese, and the former are largely skewed towards local government. Concerning the empire as a whole, we are told that the king of China has over 200 urban metropolises, each with its prince and eunuch (#33), and the king himself is described in only the vaguest of terms: as one of four kings of the world, beneath the Arab king but above the Roman king (#24), as lacking designated heirs (#54), and as secluding himself two months of the year in order to inspire awe among his subjects (#39). Concerning the functions of government at the local level, the entries are far more knowledgeable, reflecting the first-hand observations of Arab merchants. They describe local officials in some detail (#37, 38),[84] as well as taxation (incorrectly stating that the Chinese had no land taxes, only head taxes) (#40, 47), legal proceedings (#38, 58, 67), coinage (#34), schools (#48) and the documents required for travel around the empire (#43). One intriguing entry describes a public bell – to be found in every locality – that anyone who has suffered an injustice can

statements about China, most of which involve comparisons with India. This material is also treated by Park, *Mapping the Chinese and Islamic Worlds*, pp. 63–72. The Mackintosh-Smith translation in Abu Zayd al-Sirafi, *Accounts of China and India*, which I have used elsewhere, does not number these entries, so I am using Ahmad and *Akhbar al-Ṣwa-'l-Hind* for this section.

[83] This is No. 11 (Ahmad, *Arabic Classical Accounts*, p. 37; *Akhbar al-Ṣin wa-'l-Hind*, p. 6), which also mentions shipwreck, plunder while en route, and being blown off course to Yemen or other regions as other factors increasing the rarity of these goods.

[84] Although a number of the Arabic terms used cannot be linked to the Chinese names of offices, some can. A good example is *tasushi*, described as "a king ruling over a small town," which Sauvaget identified as *ts'ie-si* (*cishi* 刺史) or prefect. Ahmad, *Arabic Classical Accounts*, pp. 47, 69.

ring, and then present his grievance to the "prince." From Song Chinese sources we know that the Chinese indeed had such a public grievance system, though using drums rather than bells.[85] Finally, armies and warfare are mentioned only twice, and then briefly (#56, 72), a reflection of the largely pacific character of this world of commerce in the mid-ninth century.

The entries describing the lives of the Chinese present abroad and fascinating array of observations. Concerning appearances, we are told that the Chinese "are handsome and large," with skin "of a white hue and a tint of red" and very black hair, and also that women leave their hair uncovered, in contrast to the men, who cover theirs (#49), that all Chinese dress in silk, using multiple layers in the winter and a single layer in summer (#21) and that Chinese almost never have beards (#65). Food and the preparation of food is another common subject; the Chinese staples of wheat and rice, fruit trees, and the butchering of meat are all briefly described (#62, 72, 71). Most informative is #22, with its details of cooking and foods of all sorts:

Their food consists of rice, and sometimes they cook *kushan* [stew] which they pour over the rice and then eat it. The members of royal houses eat wheat bread and meat of all the animals and pork and even other animals. Among the fruits they have apple, peach, citron, pomegranate, quince, pear, banana, sugar-cane, melon, fig, grape, cucumber, glossy cucumber, crab-apple, walnut, almond, hazel-nut, pistachio, plum, apricot, sorb and coconuts. They do not have in their country many date-palms except a [solitary] date-palm tree in the house of one of them. Their drink consists of the intoxicating drink prepared from rice. They do not have wine in their country, nor has it been exported to them. They neither know about it, nor do they drink it. It is from rice that vinegar, intoxicating wine, sweetmeat and things resembling them are prepared.[86]

Other topics include marriage (#57, 61), illness and medicine (#46, 72), death and burial (#35), writing by all Chinese, "poor or rich, small or great" (#36), and the love of music (#55). Remarkably specific information is also given on toilet practices (#23, 71) and the males' lack of circumcision (#63), and the charge is made that Chinese "surrender themselves to sodomy with young slaves" (#59).

---

[85] See Edward A. Kracke, Jr., "Early Visions of Justice for the Humble in East and West," *Journal of the American Oriental Society* 96.4 (1976), pp. 492–498. He writes that grievance bells were attributed to various early west Asian and European rulers, including Charlemagne, the East-Roman Theodosius the Great and the Sasanian ruler Anusharvan the Just. The first reference to grievance drums in China comes from the early Zhou dynasty (c. 1000 BCE). Grievance bells also appear in east Asian records: from 647 CE in Japan and 1039 among the Khitans in north China.

[86] Ahmad, *Arabic Classical Accounts*, pp. 41–42; *Akhbar al-Şin wa-'l-Hind, p. 11.*

There are, finally, several references to Chinese religion: to their worship of statues (#64), the role of priests speaking for the statues (#70), and their practice of Buddhism, with its belief in the reincarnation of souls (#72). The most judgmental entry (#23) likens them to the Zoroastrians: "They eat carrion and other similar things, just as the Magians do; in fact, their religion resembles that of the Magians."[87] There is nothing, however, that would hint at any concern with proselytizing the Chinese.

Taken as a whole, these ninth-century descriptions of China and the Chinese reveal a remarkable breadth of knowledge, but knowledge with definite limitations. Against vague and at times fanciful ideas about the empire and monarchy, we have concrete and detailed accounts of those elements of government, law and products that one would expect from merchant observers. I would suggest that the accounts of the customs and activities of the people reflect a level of social and even personal intimacy that came from extended residence in Guangzhou, a residence which, as we have seen, included living among the Chinese and even intermarrying with them. At the same time, nothing in these accounts suggests any significant interaction with the local elite, with the exception of the "prince," probably the provincial governor, whose habits are described, perhaps as a result of official interactions, including banquets, held for the merchants.

About the interactions of the maritime merchants themselves we are almost entirely ignorant. We know from the *Account* that the Guangzhou Muslims had a chief who led them in prayers and delivered the weekly sermon (*khotba*). Whether the merchants had additional corporate practices we do not know as in southern and southeastern Asia, but Edward Schafer provides an intriguing glimpse of what he calls mutual benefit associations among Persian merchants.[88] In the three examples that he found in Tang tales, merchants gathered to socialize, compare their treasures, and in one case even to pool their resources to purchase a valuable pearl. In the most revealing story,

... the hero is invited by a group of his foreign friends in Ch'ang-an [Chang'an] to attend a meeting for the inspection of treasures: here he finds the various *hu* [Persian merchants] seated in a formal hierarchy significant of the relative value of their goods, and, as might be expected, the hero is found to have the

---

[87] Abu Zayd al-Sirafi, *Accounts of China and India*, p. 37; Ahmad, *Arabic Classical Accounts*, p. 42; *Akhbar al-Ṣin wa-'l-Hind*, p. 11.

[88] Although she is dealing with a late period, Elizabeth Lambourn provides an excellent account of Muslim corporate practices in cities on the west coast of India in "India from Aden," pp. 55–98.

most precious object of all and is honored by transference to the head of the assembly.[89]

Beyond this, we can speculate that the mechanisms for Islamic trade in west Asia and the Mediterranean were employed by the Muslim merchants in Tang Guangzhou. These included the universal and limited investment partnerships (*mufawada* and *'inan*), which offered a degree of financial security in the pooling of funds, and *commenda* contracts, in which an agent-manager was entrusted with capital or merchandise.[90] There were also corollary practices that "rendered possible the delegation of power and authority to associates, colleagues, and even strangers, as economic circumstances required," for example, by allowing an investor or merchant to entrust his goods to another, who would act for him in disposing of the goods and provide him with the proceeds at no charge.[91] Although this description is largely based upon eleventh-century sources from western Asia, it is highly likely that the Guangzhou Muslims made use of these practices – or some much like them – that relied upon trust and honor more than written contracts of the sort ascribed to the Chinese. As an example of the importance of ethics in commerce, we might cite the case of Abu'Ubayda 'Abdallah ibn al-Qasim, known as "al-Saghir" (the small), from a small Omani market town, who was involved in the China trade and traveled there, probably before 758. On one occasion, when he discovered that his partners in the aloes wood trade had disparaged a shipment of wood – probably from China – to drive down the price, and had then praised the same goods after purchasing them so as to drive up the price, he broke off the partnership.[92]

The Arab-Persian merchants in China were not simply isolated individuals pursuing wealth on their own, but part of a diaspora creating the most effective and integrated long-distance trade network that maritime

[89] Schafer, "Iranian Merchants in T'ang Dynasty Tales," pp. 416–417. As noted earlier, given the ambiguity of the term *hu* 胡, these merchants could be Sogdian rather than Iranian.

[90] Abraham L. Udovitch, "Commercial Techniques in Early Medieval Islamic Trade," in D. S. Richards, ed., *Islam and the Trade of Asia: A Colloquium* (Papers on Islamic History: II; Oxford: Bruno Cassirer, 1970), pp. 44–47. According to John H. Pryor, the *commenda* was very similar to the Muslim *qirad*, which involved a similar relationship between the provider of capital (capital-investor) and the user merchant (labor-investor), so in fact the Muslim merchants in China may have used *qirad* contracts. "The Origins of the Commenda Contract," *Speculum* 52.1 (1977), pp. 29–36. I am following Udovitch and employing the more familiar term, *commenda*.

[91] Udovitch, "Commercial Techniques in Early Medieval Islamic Trade," p. 59.

[92] M. Kervran, "Famous Merchants of the Arabian Gulf in the Middle Ages," *Dilmun, Journal of the Bahrain Historical and Archaeological Society*, No. 11 (1983), p. 21 and Tadeusz Lewicki, "Les premiers commerçants Arabes en Chine," *Rocznik orientalistyczny*, 11 (1935), pp. 178–181.

Asia had ever seen, and their success was to a large extent dependent upon shared values and mutual trust. At the same time, neither the trade nor the trading diaspora was a fixed entity. As we will see below, both underwent dramatic developments in the eighth and ninth centuries that had profound consequences for their subsequent histories in China.

The Waxing and Waning of the Settlements

Over the 700-year course of the Muslim communities that we are exploring in this book, the period of the late Tang was perhaps the most dramatic, marked by three traumatic events: the Arab-Persian raid on Guangzhou in 758, the massacre of Persians and Arabs in Yangzhou in 760 and the larger massacre of Muslims, Christians and Zoroastrians in Guangzhou in 879. These have all been mentioned earlier; here our attention will be focused upon how these events shaped the history of the west Asian communities in China.

Although there is no discernable connection between the events of 758 and 760, both occurred during the Rebellion of An Lushan 安禄山, which wracked the Tang from 755 to 763 and for a time threatened to topple the dynasty. The rebellion was fought out mainly in the north – most famously with the rebel capture of Chang'an in the sixth month of 755 and the flight of the emperor Xuanzong 玄宗 and his retinue to Sichuan – but the entire empire was profoundly affected, initially by the chaotic conditions that prevailed for the better part of a decade, since the initial rebellion spawned many local rebellions (especially after An's assassination in 757), and, in the longer run, by the multi-faceted weakening of the power of the central government.[93]

The Yangzhou massacre was in fact a product of this season of rebellion, for it occurred when so-called government troops, sent to put down the local rebellion of Liu Zhan 劉展, entered the city of Yangzhou, and in their looting and killing made the prominent Persian and Arab merchant community a particular target.[94] There is an interesting discrepancy among the four accounts of the massacre that sheds some light on the nature of that community. They are found in the biographies of the two Tang generals responsible for putting down a local rebellion. In the *Old* and *New Tang History* biographies of Zheng Jingshan 鄭景山, both state

---

[93] Among the many treatments of the rebellion, see Charles A. Peterson, "Court and Province in Mid- and Late T'ang," in Denis Twitchett, ed., *The Cambridge History of China, Volume 3: Sui and T'ang China, 589–906, Part 1* (Cambridge: Cambridge University Press, 1979), pp. 468–486.

[94] Peterson, "Court and Province in Mid- and Late T'ang," p. 482.

that "several thousand Arab and Persian merchants were killed."[95] By contrast, the biographies of Ma Shengong 馬神功 both mention only Persian merchants as having been killed.[96] Why were the Arabs omitted? I would argue that this reflects the long-standing nature of the Persian community in Yangzhou, to which Arabs were a recent addition. We know nothing about that community in the aftermath of the massacre, so we can only speculate as to length and extent of the damage visited upon it and the South Seas trade with which it was involved. There is one bit of evidence from the ninth century indicating that a discrete Persian community continued. The Japanese Buddhist monk Ennin 圓仁, who recounted a lengthy trip that he made to China (in a diary that remains an important source for information on late Tang China), described how, during his stay in Yangzhou in 839, an official solicitation for funds to repair a balcony at a local Buddhist temple resulted in a donation of 1,000 strings of cash (out of 10,000 needed for the repairs) from the "Persian state" (Bosiguo 波斯國).[97] The use of *guo* is curious, since it typically refers to a state. However, because of the local nature of the restoration project, it seems most likely that *Bosiguo* referred either to the Persians collectively (perhaps including Arabs) or else to a Persian headman who spoke for the community. In any case, Persians had clearly survived the 760 massacre.

In contrast to Yangzhou, Guangzhou in 758 was far from the scenes of rebel activity and the government was preoccupied with its campaign to take back the capital (accomplished with the help of Tibetan and Uighur soldiers), so this raid by Arabs and Persians in a frontier port seems to have elicited no reaction. The raid, an account of which began this chapter, is recounted in four places, two each in the *Old* and *New Tang Histories*. The least informative, from the *New Tang History* annals, simply says that Arabs and Persians "plundered" (*kou* 寇) Guangzhou.[98] In their treatises on Persia (and Persians), the two histories are largely in accord, describing how the two groups plundered the city, burning its warehouses and storehouses and then leaving by sea, though the *New Tang History* states that the Persians followed the Arabs in the "raid" (*xi* 襲), presumably coming from the sea, capturing the city of Guangzhou, and burning its storehouses.[99] The annals of the *Old Tang History* provide a very different account: "[Officials from] Guangzhou memorialized, [reporting] that soldiers from the countries of Arabia and Persia besieged the

[95] JTS, 110, p. 3313, and XTS, 141, p. 4655 and 144, p. 4702.
[96] JTS 141, p. 3533, and XTS, 144, p. 4702 and 144, p. 4702.
[97] Ennin, *Ennin's Diary: The Record of a Pilgrimage to China in Search of the Law*, Edwin O. Reischauer, trans. (New York, NY: Ronald Press, 1955), pp. 69–70.
[98] XTS, 6, p. 161.   [99] JTS, 15b, p. 5313, and XTS, 221B, p. 6259.

city, and the prefect, Wei Lijian 韋利見, abandoned the city and went into hiding."[100] Whatever their differences, all four accounts agree that this was indeed a raid and not a takeover of the city.

To return to the question with which we began this chapter, who were these raiders and from where did they come? Two suggestions – that they were the product of increased trade activity following the establishment of Baghdad as the Abbasid capital in 750,[101] or that they were disgruntled Arab troops sent by the Caliph to help Guo Ziyi (the loser in the Battle of Talas) to quell an insurrection – both seem highly unlikely, since neither theory explains how these groups would have made their way to the coast of China. That it was the work of unhappy traders also seems unlikely: they might have engaged in an urban riot, but the raid as described suggests plunder rather than simple destruction. Rather, the most likely explanation is that they were followers of the piratical strongman of southern Hainan, Feng Ruofang 馮若芳.[102]

In 749, the Chinese monk Ganjin, whose description of Guangzhou was quoted earlier, made unexpected landfall on Hainan Island, when the ship on which he was traveling almost sank in a typhoon.[103] Once there, he was escorted by the inspector general to Wan'an prefecture 萬安州 (modern Lingshui) in the far south, where he was entertained for three days by the prefectural chief, Feng Ruofang. According to Ganjin,

Feng Ruofang captured two or three Persian merchant ships every year, taking the goods for himself and the sailors ("equipage") as his slaves. The place where these slaves, men and women, lived was to be found three days to the north and five days to the south. The villages in that area became the home of the Persian slaves of Ruofang.[104]

This curious tale, dated just ten years before the Guangzhou raid, is supported by an entry in the early Song literary compendium, the *Taiping guangji* 太平廣記 of Li Fang 李昉, which recounts a Tang tale of one Chen Wuzhen 陳武振, whose mansion in Zhenzhou (modern Yaxian in southwestern Hainan) was filled with gold, rhinoceros horns, elephant's ivories and hawksbill turtles. The source of this wealth came from "merchants from the west" whose ships had foundered on the

---

[100] JTS, 10, p. 253.   [101] Abu-Lughod, *Before European Hegemony*, p. 199.

[102] This is the view of Schafer, *The Golden Peaches of Smarkand*, p. 16, who also describes the Guo Ziyi theory, ascribing it to Nakamura Kushirō in "Tō-jidai no Kanton," *Shigaku Zasshi*, 28 (1917), p. 354.

[103] This was in the course of Ganjin's fifth unsuccessful attempt to travel to Japan. On his sixth attempt, traveling on the ship of a Japanese emissary in 753, he finally reached Japan, where he proceeded to establish the temple (Tōshōdai-ji 唐招提寺) and found the Ritsu School of Japanese Buddhism.

[104] Takakusu, "Aomi-no Mabito Genkai," p. 462.

coast. His success in doing so was attributed to his *moude fa* 牟得法 (method of capture), which involved reciting incantations from a mountain when a merchant ship appeared so as to call up wind and waves and trap the ship on the coast.[105] This account is from the "magic" (*huanshu* 幻術) section of the compendium, and so one might question its reliability. However, the striking parallels with Ganjin's account make it likely that Feng Ruofang was the model for Chen Wuzhen, and it should be noted that the southern coast of Hainan lay right along the most common sea route from the south to Guangzhou. Perhaps most important, in recent years archaeologists have found conclusive proof of ancient Muslim communities dating to the Tang and Song periods in southern Hainan. Two abandoned Muslim cemeteries were discovered in coastal areas (one in Lingshui, the other in Yaxian) with numerous tombs and stelae with Arabic inscriptions. Although none of them provide dates, they may well be associated with an eleventh-century influx of Muslims into Hainan that will be discussed in the next chapter, some of them, stylistically at least, can be dated to the ninth century, and several have Persian titles, thus indicating a connection with the Tang community (see Figure 1.5).[106]

Returning to the raid of 758, were the Persians and Arabs shipwrecked merchants and seamen who had been captured by Feng Ruofang and perhaps operating under his command? Could they have been a group that had escaped from the clutches of Feng and were acting on their own? We can only speculate, but the very existence of these west Asians in Hainan, living outside of the normal bounds of Tang–Abbasid trade, makes them the likely candidates for those who undertook the piratelike raid of Guangzhou.

Whatever the identity of the raiders, the raid itself marked the beginning of a period of great difficult for the port of Guangzhou. Li Mian's praised tenure as governor of Lingnan, which, as we observed earlier, resulted in the increase of arriving ships from the Western Regions to over 40 per year, was the exception in the late eighth century. Earlier, in 763,

---

[105] Li Fang 李昉, *Taiping guangji* 太平廣記 (Song; Taipei: Xinxing shuju, 1962), 286, vol. 23/28a–b (p. 879). See Chen Dasheng, "Synthetical Study Program on the Islamic Inscriptions on the Southeast Coastland of China," in *Zhongguo yu haishang sichou zhi lu* 中国与海上丝绸之路 (*China and the Maritime Silk Route*), edited by Lianheguo jiaokewen zuzhi haishang sichou zhilu zonghe kaocha Quanzhou guoji xueshu taolunhui zuzhi weiyuanhui 联合国教科文组织海上之丝绸上之路综合考察泉州国际学术讨论会组织委员会 (Fuzhou: Fujian renmin chubanshe, 1991), pp. 167–168 and Chen Dasheng and Claudine Salmon, "Rapport préliminaire sur la découverte de tombes musulmanes dans l'île de Hainan," *Archipel*, Paris, 38 (1989), p. 80.

[106] Chen and Salmon, "Rapport préliminaire," pp. 75–106, and Chen, "Synthetical Study Program," pp. 165–166.

Figure 1.5 Tang Muslim tombstone from Hainan (Guangzhou Museum)

the Commissioner of Maritime Trade (a eunuch) got rid of the military governor and allowed his men to ransack the city.[107] Then, in 773, his successor was killed by a mutinous officer who held the city for three years. Order was restored in 775 when the general Lu Sigong 路嗣恭, with a force of 8000, took the city and killed 10,000 of his "fellow traitors." He also acted against the merchant community, executing those merchant ship crew members (*shangbo zhi tu* 商舶之徒) who had served the rebels and confiscating the family property of the merchants, worth several million strings, keeping that for himself rather than sending it to the capital. This displeased the emperor, who did not reward Lu for his military success.[108] Not surprisingly, it also soured the foreign merchants

[107] Wang, "The Nan-hai Trade," 81.
[108] JTS 122, p. 3500 provides the most detailed account, but it is also dealt with briefly in XTS 138, p. 4624. See also Wang, "The Nan-hai Trade," p. 81.

on Guangzhou as a port, with the result that Annan (Hanoi) became their favored port.

In 792, the court received a request from the governor of Lingnan to address the trade woes of Guangzhou by imperial fiat:

Lately, many sea-ships bearing precious and strange [goods] gone to Annan to trade in the market there. I wish to send an officer to go to Annan and close the market, and request that your imperial majesty send one central [government] official to accompany him.

Although the emperor was inclined to grant the request, it was countered by the minister Lu Zhi 陸贄, who in one of the clearest statements of market forces to be found in any Tang document, submitted that:

The merchants of distant countries merely seek profits and will come if treated with moderation, but would leave if constantly troubled. Guangzhou was always [the port] where various ships (i.e., merchants dealing in the Nanhai trade) assembled; now [the merchants] have suddenly changed their minds and gone to An-nan. If this was not due to excessive taxation and interference, it must certainly have been because [the Guangzhou officials] have not received them and guided them as they should have done.[109]

Lu argued further that, since Annan and Guangzhou were both part of the empire, it was unfair to discriminate against one in favor of the other. It is not clear whether there was an attempt to close the Annan port (the entry implies that the request was denied), but the fact is that in the ninth century Guangzhou was able to regain its dominant position in the maritime trade, and the Arabic *Account* that were analyzed above are a reflection of this, for they do not make any mention of the eighth-century troubles. Then came the massacre of 879.

Like the events of 758 and 760, the massacre came at a time of national convulsion caused by the rebellions of Wang Xianzhi 王仙芝 and Huang Chao 黃巢, which transpired during the years 874–878 and 878–884, respectively. In the judgment of Robert Somers, this lengthy period of rebellion was "... the final stage of a long period of social dislocation and widespread militarization that had begun many decades before."[110] Ironically, Guangzhou was an almost accidental victim, for when Huang Chao and his troops approached the city in the fifth month of 879, they were ending a long period of flight south from stronger

---

[109] Sima Guang 司馬光, *Zizhi tongjian* 資治通鑒 (Beijing: Zhonghua shuju, 1956), 234, pp. 7532–7533. Both translations are adapted from Wang, "The Nan-hai Trade," p. 82.

[110] Robert M. Somers, "The End of the T'ang," in Denis Twitchett, ed., *The Cambridge History of China, Volume 3: Sui and T'ang China, 589–906, Part 1* (Cambridge: Cambridge University Press, 1979), p. 179.

government forces that had begun some nine months before in Henan. After Li Tiao 李迢, the military governor of Guangzhou, refused to surrender, Huang's forces stormed the city and sacked it. Four medieval Arab authors have provided accounts of the plunder and killing, but those of Abu Zayd al-Sirafi and al-Mas'udi (896–956) are the most valuable. Abu Zayd's account is the earliest (c. 914) and the most detailed.[111] After describing Huang and the origins of the rebellion, Abu Zayd continues:

> In time, when his fighting capacity, the size of his forces, and his lust for power had grown strong enough, he marched on the great cities of China, among them Khānfū: this city is the destination of Arab merchants and lies a few days' journey from the sea on a great river where the water flows fresh. At first the citizens of Khānfū held out against him, but he subjected them to a long siege – this was in the year 264 [877–878] – until, at last, he took the city and put its people to the sword. Experts on Chinese affairs reported that the number of Muslims, Jews, Christians, and Zoroastrians massacred by him, quite apart from the native Chinese, was 120,000; all of them had gone to settle in this city and become merchants there. The only reason the number of victims from those four communities happens to be known is that the Chinese had kept records of their numbers. Huang Chao also cut down all the trees in Khānfū including all the mulberry trees; we single out mulberry trees for mention because the Chinese use their leaves as fodder for silkworms: owing to the destruction of the trees, the silkworms perished, and this, in turn, caused silk, in particular, to disappear from Arab lands.[112]

Al-Mas'udī's version largely agrees with Abu Zayd's, though it puts the number of those killed at 200,000, "a prodigious number of inhabitants." It also states that Huang's forces destroyed the mulberry plantations outside of Guangzhou, thereby striking at the silk trade, "as the destruction of mulberry stopped the export of Chinese silk to Muslim countries."[113] That the two accounts agree on Huang Chao's destruction of mulberry trees provides important testimony for the importance of silk as an export commodity during the Tang.

Although Abu Zayd's figure of 120,000 has been accepted at face value by many historians, perhaps because of the claim that they came from the Chinese census, it and al-Mas'udi's even larger figure are almost surely exaggerations. There is no suggestion in the *Account* from 851 that such

---

[111] See Levy's detailed study of the Arabic accounts of the massacre in the appendix to the *Biography of Huang Ch'ao*, pp. 109–121. The other Arabic accounts are by Mas'udi (*Muruj al-dhahab wa-ma'adin al-jawahir – Meadows of Gold and Mines of Gems*) (947), Ibn al-Athir (1160–1234), and Abu'l Fida (d. 1331).

[112] Abu Zayd al-Sirafi, *Accounts of China and India*, pp. 67–69. See, too, Levy, *Biography of Huang Ch'ao*, pp. 113–114.

[113] Abu 'l-Hasan 'Ali ben al-Husain al-Mas'udi, *Muruj al-dhahab wa-ma'adin al-jawahir*, tome I, pp. 302–305. Cited by Angela Schottenhammer, "Guangzhou as China's Gate to the Indian Ocean," pp. 135–136.

a great number of westerners had congregated in Guangzhou, a number that would have exceeded the populations of many of the leading cities in the ninth-century world. If one considers, further, that the only Tang statistic we have for the annual shipping traffic into Tang Guangzhou is for 40 ships (in the early 770s), it should be clear that there was no way for such a number to have been employed in Guangzhou, even if they could have made their way there.

That said, there can be no doubt that a tragedy of major proportions occurred at the hands of Huang Chao and his followers. For Abu Zayd, moreover, the consequences for the Arabs' maritime trade with China were profound. In his account, after describing how the Chinese appealed unsuccessfully to the Turkish King of Taghazghaz for help in putting down the rebellion, he writes of the trade:

Then [the Chinese] stretched out their hands, along with that [development], towards tyrannizing those of the [foreign] merchants who journeyed to [trade with] them. And when this happened, it combined in it the appearance of tyranny and aggression towards Arab ship captains and boat owners. Then they compelled the merchants [to do] that which was not binding upon [by legal agreement], and forcibly deprived them of their properties. They legalized that which custom had not hitherto allowed as a part of their activities. Then God, great be His name, completely stripped them of blessings. And the sea forbade its side [to passengers], and, by the decree emanating from the Almighty, blessed be His name, desolation befell the ship captains and guides [as far as] Siraf and 'Uman.[114]

Although we cannot corroborate the particulars of these Arab accounts with Chinese sources, what is important is the Arab sense of rupture, betrayal and loss (the loss of properties being no small matter for merchants). As we will see in the next chapter, they and (at least) many of their fellow merchants from across Asia departed China and moved their operations to southeast Asia. The massacre therefore marks the beginning of a period of transition that would result in the reconstitution of the Muslim communities in China, but with distinctly different parameters and practices, and quite possibly contributed to a transition to a more segmented long-distance trade, with fewer ships traversing the entire route from western Asia to China.

Reflecting on the Tang period as a whole, I would suggest that the west Asian merchants of Guangzhou occupied an anomalous position. As essential middlemen in a highly lucrative trade that fed a luxury market in China (especially at the court) and supported large-scale ceramic production well beyond southern China, they were the recipients of liberal government policies and were able to settle and flourish in

---

[114] Levy, *Biography of Huang Ch'ao*, p. 115.

Guangzhou (as well other cities like Yangzhou). Yet they were also at the mercy of extortionate demands by corrupt officials and, more seriously, they were the targets (and on occasion agents) of violence. This undoubtedly owed much to the frontier, colonial nature of Guangzhou in the Tang empire, where both eunuchs representing the imperial household, a primary consumer of imported luxuries, and the military were able to play outsized roles, the latter in both fomenting and suppressing uprisings. But the great wealth and racial and cultural foreignness of the west Asian merchants, when combined with their significant numbers, would also have made them easy targets. This element of violence seems to have been a characteristic of the period, for as we will see during the succeeding Song period (960–1279), large-scale violence involving the foreign merchants in the port cities of China was nonexistent.

2   The Reorientation of Trade

It is perhaps indicative of Tang preoccupations that the Guangzhou massacre of 879 is not mentioned in any contemporary Chinese sources. While Huang Chao's ransacking of the city is treated, if briefly, in the *Old* and *New Tang Histories*, it appears as an early part of the narrative of his rebellion, with Guangzhou another casualty of the rebels but with no acknowledgment of the economic costs that were entailed. In fact, the Huang Chao rebellion constituted a great rupture in the imperial fabric from which the Tang never recovered. By the time the rebellion was defeated in 884, the court had endured exile in Sichuan, faced the threat of other rebellions, and been forced to rely upon foreign troops in order to reestablish itself in the capital. Not only did the imperial appetite for exotic luxuries dry up, but in the south the breakup of the empire that was to result in the Ten Kingdoms of the Five Dynasties period (907–960) was under way.

For the maritime merchants of China's port cities, the massacre spelled the end of an era. As it happened, the Abbasids were facing their own challenges with the rebellion of the Zanj slaves in lower Mesopotamia in the early 870s (an event that drove Ibn Wahb out of Basra and eventually on to China) and the Qarmatian revolt, which broke out in eastern Arabia in 899.[1] However, according to G. S. P. Freeman-Grenville, the move of the capital from Baghdad to Samarra in 836 and then back to Baghdad in 892 resulted in large-scale building projects in both cities and a heightened demand for luxuries such as spices, silks, gold and slaves.[2] Thus, the maritime trade continued to flourish, with an undiminished demand for luxury items in western Asia. But through much of the ensuing century the primary maritime emporia were to be found in southeast Asia, with

---

[1] Rita Rose Di Meglio, "Arab Trade with Indonesia and the Malay Peninsula from the 8th to the 16th Century," in D. S. Richards, ed., *Islam and the Trade of Asia: A Colloquium* (Papers on Islamic History: II; Oxford: Bruno Cassirer, 1970), p. 106; and Hourani, *Arab Seafaring in the Indian Ocean*, p. 78.

[2] Buzurg, *The Book of the Wonders of India*, p. xxi.

the China trade conducted largely from afar. This had a significant impact on the states of southeast Asia and shaped the Muslim trade diaspora in important ways, so that when the merchants returned to China in numbers in the late tenth century, the new social order in Guangzhou and elsewhere differed from that of the Tang.

To be clear about what was involved, we must distinguish itinerant sojourning merchants who were constantly on the move from port to port (though, given the nature of Asian monsoons, that could still involve months of waiting in port) and those who took up residence in a port city.[3] The large numbers of west Asian merchants who, as we saw in Chapter 1, became resident in Guangzhou, Yangzhou and other Chinese cities did not do so casually. Given the vast distances involved in the Asian maritime trade and the need of large-scale merchants to warehouse goods, having a base in eastern Asia was essential, not only for their personal ventures, but for the sake of the itinerant merchants as well, both important elements of the trade diaspora. It was that base that they lost with the flight from Guangzhou.

Southeast Asian Transformations

In the wake of the Huang Chao massacre so vividly described by Abu Zayd, the Muslim merchants – and quite likely other foreign merchants as well – relocated their base of activities to southeast Asia (see Map 2). Although a number of port cities benefited from this, the most important of them was Kalah, which was probably located on the west coast of the Malay peninsula. I say "probably" because, while Kalah figures prominently in tenth-century Arabic accounts of India, China and southeast Asia, writers disagree considerably on specifics, including its location. They were agreed on its central position in maritime trade, that tenth-century Kalah served as a midpoint in the trip from Siraf and Oman to China. Writing c. 914, Abu Zayd described it as an island-city in the kingdom of Zabaj (from Java, but probably referring to Srivijaya) and "located mid-course between the land of China and the countries of the Arabs."[4] Likewise, Abu Dulaf (c. 940) described Kalah as being located

---

[3] See Kenneth R. Hall's treatment of this distinction in "Local and International Trade and Traders in the Straits of Melaka Region: 600–1500," *Journal of the Economic and Social History of the Orient* 47.2 (2004), pp. 237–238.

[4] Gabriel Ferrand, *Relations de voyages et textes géographiques arabes, persans et turks relatifs de l'Extrême-Orient du VIIIe au XVIIIe siècles*, 2 vols. (Paris: Ernest Leroux, 1913–1914), p. 83. For the identification of Zabaj with Srivijaya, see Wink, *Al Hind*, p. 341: "The term Zābaj before 860 refers to Java and the Shailendra dynasty, but after that date Zābaj is equated with Shrivijaya, the San-fo-ch'i of the Chinese, or with the entire Archipelago."

"almost halfway to China" from Oman.[5] Precisely where that was has been the subject of considerable debate, though the general consensus is that it was located somewhere on the west coast of Malaya.[6] It has also been associated with the state of Geluo 哥羅, which is mentioned in Chinese sources.[7]

Arab writers also disagreed about the political status of Kalah. As noted above, Abu Zayd described it as part of Zabaj or Srivijaya, as does the earlier *Account of India and China* (851), while Ibn Khurradadbih (d. 903) places it under the empire of Jabat al-Hindi, described by Tibbetts as a Hindu ruler in central Sumatra or even India.[8] Most different is the account of Abu Dulaf Mis'ar bin al-Muhalhil, who implausibly portrays Kalah as a virtual Chinese tributary state, albeit with a Muslim ruler: "The king is a vassal of the king of China, and makes the *khutba* in the name of the latter. The *qibla* of the king of Kalah is orientated towards him, and the house of prayer of the king of Kalah is dedicated to the king of China."[9]

Among the tenth-century writers, Abu Dulaf was one of the few who actually visited east Asia, so his writings about Kalah are important, but at the same time problematic. He was a poet from Yambo on the Red Sea who traveled to China around 940 as part of an embassy from the Saminid court in Bokhara, where he was serving. Following his return by sea (the embassy had gone to China by land), he wrote an account (*risala*) describing his travels. These were lost, so we know of them only from quotations in the writings of others. It may be, as Tibbetts has argued, that he never made the sea trip but drew his information about Kalah, which stresses Chinese elements, from Chinese traders that he

---

[5] Ferrand, *Relations de voyages et textes*, p. 96.

[6] According to G. R. Tibbetts, who meticulously compared all of the Arab accounts of Kalah, "A summary of all the information gleaned from the texts shows that Kalāh was an 'island' or kingdom situated on the sea route from India to China, some twenty or thirty days sail from south India and Ceylon and six days from the Nicobars, ten days from Tiyūma, 120 *zām* from Sribuza and two days from Bālūs." *A Study of the Arabic Texts Containing Material on South-East Asia* (Leiden and London: E. J. Brill, 1979), p. 121. The following discussion draws heavily from the extended treatment of Kalah on pp. 118–128, which includes a detailed analysis of the many theories concerning the location of the port. See, too, Michel Jacq-Hergoualc'h, *The Malay Peninsula: Crossroad of the Maritime Silk Road*, Victoria Hobson (Leiden: Brill, 2002), pp. 195–196, and Schottenhammer, "China's Gate to the South," p. 17.

[7] Geoff Wade, "Beyond the Southern Borders: Southeast Asia in Chinese Texts to the Ninth Century," in John Guy, ed., *Lost Kingdoms: Hindu-Buddhist Sculpture of Early Southeast Asia* (New York, NY: The Metropolitan Museum of Art; New Haven, London: Yale University Press, 2014), pp. 29–30.

[8] Ahmad, *Arabic Classical Accounts*, No. 15, p. 39 for *Observations*, and p. 6 for Ibn Khurradadbih; Tibbetts, *A Study of Arabic Texts*, p. 120.

[9] Tibbetts, *A Study of Arabic Texts*, p. 40.

encountered in China.[10] It also is possible that he traveled to Kalah with Chinese merchants and relied upon their linguistic knowledge and presumed expertise about the city.[11]

The most informative description of the evolving role of Kalah is that of al-Masʿudī, writing in the tenth century. Having described the Guangzhou massacre perpetrated by Huang Chao, he uses the example of an individual merchant to illustrate a new pattern of trade:

> It is said that a merchant of Samarkand, a city of Transoxiana, having left his country with a rich inventory, had come to Iraq. From there he went with his goods to Basrah, where he embarked for the country of Oman; then he went by sea to Kalāh, which is about half way to China. Today this city is the general meeting-point for the Muslim ships from Sīrāf and Oman, which encounter there ships from China. This was not so in the past, when Chinese ships reached Oman, Sīrāf, the coast of Fars (Persia), Bahrain, ʿUbullah and Basrah, and from these countries in turn [people] sailed directly to China. Because we can no longer rely on the justice of the [Chinese] rulers and the rectitude of their intentions, and because China's state has become as we described it, that [merchants] meet at this middle point. The merchant [from Samarkand] therefore embarked on a Chinese ship to go from Kalāh to the port of Khanfu.[12]

This passage is noteworthy on several grounds. The merchant's journey from Samarkand to Khanfu provides a rare glimpse of the actual route taken by a wealthy trader traveling on the ships of others. The statement about the past voyages of Chinese ships to Oman, Siraf and other ports is problematic, for there is no evidence from non-Arab sources to suggest that they had penetrated the Indian Ocean – let alone reached the Persian Gulf – by the tenth century. Following G. F. Hourani's argument that Arab references to "ships from China" referred to Persian ships that went to China, I would suggest that the "Chinese ships" referred to by al-Masʿudi could refer to ships from China making the direct voyage to the Persian Gulf, and so might be better rendered as

---

[10] *A Study of the Arabic Texts*, pp. 9–10, 124.

[11] Tibbetts' argument has its own difficulties. The Saminid embassy would have been to the Later Jin dynasty (936–947) in the north, far removed from the maritime trade, which, as we will see, was continuing in the Southern Kingdoms, so it is unlikely that Abu Dulaf would have had contact with Chinese traders in the capital of Kaifeng. On the other hand, if he made his way to the southern ports, where there assuredly were traders, then it would have made eminent sense for him to have returned home via the sea route.

[12] Abu al-Ḥasan al-Masʿudi, ʿAli ben al-Ḥusain al-Masʿudi, *Muruj al-dhahab wa-ma'adin al-jawahir*, tome I, pp. 307–308. See, too, the translation of this passage in Yokkaichi Yasuhiro 四日市康博, "Chinese and Muslim Diasporas and the Indian Ocean Trade Network under Mongol Hegemony," in Angela Schottenhammer, ed., *The East Asian "Mediterranean": Maritime Crossroads of Culture, Commerce and Human Migration* (Wiesbaden: Harrasowitz Verlag, 2008), p. 83. He identifies Transoxiana as Mawara al-Nah.

"China ships."[13] But however one understands the term, it points to a change much noted by maritime historians, from direct to segmented trade in the movement of goods between east and west Asia.[14] Finally, al-Mas'udi provides explicit confirmation of the Huang Chao massacre and subsequent unsettled conditions in Guangzhou as causing the rise of Kalah with its new pattern of trade, and in fact this argument was repeated in later Arab writings, such as those of the geographer Idrisi (c. 1156):

It is said that when state affairs in China were troubled by rebellions and when tyranny and confusion had become excessive in India, the inhabitants of China moved their commerce to Djāwaga and in other islands... It is for this reason that this island is so populous, and that it is so frequented by strangers.[15]

Idrisi's conflation of Djawaga with Kalah (or was he in fact speaking of a different port altogether?) underlines the difficulties posed by the Arabic sources, with their frequent inconsistencies and even contradictions. However, they agree in their depiction of a vibrant commercial culture in tenth-century southeast Asia, a portrayal that is supported by the less-numerous Chinese, Indian and archaeological sources. While Kalah occupied a position of primary importance, other ports flourished as well. In his *risala* the *Aja'ib al-Hind* (*Marvels of India*), the sea captain Buzurg ibn Shariyar (c. 952) frequently mentions the ports of Qaqullah, Fansur and Lambri (or Lamuri), in addition to Kalah.[16] Champa, strategically located on the sea route between China and maritime southeast Asia, was also an important location for trade and settlement by merchants, and we shall have more to say about it below.

Although not mentioned as a commercial center in Arabic sources, the Srivijayan capital of Palembang (or Sribuza) in eastern Sumatra was clearly a major port for west Asians and others, for through the ninth and much of the tenth century, Srivijaya's vassal states such as Borneo

---

[13] G. F. Hourani, *Arab Seafaring in the Indian*, pp. 46–50, especially p. 47. See, too, K. N. Chaudhuri, *Trade and Civilization*, p. 51; and Tansen Sen, *Buddhism, Diplomacy, and Trade*, p. 230.

[14] Chaudhuri, *Trade and Civilization*, pp. 37–39; Sen, *Buddhism, Diplomacy, and Trade*, pp. 178–179.

[15] Ferrand, *Relations de voyages et textes*, p. 176. Abu' Abdallah as-Sarif al-Idrisi was born in Ceuta in 1099 and studied in Cordova, and wrote his great geography for Roger II of Sicily.

[16] Buzurg, *The Book of the Wonders of India*, pp. 56, 57, 76 and 77. According to Rita Rose Di Meglio, "Arab Trade with Indonesia and the Malay Peninsula from the 8th to the 16th Century," in D. S. Richards, ed., *Islam and the Trade of Asia: A Colloquium* (Papers on Islamic History: II; Oxford: Bruno Cassirer, 1970), p. 112, the *Aja'ib al-Hind*, despite its accounts of monsters and mermaids, "does give a picture of the commercial activities of the Muslim Arabs at that time."

directed all of their trade with China through Palembang.[17] More importantly, Srivijaya's domination of the Straits of Malacca provided a ready source of revenue. The *'Aja'ib al-Hind* (c. 1000) describes the Maharaja of Sribuza levying taxes on ships sailing to China,[18] and as a likely example of this, the Jewish merchant Yishaq bin Yahuda from Siraf, whose successes in the China trade were described in Chapter 1, was ultimately killed in Sumatra after his ship was seized.[19] Given Srivijaya's power, Abu Zayd's description of Kalah as belonging to the kingdom of Zabaj makes sense, for Kalah could not have flourished had it not been a part (or at least a vassal) of Srivijaya.

Mention must also be made of Java, which with Srivijaya was the other great power in maritime southeast Asia in the tenth century. With a population accounting for as much as half of an estimated ten million inhabitants for all of the region, Java played an active role in maritime trade, especially following a move of the capital from the central to eastern part of the island in the first half of the tenth century.[20] Even more than in the case of Srivijaya, Javanese ports are little mentioned by Arab geographers, but as we shall see, Java was profoundly involved in long-distance maritime trade, especially during the tenth through thirteenth centuries when its foreign trade grew dramatically. Indeed, Javanese records from this period portray merchant associations and highly capitalized merchants within the Javanese ports.[21]

A variety of merchant groupings or trade diasporas formed the maritime merchant community of tenth-century southeast Asia. Although little mentioned in Chinese or Arabic sources, merchants from Malaya, Sumatra, Java and other parts of southeast Asia were undoubtedly among the most numerous. Their presence is dramatically reflected in two tenth-century shipwrecks found in the Java Sea (see Map 2).[22] The Intan

---

[17] Graham Saunders, *A History of Brunei* (Kuala Lumpur: Oxford University Press, 1994), p. 24.

[18] Hall, *A History of Early Southeast Asia*, p. 129.   [19] Tampoe, *Maritime Trade*, p. 129.

[20] On demographic estimates, see Horst Liebner, "Cargoes for Java: Interpreting Two 10th Century Shipwrecks," *Southeast Asian Ceramic Society, West Malaysia Chapter, Lecture Series* (Kuala Lumpur, 2009), p. 41.

[21] Jan Wisseman Christie, "Javanese Markets and the Asian Sea Trade Boom of the Tenth to the Thirteenth Centuries A.D.," *Journal of the Economic and Social History of the Orient* 41.3 (1998), pp. 341–381, especially pp. 351–353; Horst Liebner, *The Siren of Cirebon: A Tenth-Century Trading Vessel Lost in the Java Sea* (Ph.D. dissertation, University of Leeds, 2014), p. 19. For Java's move to the east, see pp. 26–31. See, too, Kenneth Hall, "Indonesia's Evolving International Relationships in the Ninth to Early Eleventh Centuries: Evidence from Contemporary Shipwrecks and Epigraphy," *Indonesia* 90 (Fall 2010), pp. 15–45, especially pp. 27–28.

[22] In addition to the Intan and Nanhan/Cirebon shipwrecks, discussed below, there is a third – the Karawang shipwreck – found in the same part of the Java Sea (north of western Java) and described by Liebner in "Cargoes for Java" along with his treatment of

shipwreck consists of the remains of a ship of southeast Asian origin (as indicated by the lack of iron nails) that was 30 meters long and 10 meters wide, with a likely displacement of around 200 tons. Discovered in the 1990s off the east coast of Sumatra in the Java Sea, presumably lost en route from Sumatra to Java, and dated to 920–960 or slightly later, the ship's cargo – most but not all of which originated in China – included "Javanese bronze fittings with grotesque animal mask motifs, Chinese glazed porcelain ceramics, Chinese lead coins, and a treasure of Chinese silver ingots, some of them inscribed." Some 5,000 *liang* (roughly 185 kilograms) of the silver ingots were recovered, which Twitchett and Stargardt have calculated to be 1.15 percent of the Song government's total silver receipts for 996.[23]

The Cirebon ship was also of southeast Asian origin, slightly smaller than the Intan ship, with a length of 25 meters and beam of 11.5–12 meters. It can be dated to the mid-tenth century on the basis of its coinage (all from southern China) and a potter's mark dated 968.[24] Its large cargo consisted primarily of some 500,000–600,000 Chinese ceramic pieces, but also glassware from western Asia, bronzes from India, raw Afghani lapis lazuli, kendi (containers) from southeast Asia, silver ingots from China and many other commodities from across maritime Asia. In his painstaking analysis of the archaeological data, Horst Liebner has argued that the ship, having come originally from the Southern Han kingdom in Guangzhou and having made stops elsewhere in southeast Asia where it had picked up its non-Chinese cargoes, was en route to its destination in eastern Java. He further argues that the distribution of the ceramics points to a single owner, and still further that the quantity of ceramics was such that the entire population of Java – estimated at around five million – could not have absorbed more than four to five such shiploads per year, the ceramics being used for Hindu rituals and mortuary practices as well as daily use.[25]

For our purposes, the most significant artifacts recovered from the Cirebon shipwreck are artifacts associated with Islam. There is a jewelry mold, probably used to cast a protective charm or *wafaq* using metals like gold or silver and inscribed with the Arabic words *al-malk lillah al-wahid al-qahhar*, which has been translated as "all might is owned by Allah, the One and Omnipotent." There are also a large number of Muslim wooden beads, most of which carry inscriptions invoking Allah.[26] These objects

Nanhan/Cirebon. Because the findings from the latter give far more information, I have chosen to focus on it along with the Intan wreck.

[23] Twitchett and Stargardt, "Chinese Silver Bullion," pp. 14–16, 29.

[24] Liebner, "Cargoes for Java," pp. 33–35.   [25] Liebner, "Cargoes for Java," pp. 41–46.

[26] Horst Liebner, *The Siren of Cirebon*, pp. 188–191. There are also two hilts, probably for swords, made of gold-sheeted resin, which have markings that may be Arabic, though

strongly suggest the existence of a Muslim community in Java, the members of which would almost certainly have been merchants, thus indicating that the Muslim trade diaspora extended into the southern reaches of maritime southeast Asia.

Returning to Abu Dulaf's description of Kalah, the Chinese ships that he mentions point to another group, namely Chinese merchants. Acceptance of this claim demands some caution, for while Chinese merchant activities in southeast Asia are well documented for Song times, there is no evidence that they had ventured into the South Seas at all during the Tang, and we lack Chinese sources to confirm it. I am inclined to accept Abu Dulaf on this point, in part because, assuming that he returned home by sea, the presence of Chinese ships in Kalah was something that he would have observed directly without reliance on a translator, but also because the vacuum created by the departure of the foreign trades from Guangzhou could very plausibly have served as the impetus for Chinese ships to venture south.

Yet other groups are referenced by the Fatimid writer al-'Aziz, who, writing in the late tenth century, described Kalah as a "prosperous town" inhabited by Muslims, Hindus and Persians.[27] The presence of Hindu merchants should not surprise us, given the lengthy history of Tamil mariners in southeast Asia and the presence of the thriving port of Nagapattinam across the Bay of Bengal, which during the course of the tenth century was annexed by the sea-oriented Chola empire, and the thriving merchant guilds of southern India.[28] The juxtaposition of Muslims and Persians, however, is curious, mixing as it does ethnicity and religion. Perhaps Persians were singled out because of their linguistic and physical distinctiveness in maritime Asia, even though many of them were Muslim, as we noted in Chapter 1. As for "Muslims," as Andre Wink has documented, by the tenth century permanent Muslim communities had established themselves in such far-flung communities as the Sind, Gujarat, Sri Lanka (Sarandib) and Ma'bar (Malabar) – not to mention China before 879 – and while these may have had Arab roots, intermarriages or "temporary marriages" (mut'a) undoubtedly attenuated the Arab

---

they can also be taken as Old-Javanese or "Malay" Kawi and their workmanship is more southeast Asian than west Asian (pp. 188–189).

[27] Wink, *Al Hind*, p. 84.

[28] See Gokul Seshadri, "New Perspectives on Nagapattinam: The Medieval Port City in the Context of Political, Religious, and Commercial Exchanges between South India, Southeast Asia and China," in Herman Kulke, K. Kesavapany, and Vijay Sakhuja, eds., *Nagapattinam to Suvarnadwipa: Reflections on the Chola Naval Expeditions to Southeast Asia* (Singapore: Institute of Southeast Asian Studies, 2010), pp. 118–123; and Noboru Karashima, "South Indian Merchant Guilds in the Indian Ocean and Southeast Asia," in Hermann Kulke et al., *Nagapattinam to Suvarnadwipa*, p. 137.

identities of their members.[29] Thus it could have been the ethnic diversity of the Muslims of Kalah that prompted Al'Aziz to use "Muslim" rather than "Arab."

Champa – Zhancheng 占城 in the Chinese sources – was another southeast Asian locale for which the evidence, although circumstantial, points to an active Muslim mercantile community in the tenth century and beyond. Crucial in this regard was its proximity to China, which made it a natural port of call for ships traveling between China and the South Seas. Describing the port of Champa as "only one of the links in a long chain, which connected the Middle East with Africa and China," Pierre-Yves Manguin has argued that "nothing could be more normal than this settlement."[30] Champa, as one of the most active tributary states during the Song, regularly sent tribute that consisted in large part of goods from western Asia, such as rosewater, glass and embroidered textiles.[31] There is an observation concerning Champa, made first in Five Dynasties sources but repeated in Song sources, that "its customs and clothing are similar to those of the country of Dashi (Arabia)," suggesting significant Muslim influence on Champa culture.[32] Geoff Wade has also proposed a direct point of religious influence: "...a fascinating reference to the killing of mountain cattle in sacrifice notes that 'when they are about to be slaughtered, a "medium" is instructed to offer prayers, which sound thus: 'A-luo-he-ji-ba'." He goes on to explain that this is the beginning of the prayer uttered by Muslims when killing animals for food.[33]

For evidence, Manguin cites Champa's sending of an ambassador to China in the Later Zhou and early Song by the name of Pu Hesan 蒲可散, whom he identifies as Abu Hassan (Pu serving as a common shortening

[29] Wink, *Al Hind*, pp. 67–86. On the spread of Islam through much of the western Indian subcontinent, see Brajesh Krishna, *Foreign Trade in Early Medieval India* (New Delhi: Harman Publishing House, 2000), p. 65.

[30] Pierre-Yves Manguin, "The Introduction of Islam into Champa," in Alijah Gordon, ed., *The Propagation of Islam in the Indonesian-Malay Archipelago* (Kuala Lumpur: Malaysian Sociological Research Institute, 2001), p. 290.

[31] See the detailed analysis of Champa tribute goods in Geoff Wade, "The 'Account of Champa' in the *Song Huiyao Jigao*," in Tran Ky Phuong and Bruce M. Lockhart, eds., *The Cham of Vietnam: History, Society and Art* (Singapore: NUS Press, 2011), pp. 138–167.

[32] Wang Pu 王溥, *Wudai huiyao* 五代會要 (Beijing: Zhonghua shuju, 1998) 30, p. 367; *Song huiyao jigao* 宋會要輯稿 (Taipei: Shijie shuju, 1964), Fanyi 4, p. 61a (hereafter cited as SHY); and Tuo Tuo 脱脱, *Song shi* 宋史 (Beijing: Zhonghua shuju, 1977), 489, p. 14078 (hereafter cited as SS). Cited by Tazaka Kōdō 田坂興道, *Chūgoku ni okeru kaikyō no denrai to sono gutsū* 中國における回教の傳來とその弘通 (Islam in China: Its Introduction and Development) (Tokyo: Tōyō Bunko, 1964), p. 305, who makes a strong case for a significant Muslim presence in tenth- and eleventh-century Champa (pp. 305–307).

[33] Wade, "Account of Champa," p. 143 and n. 14.

for the Arabic Abu), and bearing, among other things, Arabian bottles and rosewater, a product of the western regions.[34] This use of Arabs – presumably merchants – by southeast Asian monarchs for tribute missions to China is a point to which we will return. However, Manguin also cites a set of dramatic events from the 980s, which he believes to have consisted of the flight of hundreds of Muslims out of Champa:

Following the usurpation of the crown by the Vietnamese Luu Ky Tong, an emigration developed from 986 from Champa to South China. Some hundred "foreigners from Champa" arrived in that year in Hainan, led by a certain Pu Lo E. Nearly 500 others at Canton demanded the protection of China; they had at their head Li Nian Bing in 987 and Hu Xuan in 988. If it is admitted, as has several times been proposed, that the restoration of Hu Xuan is Husayn (the *hu* easily renders the 'Arabic *h*), then again it is a question of Muslims having come from Champa. This is confirmed by various written sources, amongst which is the genealogy of the Pu family of Sanya shi, which states that these "foreigners" of South Hainan came from Champa.[35]

The references to Pu Hesen and Pu Lo E (Pu Luoe) raise an issue of considerable importance for this study, namely the assumption that the surname "Pu 蒲" was a transliteration of the Arabic "Abu" and therefore an indicator of Arabic, or at least west Asian, origins. During the Five Dynasties and especially the Song, numerous tribute missions from southeast Asia as well as western Asia were led by individuals identified as Pus, and then during the Song there are a references to foreign merchants surnamed Pu in the ports of Guangzhou and Quanzhou. We will return to these cases in Chapter 3, but to address the issue of translation the presumption, with which I agree, is that these individuals were west Asian – probably Muslim – merchants. The issue is controversial. A number of scholars have rejected this hypothesis, arguing first that because Pu is a Chinese surname of longstanding, one can make no assumption about foreign – especially Muslim – origins of so-named individuals, second that "Pu" could be a transliteration for other non-Chinese designations such as *pu/mpu/pŏ*, a title in Nusantaran (Indonesian) languages, and third that "Pu" with its explosive "p" is a poor transliteration for "Abu."[36] In response, it should be noted that

---

[34] Manguin, "The Introduction of Islam into Champa," p. 291. For the embassies, see SS 489, p. 14079.

[35] Manguin, "The Introduction of Islam into Champa," p. 292. The source for this account is SS 489, p. 14080.

[36] See Manguin's discussion of this issue in "The Introduction of Islam into Champa," p. 291, and especially n. 18–19 (pp. 312–313). See, too, Sen, *Buddhism, Diplomacy, and Trade*, pp. 167–168. The suggestion about *pu/mpu/pŏ* was made by Gabriel Ferrand in 1922. I should also reference an extensive personal correspondence with Stephen Haw, who strenuously objects to the assumption that "Pu" designated west Asians or Muslims.

while "Pu" is indeed a Chinese surname that long predated this period, it was rare, and certainly not an explanation for the many Pu tribute emissaries from abroad.[37] Concerning other proposed transliterations of Pu, while this is a possibility that might account for some of the Srivijayan or Javanese emissaries, against this we have the numerous individuals surnamed Pu either representing west Asian states or identified as Arab (Dashi), not to mention the fact that most of the Pus have given names that lend themselves to plausible transliterations of Arabic names. Finally, concerning the suitability of "Pu" as a transliteration for "Abu," while one could point to the case of Bu Luohai 不囉海, an Arab envoy to the Song court in 974, the advantage of Pu 蒲 is that it was the most recognized Chinese surname that is pronounced as either "Pu" or "Bu," and as such a logical choice for whoever made the transliteration of the foreign name into Chinese (probably an official or clerk). In summary, this is an issue for which proof is not to be had, but here I join most of the scholars working in this area in accepting the Pu/Abu connection in most cases.

Thus, while not conclusive, the evidence concerning a Muslim maritime presence in tenth-century Champa is, I believe, both plausible and persuasive,[38] especially given Champa's key position along the trade routes between China.

The presence of Muslim and other foreign merchant groups in Kalah and other ports of tenth-century southeast Asia, as detailed in the preceding pages, had important consequences for both southeast Asia and China. Kenneth Hall, while rejecting simplistic models in which foreign merchants functioned as autonomous agents of change in southeast Asian societies, proposes a far more interactive model of change, but one that was nevertheless receptive to outside influences. In contrast to the territorially defined polities of China (and other land-based empires),

Southeast Asia's polities were relatively open, people-centered realms in which non-contiguous population clusters were afforded some degree of autonomy, including, if they wished, the opportunity to participate in external commercial and cultural networks. Appropriately, local clusters welcomed the periodic influx

---

[37] For example, Chang Bide's *Song Biographical Index* gives just 6 pages to 26 Pus out of 4,509 pages of biographical entries. Chang Bide 昌彼得, Wang Deyi 王德毅, Cheng Yuanmin 程元敏 and Hou Junde 侯俊德, eds., *Songren zhuanji ziliao suoyin* 宋人傳記資料索引, 6 vols. (Taipei: Dingwen shuzhu, 1974–1975).

[38] I am not including in the supporting evidence two eleventh-century Kufic inscriptions allegedly from southern Champa published by Paul Ravaisse in 1922 (Paul Ravaisse, "Deux Inscriptions Coufiques Du Čampa," *Journal Asiatiques* (Paris), Série II, 20.2 (1922), pp. 247–289). They were controversial from the outset, for Ravaisse was relying on rubbings that he had obtained from intermediaries.

of new resident "foreigners," who became community resources but also brought their own cultural practices.[39]

Hall suggests, further, that these new commercial realities led to "a consequential generalized prosperity that improved the lives and psychological well-being of Southeast Asian courtiers as well as commoners."[40] Although he is not writing specifically about the tenth century, I believe that his characterization works well for that period, when the long-standing dominance of Srivijaya was challenged by state-building ventures in Burma, the Malay peninsula, Java and southeastern India.

For the Chinese, the vitality of Asian maritime trade in which the role that they played had become peripheral offered promising economic opportunities, and, as it happened, the sea-oriented kingdoms along the southeastern coast of China during the Five Dynasties period (907–960) were well placed to begin taking advantage of that opportunity, and so to initiate a new era of maritime activity for the Chinese.

The Southern Kingdoms and the Revival of Trade

In many ways the nadir in China's trade relations with the Nanhai occurred in the late ninth century, in the years following the Huang Chao massacre. Brief as Huang's southern expedition may have been, it left Guangzhou devastated and also severely demoralized local officials and governing structures throughout the south. In terms of the ensuing political fragmentation, the Tang had effectively ended in the south, even though most of the warlords who dominated most of the southern regions in the years leading up to the dynasty's formal demise in 907 continued to give lip service to Chang'an.

As the name suggests, the period of the Five Dynasties and Ten Kingdoms was one of two histories. In the north, a sequence of five dynasties dominated the considerable reaches of the Yellow River Valley during the 53 years between the end of the Tang and establishment of the Song (907–960). By contrast, the nine kingdoms (the tenth being in the far north) in south China were much smaller than any of the northern dynasties, but in most cases longer lasting, especially since the Song conquest of the south was not completed until 978. With their beginnings in the chaotic conditions of the late ninth century, most of these kingdoms were founded by men who had their beginnings in banditry. It is the three

---

[39] Hall, "Local and International Trade and Traders," p. 231.
[40] Hall, "Local and International Trade and Traders," p. 214.

on the coast that concern us here, since they were the states directly involved with overseas trade.[41]

The coastal kingdoms of Southern Han 南漢 in Guangdong, Min 閩 in Fujian and Wuyue 吳越 in Zhejiang had similar histories in which local authorities (in the case of Min and Wuyue, ex-bandits) brought order to troubled regions in the late ninth century and created relatively stable and prosperous regimes that lasted through much of the tenth century.[42] They also shared access to maritime trade and dependence upon it as a vital source of revenue. Their role primarily involved the transshipment of goods, for the demand for luxuries of the Nanhai in the many courts of the tenth-century states was reportedly huge. In 977, just prior to the incorporation of Wuyue and Quanzhou into the Song empire,[43] the Song government attempted to ban private trade in the Nanhai commodities of "spices, medicinal ingredients, perfumes, rhinoceros horn and ivory" from "Guangnan, Champa, Srivijaya, Jiaozhou (i.e., Vietnam), Quanzhou, Liangzhe, or foreign countries," thereby underlining the role that had been played in overseas trade by Southern Han (Guangnan), Min (Quanzhou) and Wu-yue (Liangzhe).[44]

References to that activity in the poorly documented histories of the southern kingdoms are few, but highly suggestive. In 918 Guangzhou was described as collecting the pearls and other precious goods that made their way as far west as Sichuan and Guizhou, and that such were the "excessive pleasures and luxurious desires" associated with them that these goods were used in gift-giving between states. Indeed, when the

[41] See Hugh R. Clark, "The Southern Kingdoms between the T'ang and the Sung," in *The Cambridge History of China, Volume 5 Part One: The Sung Dynasty and Its Precursors*, Denis Twitchett and Paul Smith, eds., pp. 133–205. Naomi Standen's chapter in the same volume, "The Five Dynasties," pp. 38–132, provides an excellent introduction to the dynasties in the north.

[42] Wuyue, the most prosperous and long-lived of the southern kingdoms, included the Yangzi Delta and modern Zhejiang province and the cities of Hangzhou and Mingzhou, the latter an important port. Its founder, Qian Liu 錢鏐 (852–931) was a bandit leader turned militia commandant from a poor rural village who managed to vanquish his rivals by 895, and then in 902 claimed the title of King of Wuyue. The kingdom of Min in Fujian was established by Wang Chao 王潮, a brigand from the north who arrived in Fujian with a group of five thousand mercenaries in 884, and with their help established his hegemony in 892 and the Kingdom of Min in 909. Liu Yin 劉隱, the founder of the Southern Han with its capital in Guangzhou, was not a bandit but the son of one Liu Qian 劉謙, a Tang official who came from the non-Han Man people of the far south and who restored order to the region following the Huang Chao massacre. A loyal subject of the Tang until the end, Liu Yin established the Southern Han in 909 and took the title of emperor in 917.

[43] Southern Han submitted in 971 and Southern Tang, the Jiangxi kingdom, which by then included the rest of Fujian, in 975.

[44] *SHY, Shihuo*, 36/1b-2b, cited by Robert Hartwell, *Tribute Missions to China, 960–1126* (Philadelphia, 1983), p. 34.

founding emperor of the Later Tang received an envoy from the Southern Han shortly after his seizure of power (from the Later Liang) in 923, his main concern was to learn about the conditions of the Nanhai trade and express his concerns about the prompt arrival of Southern Han tribute in the form of Nanhai goods. Moreover, so large did the maritime world loom in Guangdong that the ruler of the Southern Han in 925 changed the regime's reign name to "Bailong" 白龍 (white dragon) after receiving a report of a white dragon in the Nanhai.[45] Another source describes the flourishing trade in Quanzhou:

Wang Yen-pin 王延彬 (Wang Yanbin) [the nephew of Wang Shen-chih 王審知 (Wang Shenzhi) and autonomous governor of Ch'üan-chou] governed for thirty years (904–34). Year after year the harvests were good and the trading ships of the southern barbarians never failed to stop.[46]

"Ships of the southern barbarians" (*manbo* 蠻舶) strongly suggests southeast Asian traders, so we can only speculate about the presence or absence of Arabs and other west Asians.

The most remarkable feature of this trade along the southeastern coast was not its volume so much as the role of the states in promoting it. According to Angela Schottenhammer, the southern rulers "sought to use the profits derived from this trade not only for their own private consumption needs, but to pay for the political and economic maintenance of the state. Maritime trade thus came to be used primarily for *politico-economic* purposes rather than private interests."[47] In support of this, Schottenhammer has argued that the rulers of tenth-century Quanzhou refrained from taxing trade at its national borders and sponsored the development of kilns for largely export-oriented ceramic production.[48] In the Min port city of Fuzhou, the Monopoly Tax Bureau (Quehuowu 榷貨務) was responsible for the taxation of imports from abroad, and a contemporary source describes the director, Zhang Mu 張睦, as "gentle and not extortionate to the foreign merchants who responded [to Wang Shen-chih's invitation to trade in Fuzhou]. Thus the state's revenues grew daily."[49]

---

[45] Xue Juzheng 薛居正, *Jiu Wudai shi* 舊五代史 (974; Beijing: Zhonghua shuju, 1976) 135, p. 1808.

[46] Clark, "The Southern Kingdoms," pp. 184–185, citing *Wuguo gushi* 五國古史 in *Zhibuzu zhai congshu* 知不足齋叢書 (Shanghai: Gushu liutongchu, 1921), 2, pp. 9b–10a (col. 4, pp. 368–936, in *Zhibuzu zhai*).

[47] Angela Schottenhammer, "China's Emergence as a Maritime Power," in *The Cambridge History of China*. Vol. 5, Part 2: *The Sung Dynasty* (Cambridge and New York: Cambridge University Press, 2015), pp. 462–463.

[48] Angela Schottenhammer, "Local Politico-Economic Particulars of Quanzhou during the Tenth Century," *Journal of Sung-Yüan Studies* 29 (1999), pp. 24–25.

[49] Clark, "The Southern Kingdoms," p. 185, citing Wu Renchen 吳任臣, *Shiguo chunqiu* 十國春秋 (Beijing: Zhonghua shuju, 1983), 95, p. 1377.

The active role played by the coastal states during this period was significant on two counts. Their pro-trade policies undoubtedly helped reassure the maritime traders that it was safe to trade and even settle in China, since according to the Arab writers cited earlier, the main reason that traders moved the base of their operations from China in the late ninth century had to do with their perception of the oppressive role of the Chinese authorities. It is therefore plausible to believe that the regeneration of the west Asian community in Guangzhou commenced during the reign of the Southern Han. Second, the example set by the southeastern kingdoms with their pro-trade policies was an important one for the Song, which proved to be the most trade-friendly of all Chinese dynasties, although as we shall see it required a couple of generations for the Song to become set in their approach to overseas trade.

Trade and Tribute in the Early Song

The imperial line that established itself in 960 under the Later Zhou general Zhao Kuangyin 趙匡胤 (927–976) as the Song dynasty was initially simply the sixth dynasty to rule north China in the 53 years since the demise of the Tang. Only gradually, following the conquest of the south, which was completed in 978, did it become clear that this was a great dynasty with staying power, and even then the failure to incorporate sixteen disputed border prefectures from the Khitan Liao to the northeast, with whom they engaged in an unsuccessful 25-year war, qualified the dynasty's success in the eyes of many.

Northern dynasty that it was, in the south the Song followed the lead of the southeastern kingdoms in actively encouraging trade. In 971, the year after the conquest of the Southern Han, the Song established a maritime trade office (*shibosi* 市舶司) in Guangzhou as a clear indication of their desire to encourage the maritime trade, and of course, to tax it and control it. The latter was evident two years later when the government banned Chinese merchants from venturing overseas to engage in trade, a ban that seems to have been maintained into the eleventh century.[50] Then in 987, the emperor Taizong 太宗 (r. 976–997) sent eight eunuch attendants in four missions out into the Nanhai to invite traders to come to China. Two years later, a second maritime trade office was opened in Hangzhou, followed by a third in Mingzhou in 992. According to the *Song History*, the result of these trade offices was that foreigners from Arabia, Guluo,

---

[50] SS 6, p. 76. See Billy K. L. So's clear summary to early Song policies towards the maritime trade in *Prosperity, Region, and Institutions*, pp. 44–45.

Java, Champa (southern Vietnam), Borneo, the Philippines and Srivijaya (in Sumatra) all came to trade.[51]

Although this official interest in maritime trade marked a sharp contrast with the Tang, in two regards Tang practices remained influential. First, the Song court vacillated between recognizing this trade as operating within the parameters of regular government supervision, through the mechanism of the maritime trade offices, and attempting to make the trade – and especially the coveted aromatics and incenses – an inner-palace activity under the control of eunuchs. Second, the Song clearly attempted to recentralize the maritime trade, which had involved multiple ports during the Tang–Song interregnum, to Guangzhou with its maritime trade office, and subsequently Hangzhou and Mingzhou, where trade with Korea, Japan and the Ryukyu Islands predominated. In the long run, the Nanhai trade could not be monopolized by the palace or limited to Guangzhou, and in fact at one time or another ten cities hosted maritime trade offices or superintendencies (*shibo tiju si* 市舶提舉司).[52] The superintendencies and the system of free trade that came to characterize Song maritime policy are the subject of Chapter 3. Here, our concern is with the first 60 years of the dynasty, when imperial interests and the role of Guangzhou were both marked.

Among the best-documented activities related to the Nanhai trade during the early Song period are the 88 tribute missions that arrived from the Nanhai region during the reigns of the first three Song emperors, from 960 to 1022 (see Table 2.1).[53] Much has been written about the unique character of Song foreign relations. It alone of the major dynasties in Chinese imperial history was forced to come to terms with reality of a multi-state east Asian region; in its relations with the Liao after 1005, and even more so with the Jin after 1142, the Song emperors were forced to send tribute, and in the latter case to address the Jin emperors as "elder brothers," thus giving the lie to the claim of the emperor to be the "Son of Heaven."[54] Song tribute relations with the states of the Nanhai, which of course posed no military threat to the dynasty, were traditional in form and content, in many ways constituting a revival of the Tang system. As in the Tang, the fact that the tribute goods consisted largely of highly desired luxury goods meant that it was in many ways a tribute-trade arrangement.

---

[51] SS 186, pp. 4558–4559.
[52] This has been treated in detail by Schottenhammer, "Emergence of China."
[53] These statistics are drawn from Hartwell, *Tribute Missions to China.*
[54] See Morris Rossabi, ed., *China among Equals: The Middle Kingdom and Its Neighbors, 10th–14th Centuries* (Berkeley: University of California Press, 1983).

Table 2.1 *Northern Song tribute missions*

	Maritime SE Asia	South Asia	SW Asia	Nanhai totals	Continental SE Asia	NE Asia	Inner Asia	Continental totals
Taizu 960–975	18	4	4	**26**	2	16	24	**42**
Taizong 976–997	21	2	8	**31**	14	18	25	**57**
Zhenzong 998–1022	13	6	12	**31**	16	12	74	**102**
Renzong 1023–1063	7	4	2	**13**	13	1	54	**68**
Yingzong 1064–1067	0	0	0	**0**	1	0	1	**2**
Shenzong 1068–1085	8	3	7	**18**	6	7	25	**38**
Zhezong 1086–1100	5	1	3	**9**	4	5	26	**35**
Huizong 1101–1126	5	0	1	**6**	11	10	8	**29**
Totals	31	20	37	**134**	113	69	237	**373**

SOURCE: Robert Hartwell, *Tribute Missions to China, 960–1126*

During this early Song period, Nanhai tribute missions had three salient characteristics: they were channeled through the city of Guangzhou; they involved a relatively small number of states; and the role of maritime merchants, especially Arab merchants, was substantial. After the Song defeat of the Southern Han in 970, the Nanhai tribute missions would enter Chinese waters off the coast of Guangdong, enter the port of Guangzhou under escort, and then, after a stay there, make the trip to the capital in Kaifeng. This practice, when combined with the opening of the maritime trade office in Guangzhou in 971, had the effect of recentralizing the activities of the maritime traders into Guangzhou. Ports like Quanzhou and Fuzhou further up the coast undoubtedly continued to trade, but by law, ships were required to stop at a maritime trade office (in Mingzhou or Hangzhou, if not in Guangzhou) in order to have their cargoes assessed and taxes collected.

During this period of 960–1022, ten Nanhai states sent missions to the Song, but three of them accounted for the vast majority of the 57 missions: Arabia (Dashi 大食; presumably the Abbasid empire) with 21, Srivijaya (Sanfoqi 三佛齊) with 16 and India (Tianzhu 天竺) with 10. If one includes continental southeast Asia, a similar pattern pertains; of the 67 missions from that region during this period, Champa accounted for 37 of them and Dai Viet (Vietnam) for 26. We can see, therefore, that a handful of states distributed across the breadth of maritime Asia dominated Nanhai diplomatic activity with the Song during the early years of the dynasty.

Our information concerning the envoys themselves is striking. First, while the envoys for Arabia and the other west Asian states all have apparently Arabic names, as we would expect, so do many of the envoys from other states – specifically, seven envoys in five missions from Srivijaya (for 976, 983, 988, 1008 and 1017), five from Champa (960, 960, 972, 999 and 1011) and one from Borneo (977) – in the 960–1022 period. Second, there appears to have been considerable continuity in these diplomatic services, for four of these Arabic envoys served three or more times as envoy or vice-envoy. Pu Tuopoli 蒲陀婆離 (Abu Mahmud Dawal?) represented Arabia in 995, 1011 and 1019, and Pu Hesan 蒲訶散 (Abu-I-Hassan?) represented Champa in 961, 972 and 990. Especially intriguing were Pu Yatuoli 蒲押陀黎 (Abu Adil?), who led a mission from Srivijaya in 988, and then from Arabia in 995 and 998, and Pu Jiaxin 蒲加心 (Abu Kasim), who represented Arabia as a "foreign guest" in 1004, served as envoy for Muscat (Wuxun 勿巡) in 1011, and then as vice-envoy, first for the south Indian state of Chola (Zhunianguo 注輦國) in 1015 and then again for Arabia in 1019.[55] There is also an intriguing account about one Pu Luxie 蒲盧歇, a merchant (*shangren* 商人) and presumably an Arab, which provides insight into the role of such merchants in tribute missions.[56] En route from China to Java, his ship was damaged in a storm and found anchorage in Brunei (Boni 勃泥). When the king of Brunei, Xiangda, learned that Pu had come from China, he had a ship built and ordered Pu to guide the embassy (he was not designated as an envoy), which reached the capital in 977.[57]

---

[55] The Arabic names in parenthesis represent speculative attributions by Robert Hartwell in *Tribute Missions to China*, and are therefore followed by question marks.

[56] See Tazaka, *Chūgoku ni okeru kaikyō*, p. 302, on the likelihood that Pu was an Arab.

[57] SS 248, p. 14,095; Hartwell, *Tribute Missions*, p. 184. The desire by the Bruneians to have Pu guide the mission may be explained by the fact that, once at the capital, the envoys petitioned the Song emperor to order Champa to give tribute ships from Brunei safe passage in the future, should winds drive them into Champa territory, which the emperor then did. It is quite possible that fear of Champa had previously kept Brunei from sending missions. It should be noted that the vice envoy of this mission from Brunei was another

As discussed above, while there has been disagreement among scholars as to whether these envoys were ethnically Arabs, current scholarship and the weight of the evidence strongly suggests that they were. I would suggest, further, that their presence in the tribute missions reflects the remarkable extent to which the residence and trading activities of the Arab trade diaspora port cities of south and southeast Asia, which we examined above, resulted in their penetration of the most elite levels of those polities, at least insofar as interstate relations were concerned. Tribute missions were, after all, formidable undertakings, requiring lengthy and often dangerous travel, a knowledge of the Chinese bureaucracy, and the formidable ritual demands of the court audience, so it is not surprising that southeast Asian rulers turned to Arab merchants whom they had grown to know and trust.

The kind of entrée that Muslim traders had to southeast Asian rulers is illustrated by Buzurg in an account of an audience that an elderly Muslim shipmaster by the name of Jahud Kuta had with the King of Zabaj (Srivijaya).[58] Towards the end of a lengthy conversation, Jahud violated court etiquette by departing from the required cross-legged sitting position (*birsila*) and stretching out a leg – to demonstrate the length of a kind of fish but also because he was uncomfortable. After a conversation with his vizier, who noted Jahud's age and obvious fatigue, the king decreed that Muslims would be dispensed from the custom, and Buzurg adds that Muslims henceforth were able "to sit in front of the king as they like."[59]

Returning to tribute missions, the Arab merchant and envoy Pu Ximi 蒲希密 (Abu Hamid) is by far the best documented of the early Song envoys, and his story is informative. We first learn of him in 976, when he appeared at court bearing tribute from the Arab king Helifo 珂黎拂.[60] Seventeen years later we hear of him again, the designated envoy from Arabia but also described as a "ship owner" (*bozhu* 舶主). Because of old age, Pu was unable to make the trip north from Guangzhou, sending in his place the vice-envoy Li Yawu 李亞勿 and a remarkable letter to the emperor, which has been largely preserved in the *Song History*.[61]

---

likely Arab, Pu Yali 蒲亞里 (Abu Ali?), suggesting an Arab, probably Muslim, presence in Brunei even before the arrival of Pu Luxie.

[58] According to Wink, *Al-Hind*, p. 341, Zabaj referred to Java in Arab texts prior to 860, but later was used for Srivijaya. Since Buzurk was writing in the mid-tenth century, I have taken this as Srivijaya.

[59] Buzurg, *The Book of the Wonders of India*, p. 90.

[60] Hartwell, *Tribute Missions*, p. 195, identifies him as Al-Muti, "caliph of Baghdad at this time." Since Moussa Ibn Ollai Ibn Rabah al-lakhmi was caliph from 972 to 978, I have been unable to verify Hartwell's statement. Perhaps Helifo stands for the title "caliph."

[61] SS 249, pp. 14118–14119. Pu's letter is quoted, in part, in Hirth and Rockhill, *Chau Ju-kua*, p. 123. I am indebted to Professor Zu-yan Chen for his help in deciphering some of the more obscure passages in this letter.

The letter provides a unique entrée into aspects of the world of Nanhai tribute, and I quote it in its entirety. It begins with rhetorical flourishes lauding the Song tribute system, describes the origins of the mission and his disappointment at being unable to make the trip to the imperial court, and finally details the tribute goods that he, Pu, is sending via Li Yawu.

The myriad stars droop down as they return and bow to the North Star. The springs of the hundred valleys flow downstream to the Eastern Sea. The emperor sends envoys on the road to make peaceful the distant, treating them not as foreign but making them feel at home. I consider that it is your majesty the emperor whose virtue unites Heaven and Earth, whose brightness equals the seven rulers (i.e., the sun, moon and five planets), who humanely assists the myriad kingdoms, and whose light illumines the four barbarians. Continuous songs harmonize these people who beat the earth; they honor translators and walk to present this tribute of pearls. Although my customs are foreign, I admire the Central Region (i.e., China), and my heart has long been inclined towards the sun, and the abundance of the celestial court.

This is remarkable language to issue from an Arab Muslim in the tenth century. Not only do its references to the North Star and the emperor as uniting Heaven and Earth draw on Chinese cosmology, but it also contains a classical allusion. "The people who beat the earth" is a translation of *jirang zhi min* 擊壤之民, literally to strike into the earth, and signifies a game (pushpin?). According to the *Cihai* 辭海, the locus classicus for *jirang* ("to strike the earth") is the Han *Diwang shiji* 帝王世記 (record of the lives of emperors and kings), which described the time of the sage emperor Yao as one when "the world was at peace and the people had no (contentious) affairs, and 80 and 90 year-old men beat the earth and sang."[62] Pu most likely had the services of a Chinese literatus in its composition; nevertheless, it is noteworthy that he chose to begin his letter with this language. The letter then continues:

Formerly when I was in my home country, I received a letter from the foreign headman (*fanzhang* 蕃長) of Guangzhou reporting that [the Arabs] have been ordered to [send a mission] go to the capital and offer tribute. He praised the sagely virtue of the emperor, who has announced [a policy of] magnanimous favor [towards the foreigners], commanding [the officials] in Guangnan to honor and comfort the foreign merchants [so as to] make abundant the goods from distant countries.[63] I then engaged passage on a sea-going ship and collected agricultural products.

---

[62] *Cihai* 辭海 (Taipei: Zhonghua shuju, 1971), p. 1282. *Jirong* also became the name of a game known as pushpins.

[63] Hirth's rendering of this last passage: "Formerly when I was at home, I received a letter from the foreign headman of Guangzhou urging me to go to the capital and offer tribute. He said much in praise of the emperor's virtues, who had commanded a liberal treatment

This passage provides us with a rare view of the genesis and implementation of a tribute mission, and what we see is the work of multiple agents: a Song court that requests the mission and is concerned that local officials "honor and comfort the foreign merchants [so as to] make abundant the goods from distant countries"; the Arab headman (*fanzhang* 蕃長) in Guangzhou, who conveyed the request to Pu Ximi, ship owner and ex-envoy; and Pu himself, presumably with the blessing of the caliph in Baghdad, but personally undertaking the collection of the tribute goods and their transportation. The letter then concludes with Pu explaining his inability to make the trip to Kaifeng, designating his assistant, Li Yawu, to go in his place, and detailing the tribute goods that he is sending:

It has been my long cherished goal to experience the hall of the Dragon King, survey the surroundings of the Jade Emperor, and to honor [Daoist] moral cultivation. Having now arrived at the City of Five Rams (i.e., Guangzhou), I am still far from the imperial palace. I am also old and feeble, sick and unable to flourish, dreaming of the red gates [of the palace], impaired in vision and broken in heart. I have now prevailed upon Li Yawu to bring the tribute, and have respectfully prepared foreign silks and medicines to supplement the offerings. Your subject Ximi presents fifty elephant tusks, 1800 *jin* of frankincense, seven hundred *jin* of wrought iron, a roll of red-threaded cotton, four rolls of five-colored flowered foreign silk, two rolls of white *yuenuo* cloth, a glazed bottle, an unusual stone, and one hundred rosewater bottles.

Again we see a fluent application of Chinese cultural rhetoric, used to express Pu's regrets over being unable to make the trip to the capital, his designation of Li Yawu (who is identified in one source as the foreign headman and thus perhaps the one who wrote to Pu in the first place) and an inventory of the tribute goods.[64] The last is an impressive list, with those foreign luxuries that the court and wealthy individuals found especially desirable – ivory, rhinoceros horn, incense and rosewater bottles, but it also included silks and wrought iron, goods that the Chinese had in abundance, a testimony to the high level of west Asian craftsmanship. We are informed that in response to the tribute that he had sent, Pu Ximi was given imperial calligraphy, a silk robe and a variety of silver and silk goods.[65]

There is a postscript to this story. In 995, two years after Pu Ximi's letter was received, Pu Yatuoli 蒲押陀離 (Abu Adil) led a tribute mission to court, and as in 993 there was a letter and even more lavish tribute gifts

---

towards the foreigners to the viceroy of Guangnan, in order to console the foreign traders and make them import things from distant countries."

[64] Ma Duanlin 馬端臨, *Wenxian tongkao* 文獻統考 (Taipei: Xinxing shuju, 1964), 340, p. 2665.

[65] SS 249, p. 14119.

from Pu Ximi. During his imperial audience in the Chongwen Hall, Pu Yatuoli explained through an interpreter: "My father Pu Ximi, seeking commercial profits, took ship and came to Guangzhou, and when five years had passed without his return, my mother sent me this long distance to see him. Upon my arrival in Guangzhou I saw him." He then conveyed Ximi's gratitude for the imperial gifts bestowed upon him two years before and offered the new gifts as a token of his thanks. In response, the emperor Taizong gave Yatuoli clothing, cap and belt, and even bedding, held a feast for him and had him rest a few months before returning. He also sent Pu Ximi quantities of gold equaling the value of Ximi's gifts.[66]

Pu Ximi and Yatuoli, father and son, together accounted for five tribute missions spanning the years 976 to 998 and including one from Srivijaya (988). We also know from this last account that Yatuoli's mother (and a wife of Ximi) was still in Arabia, from whence Yatuoli had just come, as Ximi had prior to the mission of 993. Here we see manifest the fluid nature of the Arab merchant diaspora at its very highest levels, involving long-term engagement in China, political importance in Srivijaya and continued trips to and from Arabia. The reference to the foreign headman in Guangzhou is also important, for not only is it the first post-Tang reference to an Arab residential presence in that city but it also illustrates the headman's role in communicating with his homeland to promote tribute and trade.

At about the time of the death of Emperor Zhenzong in 1022, the Nanhai tribute missions largely halted. Following the Arab mission of 1019, there was a 36-year hiatus until the next mission in 1055. Srivijaya's mission of 1017 was followed by another in 1028, but then there was a 49-year gap until their next mission in 1077. India and Chola each had a mission in the 1030s, but then had 36- and 34-year gaps in missions, respectively. A similar pattern can be seen with Korea: six missions between 1014 and 1021 were followed by one in 1030 and then not another until 1068. By contrast, missions from such western and northwestern states as Tibet, Khotan and Kucha continued with high frequency throughout the eleventh century, as did those from Champa and Vietnam in continental southeast Asia.[67]

It is not my intention to attempt an explanation of all these findings, but the general cutoff in maritime missions begs for explanation. One reason was economic. By the early eleventh century, the ever-increasing volume

---

[66] SS 249, pp. 14119–14120; Ma Duanlin, *Wenxian tongkao*, 339, pp. 2663–2664. The translation follows, in part, that given in Kuwabara, "On P'u Shou-keng," Part 1, p. 78.
[67] These data on the tribute missions are all drawn from Hartwell, *Tribute Missions to China*.

of trade between China and the Nanhai was placing a strain upon the tribute system. In 1016 the prefect of Guangzhou, Chen Shiqing 陳世卿, proposed that limits be set on the size of tribute missions:

The embassies with their envoys, vice-envoys, subordinate officials (*panguan* 判官), and assisting officials (*fangshouguan* 防援官) should be limited to 20 for Arabia, Chola, Srivijaya, and Java, and 10 for Champa, Tambralinga (Danliumei 丹流眉), Borneo, Guluo 古邏, and the Philippines (Moyi 摩逸), and they should be given documents for their travel. Guangzhou foreign guests (*fanke* 蕃客) who falsely substitute for them should be found guilty.[68]

Since we know that Guangzhou-based foreign merchants had in the past participated in tribute missions, this proposal, which was accepted, was probably not aimed at them as such. Rather, it seems likely that the missions had been used as excuses for large numbers of Guangzhou merchants to pile on and use the opportunity to engage in their own trade; thus the numerical limits.

Another reason for the hiatus in tribute missions from the late 1020s on is that the emperor Renzong 仁宗 (r. 1022–1063) may simply have been less interested in overseas tribute missions than his three predecessors, who all evinced a lively interest in them. Indeed, one of the clear high-points of the Song tribute system occurred in the years following 1007, when the mysterious discovery of "Heavenly Texts" (*Tianshu* 天書) – and subsequently of other auspicious omens – led to Zhenzong 真宗 (r. 997–1022) to carry out ancient sacrifices on a vast scale and with international dimensions. In 1008, not only did the Arab envoy and ship-master Pu Mawu Tuopoli 蒲麻勿陀婆 離 [Abu Mahmud Dawal?] accompany the court to Mount Tai to carry out the Fengshan 封禪 sacrifices, but Li Mawu 李麻勿, a member of the mission, presented the emperor with a jade tablet measuring a foot and two inches in length, explaining that his fifth-generation ancestor had obtained it in western India (Xitian 西天) and had sent it with the instruction that it was to be presented in tribute when "a sage emperor of China" performs the Fengshan sacrifices.[69] Not surprisingly, when Zhenzong performed the

---

[68] SHY, Fanyi 7, p. 20b; Li Tao 李燾, *Xu zizhi tongjian changbian* 續資治通鑑長編 (Beijing: Zhonghua shuju, 1979), 87, p. 1998.

[69] SHY, Fanyi 7, p. 19b; SS 249, p. 14120. For an excellent study of the Heavenly Texts affair and Zhenzong's performance of the Feng-shan sacrifices, the most ancient and prestigious of imperial sacrifices, see Susan Cahill, "Taoism at the Sung Court: The Heavenly Text Affair of 1008," *Bulletin of Sung Yuan Studies* 16 (1980), pp. 23–44. See also Lau Nap-yin and Huang K'uan-chung, "Founding and Consolidation of the Sung Dynasty under T'ai-tsu (960–976), T'ai-tsung (976–997), and Chen-tsung (997–1022)," in Denis Twitchett and Paul Smith, eds., *The Cambridge History of China, Vol. 5, Part One: The Sung Dynasty and Its Predecessors, 907–1279* (Cambridge: Cambridge University Press, 2009), pp. 270–273.

sacrifice to earth three years later at the Fen 汾 River in Shanxi, the Arabs accompanied the court again, this time in the company of envoys from other countries – among them three west Asian states that had never sent missions before.[70] Whatever one makes of this curious incident in Song history, it was clearly driven by Zhenzong's desire to be accorded the legitimacy and prestige due a true Son of Heaven in the wake of the humiliating peace treaty that had been signed with the Liao in 1005, and in this context all tribute missions served a useful purpose.

By contrast, Zhenzong's reign was followed by an 8-year regency by Empress Liu, with the young Renzong only beginning his personal reign in 1031. It is quite possible, therefore, that the hiatus in tribute missions reflected a generational shift to a political culture less concerned with issues of dynastic prestige and legitimacy.[71] Such an interpretation would also accord with the fact that the resumption of frequent maritime missions in the 1070s corresponded with the muscular foreign policy that characterized the reign of Shenzong 神宗 (r. 1067–1085).

The historian Hermann Kulke has noted the synchronous emergence of three powerful new dynasties across Eurasia: the Fatimids in Egypt in 969, the Cholas on the east coast of India in 985, and the Song in 960, regimes that "began to interfere with the Indian Ocean trade system." The Fatimids challenged the declining and fragmenting Abbasids,[72] increasing the importance of the Red Sea and therefore the role of the Malabar (Ma'bar) coast in southwestern India, to which their ships sailed directly; the Cholas challenged the long-standing supremacy of Srivijaya in southeast Asia through their naval expedition against it in 1025; and the Song "from the outset began to promote and control maritime trade more successfully than any other Chinese dynasty."[73] Without

---

[70] XCB 70, p. 1570; SS 490, pp. 14120–14121; Hartwell, *Tribute Missions to China*, pp. 198–199. The other west Asian states were Muscat (Wuxun 勿巡) and two others of uncertain identity: Pupoluoguo 蒲婆羅國 and Sanmalanguo 三麻蘭國.

[71] Jan Wisseman Christie, "The Medieval Tamil-Language Inscriptions in Southeast Asia and China," *Journal of Southeast Asian Studies* 29.2 (1998), p. 254, argues that the hiatus in tribute missions was the result of a Song decision and not a reflection of the decline of Srivijaya, as some have argued.

[72] The Persian and Shiite Buyid dynasty (934–1062), which controlled most of Iraq and Persia while leaving the caliphate intact but powerless, actively supported maritime trade through its port Siraf. However, its lively trade in the tenth century declined precipitously in the eleventh. Mukai Masaaki, "Transforming Dashi Shippers: The Tributary System and the Trans-National Network during the Song Period," Harvard Conference on Middle Period China, 2014; David Whitehouse, "Chinese Stoneware from Siraf," pp. 241–256, especially 242.

[73] Hermann Kulke, "The Naval Expeditions of the Cholas in the Context of Asian History," in Hermann Kulke, K. Kesavapany, and Vijay Sakhuja, eds., *Nagapattinam to Suvarnadwipa: Reflections on the Chola Naval Expeditions to Southeast Asia* (Singapore: Institute of Southeast Asian Studies, 2010), pp. 2–3.

disagreeing with this formulation, I would qualify Kulke's characterization of the Song and say that Zhenzong with his grand ceremonial schemes represented the ending of a Song attempt to recreate the Tang tributary order in its relations with maritime Asia. The earlier dominance of Abbasid and Tang had given way to a new trade system that was truly multipolar, with the Persian Gulf and Red Sea, the east and west coasts of India, Sri Lanka, Srivijaya and Champa, and also Japan and Korea all playing roles. The Song response, belated but successful, was to move from tributary trade to a relatively free trade in which the government's primary function was the collection of revenue derived from the maritime trade. As we shall see in Chapter 3, this ushered in a new period in the history of Muslim merchant communities in the port cities of China, communities that were part of a Muslim trade diaspora that was no longer simply anchored in China and west Asia, but included numerous communities throughout the Indian Ocean and southeast Asia.

3   The Maturation of Merchant Communities

From the early eleventh century to the rise of the Mongol empire in the thirteenth century, maritime Asia was interconnected through a flourishing multi-polar trading system that proved to be a powerful influence on the development of states across Eurasia. Less focused than the luxury trade of earlier centuries (though luxuries continued to be traded), it included new products, bulk commodities, and new kinds of ships. The Muslim trade diaspora was challenged by an array of merchant groups but also evolved in important ways, as its increasing ethnic and geographic diversity decreased the importance of west-Asian ports as diasporic anchors. As a result, the maritime communities in the port cities of southeastern China created a vibrant culture that differed considerably from that of their Tang predecessors.

The New Maritime Trading System

The emergence of the Fatimid, Chola and Song empires in the late tenth century, which we discussed at the end of Chapter 2, clearly introduced forces into maritime Asia that created new commercial configurations, but in contrast to the Tang–Abbasid age, and thanks in considerable part to the changes described in Chapter 2, they were all operating in a multi-state context. When combined with the pro-trade policies of the Song, with the world's largest and most dynamic economy, the result was that throughout the maritime world there were more states participating in long-distance commerce, more merchants' groups, and more goods being traded.

In western Asia, although the rise of Egypt served to alter trade routes and led to the emergence of Aden and Jidda in the Red Sea and the active role of the Jewish Karimi merchants in the Indian Ocean, it took a century or two for the possibilities of that trade to be realized.[1] More immediately,

---

[1] S. D. Goitein, "Portrait of a Medieval Indian Trader: Three Letters from the Cairo Geniza," *Bulletin of the School of Oriental and African Studies* 50.3 (1987), pp. 449–464.

the disintegration of the Abbasid Caliphate resulted in the overshadowing of Basra and other ports in the western Persian Gulf by Siraf on the Persian coast and Oman in the tenth century, though this in turn was followed by the ascendance of Kish in the eleventh century and Hormuz in the twelfth century. To the south, Egyptian trade with the Indian Ocean and beyond developed under the Fatimids (979–1175) and Ayyubids (1175–1250), enhancing the power of the Karimi merchants in Aden, whose ships were known to venture as far as China.[2]

These new political and commercial patterns did not put an end to direct trade with China. The Arabic accounts of the China trade from this period, though rare, speak to its reputation for generating enormous wealth. In 1138, an agent of great merchant and shipowner Ramisht returned from a trip to Guangzhou with a cargo valued at half a million dinars. There is no evidence that Ramisht himself went to China, but as a philanthropist who had earlier endowed a hospice in Mecca, Ramisht was said to have provided for a covering of the entire Ka'ba in Mecca with Chinese silk following the arrival of his agent's ship.[3] While not as spectacular, two other accounts reveal important details of this long-distance trade. In his description of the merchant Ahmad ibn 'Umar al Sirafi, whom he had met in Basra around 961, the writer Ibn Hauqal offers a glimpse of a trade network extending from China to the coast of Africa:

This man, prouder than a prince, possessed a considerable fortune; a manager handled his business affairs; he had contacts with partners and agents far away; his warehouses were overflowing with spices, precious stones and perfumes; his vessels sailed for India and China, as well as the coast of Zanzibar.[4]

The thirteenth-century writer Saadi described a merchant from Qais with a command of commodities markets from China to Greece. The merchant, said to have 150 camel loads of merchandise and 40 slaves, told Saadi:

I wish to carry Persian saffron to China where I understand that it has a high price, and then take the dishes from China to Greece, Greek brocade to India, Indian steel to Aleppo, glass of Aleppo to Yemen, and the striped material of Yemen to Persia.[5]

---

[2] Di Meglio, "Arab Trade with Indonesia and the Malay Peninsula," pp. 106–108.

[3] S. D. Goitein and Mordechai Akiva Friedman, *India Traders of the Middle Ages: Documents from the Cairo Geniza ("India Book")* (Leiden: Brill, 2008), pp. 144–145; M. Kervran, "Famous Merchants of the Arabian Gulf in the Middle Ages," *Dilmun, Journal of the Bahrain Historical and Archaeological Society*, No. 11 (1983), p. 121. Goitein and Friedman cite two stone inscriptions preserved in Mecca, one from 1135 and the other after Ramisht's death in 1140.

[4] Kervran, "Famous Merchants of the Arabian Gulf," p. 22.

[5] Kervran, "Famous Merchants of the Arabian Gulf," pp. 22–23; Moira Tampoe, *Maritime Trade between China and the West: An Archaeological Study of the Ceramics from Siraf (Persian Gulf), 8th to 15th centuries A.D.* (BAR International Series 555, 1989), p. 126.

Further to the east, the impact of Chola was quite different. On a subcontinent where the great empires were typically landlocked, the Cholas faced the sea. According to Tansen Sen, the Chola rulers worked to connect their agricultural base to inter-regional and maritime commercial networks, wooed merchants from abroad and used their naval might in the expeditions of 1025 and 1067 to end the historical dominance of Srivijaya in the eastern Indian Ocean.[6] Their position at the center of east-west trade both benefited them and profoundly shaped the structure of the trading system. Sen writes that "the Chola trading emporium provided both the natural setting and economic structure that greatly facilitated the movement of merchants and commodities across the Indian Ocean and contributed to the subsequent emergence of the 'world economy' by linking the major markets of the maritime world."[7]

In southeast Asia, the Chola naval expeditions (that of 1025 in particular) effectively ended the Srivijayan hegemony over maritime trade and were a factor behind the southward expansion of both the Cambodian Khmer and Burmese Pagan empires, though one can also point to the impact of expanding Chinese trade.[8] Kenneth Hall has argued that the upsurge in trade caused by Song pro-trade policies had a profoundly unsettling effect on maritime southeast Asia, as Sri Lankans, Burmese and Malays came to challenge Srivijaya's longtime dominance of southeast Asia's maritime trade, and he identifies five discrete trading commercial zones that had come into being by the beginning of the fourteenth century.[9]

Further to the east, the Ly family's establishment of Dai Viet (Vietnam) in the late tenth century marked what was to become a permanent separation from the Chinese empire. Vietnamese hostilities with the Chams to the south made for somewhat unsettled conditions until the middle of the eleventh century, when a strong Champa monarch stabilized his relations with his neighbors to the north.[10] Here again, the role of trade was powerful. Momoki Shiro's study of Dai Viet from the tenth to fifteenth

[6] Sen, *Buddhism, Diplomacy, and Trade*, pp. 220, 227.
[7] Sen, *Buddhism, Diplomacy, and Trade*, pp. 160–161.
[8] Kulke, "The Naval Expeditions of the Cholas," pp. 10–11; Kenneth R. Hall, *Maritime Trade and State Development*, pp. 197–202.
[9] Hall, *Maritime Trade and State Development*, pp. 192–197, 222–231; Jan Wisseman Christie on the impact of maritime trade on Java: "Javanese Markets and the Asian Sea Trade," pp. 344–381. See also Geoff Wades's argument that the period of 900 to 1300 C.E. marked Southeast Asia's first great age of commerce, a development spurred by the Song "economic revolution." "An Earlier Age of Commerce in Southeast Asia: 900–1300 C.E.?" in Fujiko Kayoko, Makino Naoko, and Matsumoto Mayumi, eds., *Dynamic Rimlands and Open Heartlands: Maritime Asia as a Site of Interactions.* Proceedings of the Second COE-ARI Joint Workshop. (Osaka: Research Cluster on Global History and Maritime Asia, Osaka University, 2007), pp. 71–75.
[10] Hall, *Maritime Trade and State Development*, pp. 181–188.

centuries has shown how that state flourished through the eleventh and twelfth centuries, by virtue both of its transshipment of commodities between various southeast Asian countries and China and of a growing domestic production of precious export commodities.[11] He also argues that the volume of Dai Viet's non-tributary trade exceeded that of the well-documented tributary trade between them and the Song, this despite some of the Song court's restrictions on Nanhai trade during the tenth and eleventh centuries.[12]

In east Asia, the Song had to contend with powerful continental neighbors – the Khitan Liao and Tangut Xixia to the northeast and northwest, and then, after 1127, the Jurchen Jin, whose empire included not only Manchuria but virtually all of northern China. The Song's inability to control the Silk Route as it led into central Asia (as had the Han and Tang) gave special importance to maritime trade, not only with the countries of the Nanhai but also with Japan and Korea, both of which could be reached only by sea.[13] Momoki Shiro and Hasuda Takashi have written that "Northeast Asia was deeply incorporated into international trade networks for the first time" during the eleventh through fourteenth centuries, while Yamauchi Shinji calls this "the age of Japan-Song trade" in which "there were active exchanges of people, commodities and information through frequent maritime trade with the Asian continent."[14,15]

The dramatic changes in the political character of the states of maritime Asia from the eleventh to thirteenth centuries that we have discussed above were paralleled by transformations of the trade itself. Although the luxury goods that had dominated Tang-Abbasid trade continued to

---

[11] Momoki Shiro, "Dai Viet and the South China Sea Trade: From the Tenth to the Fifteenth Century," *Crossroads: An Interdisciplinary Journal of Southeast Asian Studies* 12.1 (1999), p. 15.

[12] Momoki Shiro, "Dai Viet and the South China Sea Trade," p. 12.

[13] This is more fully treated in my article, "Songdai yu Dong Ya de duoguo xiti ji maoyi shijie 宋代与东亚的多国係提及贸易世界," *Beida xuebao* 北大学报 *(Zhexue shehui kexue ban)* 46.2 (2009), pp. 99–108; the English version was published as "Song China and the multi-state and commercial world of East Asia," *Crossroads: Studies on the History of Exchange Relations in the East Asian World* 1 (2010), pp. 33–54.

[14] Momoki Shiro 桃木至朗 and Hasuda Takashi 蓮田隆志, "A Review of the Periodization of Southeast Asian Medieval/Early Modern History, in Comparison with That of Northeast Asia," in Fujiko Kayoko, Makino Naoko, and Matsumoto Mayumi, eds., *Dynamic Rimlands and Open Heartlands: Maritime Asia as a Site of Interactions.* Proceedings of the Second COE-ARI Joint Workshop. (Osaka: Research Cluster on Global History and Maritime Asia, Osaka University, 2007), p. 5.

[15] Yamauchi Shinji 山内晋次, "The Japanese Archipelago and Maritime Asia from the 9th to the 13th Centuries," in Fujiko Kayoko, Makino Naoko, and Matsumoto Mayumi, eds., *Dynamic Rimlands and Open Heartlands: Maritime Asia as a Site of Interactions.* Proceedings of the Second COE-ARI Joint Workshop. (Osaka: Research Cluster on Global History and Maritime Asia, Osaka University, 2007), pp. 83, 93.

be in great demand, they were joined and at times overshadowed by a vast range of commodities. In his classic study of Song maritime trade, Paul Wheatley drew on Chinese sources to describe ninety-one commodities that were traded.[16] Chief among China's export commodities were ceramics. As evidenced by archaeological finds from all parts of maritime Asia, the demand for Song ceramics – which often did double-duty as ballast for outbound ships – was global in character and it further expanded the Tang export industry that was described in Chapter 1, with large-scale kiln complexes centered on the southeastern port cities of Guangzhou and Quanzhou, but extending inland as far as Jiangxi. Besides ceramics, Song exports included silks, foodstuffs (often in large ceramic containers), manufactured goods (including books), and – in the thirteenth century especially – large quantities of copper and tin. Indeed, such was the demand for copper coins that the government repeatedly (though ineffectually) tried to ban their export. As for imports, Song urban consumers developed a great appetite for *xiangyao* 香藥, a term usually translated as aromatics but which included incense, scented woods, perfumes and medicines, but also for pearls, ivory, rhinoceros horn, cotton fabrics, ebon, sappan woods, pepper and cloves, among other commodities. Many of these goods came from southeast Asia, though there were some, including the highly sought-after frankincense, that came only from west Asia.[17]

Derek Heng's work on Chinese trade with southeast Asia in the Song and Yuan periods offers important insights into its increasing sophistication. Not only does he amply document the earlier-mentioned transition from a luxury trade to a higher-volume trade in bulk commodities, but he also identifies a change in the marketing of commodities. Beginning in the late eleventh century, the trade was characterized by "large volumes of product shipments, direct participation in the shipping trade by Chinese traders, and the possession of knowledge of the gradations of the products in question."[18] The last point is critical, for Heng shows how in both southeast Asian exports to China like aromatics, and imports from China

---

[16] Paul Wheatley, "Geographical Notes on Some Commodities Involved in the Sung Maritime Trade," *Journal of the Malaysian Branch of the Royal Asiatic Society* 32.2, no. 186 (1959), pp. 1–140. See also the detailed treatment of the majority commodities by Angela Schottenhammer in "China's Emergence as a Maritime Power," pp. 492–523.

[17] Schottenhammer, "China's Emergence as a Maritime Power," especially pp. 512–518. Other imports exclusively from west Asia included alum, ambergris, asafetida (a gum resin). That region also supplied ivory, tortoiseshells, pearls, and even black slaves, though these also came from other parts of Asia.

[18] Derek Thiam Soon Heng, *Economic Interaction between China and the Malacca Straits Region, Tenth to Fourteenth Centuries A.D.* (Ph.D. dissertation, University of Hull, 2005).

like silk and especially ceramics, sources point to increasing gradations of goods (high vs. low quality, and levels in between), suggesting increasingly complex commercial networks and improvements in commercial intelligence, for gradations would only make commercial sense if there were assurances that the market for different grades existed.[19]

One of the factors underlying the expansion of commerce was the spreading use of Chinese ocean-going ships, or junks (from the Malay *jong*), throughout east and southeast Asia, typified by their use of iron nails (in contrast to the bindings of the Arab dhow and the lashed-lug/doweled construction of many southeast Asian ships) and employing sternpost rudders and the magnetic compass as an aid to navigation. In Chapter 2 we encountered Arab references to Chinese ships in tenth-century southeast Asia, but those cannot be substantiated by other evidence. By contrast, there is ample documentation for the Song turn to the sea, both in the development of a navy that protected the dynasty from Jurchen and then Mongols, in the twelfth and thirteenth centuries, and in the emergence of a large merchant fleet.

Thanks to the pioneering work of Jung-pang Lo, the role of Chinese junks during the Song is well documented. There were 43 Song localities (9 of them with major shipyards) that produced ships of all sorts. Among these were the "whales" (*haiqiu* 海鰍), so called because of their great size, which had beams of 25 to 30 feet and were a specialty of Quanzhou. According to Lo:

Chinese junks were sturdy: their hulls were constructed with several layers of planking; they were commodious: they had cabins, common rooms for the passengers, and ample cargo space; and they were safe: they had water-tight bulkheads, fire-fighting equipment and life-boats. Some of them were said to be capable of carrying a thousand passengers and crew.[20]

---

[19] Heng, *Economic Interaction between China and the Malacca Straits Region*, pp. 210–214. See, too, Heng's article on these changes in the ceramics trade, though in it his focus is on the early Yuan: "Economic Networks between the Malay Region and the Hinterlands of Quanzhou and Guangzhou: Temasek and the Chinese Ceramics and Foodstuffs Trade," in Ann Low, ed., *Early Singapore, 1300s–1819; Evidence in Maps, Text and Artifacts* (Singapore: Singapore History Museum, 2004), pp. 73–85.

[20] Lo Jung-pang, "Chinese Shipping and East-West Trade from the Xth to the XIVth century," in *Sociétés et companies de commerce en Orient et dans l'Océan Indien. Actes du Huitième Colloque International d'Histoire Maritime*, ed., Michel Mollat (Paris: S.E.V.P.E.N., 1970), pp. 169–170. See, too, Angela Schottenhammer, "China's Emergence as a Maritime Power," pp. 450–454. For a comprehensive treatment of Chinese naval development, with special emphasis on the Song, see Lo's posthumously published *China as a Sea Power, 1127–1368: A Preliminary Survey of the Maritime Expansion and Naval Exploits of the Chinese People during the Southern Sung and Yuan Periods* (1957; Hong Kong: Hong Kong University Press, 2012), edited by Bruce A. Elleman, 2007.

Ship building itself became multinational, in that many of the essential materials came from abroad:

Cotton for sailcloth; gums and rosin for caulking; verdigris, yellow lead and cinnabar for pigments; dragon blood for varnish; not to mention borax, gold leaf, rawhide and rattan, all of which came from abroad. Items such as coir palm fibers for cordage and isinglass came from as far as the Near East and the islands of the Indian Ocean.

As shipbuilding began to deplete the forest resources of southeastern China, even timber came to be imported from Japan, with pre-sawn fir, cedar and horse chestnut wood planks shipped to the shipyards of China.[21]

This attention to the development of junks should not obscure the fact that they did not supplant the dhows and other vessels that had long plied Asian waters. To the contrary, there is every reason to believe that they coexisted, with interactions that resulted in the appearance by the thirteenth century in southeast Asia of hybrid junks combining features (and technologies) of the Chinese with distinctly non-Chinese elements.[22] The rise of the Chinese junk was clearly linked to the movement of Chinese merchants into the Nanhai – a subject to which we shall return – but the two were not synonymous. We have at least one example of a Muslim merchant having a junk built for him.[23] Moreover, merchants of any nationalities freely purchased passage on ships, Chinese or otherwise.

These points are supported by the archaeological record stemming from the excavations of two junks dating to the early and late Southern Song, respectively. The Nanhai No. 1 wreck was discovered in off the coast of Taishan 台山 (Guangdong) in 1987. The ship was 21.8 meters in length, making it comparable in size to the Belitung and Cirebon wrecks in the Java Sea, and had thirteen compartments (utilizing the bulkhead construction of junks). The ship was outbound from China with a cargo of 60,000 to 80,000 pieces, which included gold, brass and iron objects, relics, silver ingots and large quantities of porcelain and coins. The majority of the porcelain was from Fujian kilns – suggesting a Fujian, probably Quanzhou, departure – but included pieces from the

---

[21] Lo, "Chinese Shipping and East-West Trade," p. 172. See also, Wang Zengyu 王曾瑜, "Tan Songdai zaochuanye" 宋代造船业, *Wenwu* 文物 1975, No. 10, pp. 24–27, and So, *Prosperity, Region and Institutions*, pp. 84–85.

[22] Yves-Pierre Manguin, "Trading Ships of the South China Sea," *Journal of the Economic and Social History of the Orient* 36.3 (Aug. 1993), pp. 270–274.

[23] This was in 1136 and involved one Pu Luoxin 蒲羅辛 (Abu al-Hassan?), who had been rewarded by the Song government for his contribution to China's import trade. SHY, *Fanyi*, 7, p. 9a, cited by Lo, "Chinese Shipping and East-West Trade," p. 169.

famous Jingdezhen 景德鎮 and Longquan 龍泉 kilns in Jiangxi and Zhejiang, respectively. Its 6,000 coins ranged in date from the Eastern Han to the Shaoxing period of the early Southern Song. There were also some luxury objects, including a silver waist belt of distinctly non-Chinese design, suggesting foreign merchant passengers (if not the ship owner).[24]

The second shipwreck was found at Houzhu 后渚, a former port of Quanzhou, and excavated in 1974 (Figure 3.1). A large ship, 24 by 9 meters in length and beam, with 12 bulkheads, it can be dated precisely to 1277, just after the surrender of Quanzhou to the Mongols. Many of the containers aboard the ship bear labels of the Song imperial clan, indicating that the ship may have been owned by the Song imperial clan, and raising the possibility that it was purposefully foundered when it arrived in Quanzhou only to discover that the city had fallen to the Mongols.[25] That it was arriving in China is significant (and rare among shipwrecks of the era), for the ship's cargo was filled with goods from abroad: cowries, pepper, betel nut, tortoiseshell, cinnabar, Somalian ambergris and 2,300 kilograms of fragrant southeast Asian woods and incense.[26]

These two shipwrecks therefore confirm the findings of the written record concerning the importance of ceramics and metals for Song exports and spices and aromatics for imports.

The Song Promotion of Trade

To the mix of developing state systems and growing commercialization across the breadth of maritime Asia along with advances in shipbuilding

[24] Angela Schottenhammer, "China's Increasing Integration into the Indian Ocean World up to Song Times: Sea Routes, Connections, Trade," in Angela Schottenhammer, ed., *Transfer, Exchange, and Human Movement across the Indian Ocean World* [Palgrave Series in Indian Ocean World Studies], 2 vols. (London: Palgrave Macmillan, forthcoming); Li Qingxin, *Nanhai 1 and the Maritime Silk Road* (Beijing: Wuzhou chuanbo chubanshe, 2009). This shipwreck was also remarkable because the Chinese used the "whole salvage method", whereby the entire was encased on a huge container, lifted from the ocean bed and deposited a prepared facility, thus preserving the 800-year old hull while excavating its contents.

[25] Fu Zongwen 傅宗文, "Houzhu guchuan: Song ji nanwai zongshi haiwai jingshang di wuzheng" 后渚古船：宋季南外宗室海外经商的物证, *Haiwai jiaotong yanjiu* 海外交通研究 2 (1989), pp. 77–83. See also, Chaffee, "Impact of the Song Imperial Clan," pp. 33–35, *Branches of Heaven*, pp. 236–238, and Heng, *Sino-Malay Trade and Diplomacy from the Tenth through the Fourteenth Century*, Ohio University Research in International Diplomacy, Southeast Asia Series No. 121, (Athens, OH: Ohio University Press, 2009), pp. 126–127, 204.

[26] Jeremy Green, "The Song Dynasty Shipwreck at Quanzhou, Fujian Province, People's Republic of China," *International Journal of Nautical Archaeology and Underwater Exploration* 12.3 (1983), pp. 253–261; Chaffee, *Branches of Heaven*, pp. 216–217.

Figure 3.1 Houzhu ship, Quanzhou – photo of the wreck
(courtesy of John Meckley, 2006) and ship model (Shanghai Maritime
Museum, 2015)

and nautical technology that we had described so far, we must add the role of the Song government. Its remarkable pro-trade policies set it apart not only from other Chinese dynasties but also from other states in the eleventh- and twelfth-century maritime world, and were crucial to the development of the maritime trade system.

According to Zhu Yu 朱彧 (early twelfth century), who in his youth had accompanied his father to Guangzhou and seen the activities of the maritime merchants first hand, foreign ships entering Chinese waters from the south typically encountered Song authorities at Ru Island, where officials at the Inspectorate for Observing Ships (Wangbo xunjiansi 望舶巡檢司) would welcome them with gifts of wine and meat and provide troops to escort them to Guangzhou. They were then escorted to Guangzhou or one of the other officially sanctioned ports. After they had docked, the ships were placed under armed guard at an island near the superintendency of maritime trade, where officials had a chance to inspect and tax their goods (including the compulsory purchase of certain commodities), after which the foreign merchants were permitted to market them.[27]

Although Zhu Yu limits his discussion to trade in Guangzhou, which he observed as a child, there were by his time a number of ports with maritime trade offices (shibosi 市舶司) or, after 1080, superintendencies (shibo tijusi 市舶提舉司). In addition to three that were established in the early Song at Guangzhou (971), Hangzhou 杭州 (989) and Mingzhou 明州 (992), four others were created later in the Northern Song (Shanghai 上海 in 1074, Quanzhou 泉州 in 1087, Mizhou 密州 on the Shandong Peninsula in 1088 and Xiuzhou 秀州 in 1113) and another two in the early years of the Southern Song.[28] Among the later superintendencies, that of Quanzhou was most important, since it quickly assumed the position of the premier port for overseas commerce, and in fact the vast majority of our information about the merchant communities comes from it and Guangzhou.[29] The multiple superintendencies provided overseas merchants with a choice of ports at which to do their business,

---

[27] Zhu Yu 朱彧, *Pingzhou ketan* 萍洲可談 (Shanghai: Shanghai guji chubanshe, 1989), 2, p. 25.

[28] Schottenhammer, "China's Emergence as a Maritime Power," Table 13, p. 474. These two Southern Song superintendencies were Liangzhe, near the capital of Lin'an (Hangzhou).

[29] As Hugh R. Clark has shown, Quanzhou's role as a major port for maritime trade dates back to the tenth century, and although in theory ships from overseas either had to stop first at one of the other trade offices or risk being caught for smuggling, officials seem to have often looked the other way. *Community, Trade, and Networks: Southern Fujian Province from the Third to the Thirteenth Centuries.* (Cambridge, MA: Cambridge University Press, 1991), pp. 376–381.

while the superintendencies themselves provided a remarkable attention to a wide range of trade-related activity.

The maritime trade superintendencies were unique institutions in the medieval maritime world. The superintendents were generally ranking officials from the Finance Commission, in some cases concurrently appointed as prefects of the host prefectures, but answering to the Finance Commission for their activities. Those activities naturally centered upon revenue collection, to which we shall return, but their responsibilities included providing for the welfare of foreign merchants. According to Zhou Qufei 周去非 (late twelfth century), the maritime trade superintendencies were established "in order for the country to peacefully nourish the foreign barbarians"; the superintendencies "tax the merchants and protect them."[30] "Foreign ships, damaged or without their owners on board when drifting on shore because of [strong] wind, would be saved by local officials who would make records of the cargoes and allow the owners' relatives to reclaim them."[31] In the Southern Song provisions were made for those in urgent need, such as shipwrecked seamen, who were given allowances while they awaited repatriation.[32] In addition, in the tenth month of every year, the Quanzhou and Guangzhou maritime trade superintendencies each hosted the foreign merchants at a great feast, at the substantial cost of 300 strings of cash in each locality.[33]

The revenues collected by the superintendency were of two sorts. A number of commodities were subject to compulsory purchase by the government, which paid the merchants in copper, gold, silver or trade commodities such as porcelain and silk.[34] These purchases, made at below-market prices, which allowed the government to resell the goods at a profit, typically accounted for between 40 and 60 percent of a ship's cargo. The basic tariff on all imported goods, including those subject to compulsory purchase, was 10 percent, and with the exception of a brief increase to 20 percent in the 990s it remained so for most of the Northern Song. However, in the early twelfth century, a further distinction was

---

[30] Zhou Qufei 周去非. *Lingwai daida jiaozhu* 嶺外代答校注. Yang Wuquan 楊武泉, ed. (Beijing: Zhonghua shuju, 1999) 3, p. 126.

[31] Cited by Laurence J. C. Ma, *Commercial Development and Urban Change in Sung China (960–1279)* (Ann Arbor: Department of Geography, University of Michigan, 1971), p. 33.

[32] SS 491, p. 14137. The citation specifically concerns Japanese sailors, but presumably sailors from other countries would have been similarly treated.

[33] SHY, *Zhiguan* 44, pp. 24a–b; Zhou, *Lingwai daida* 3, p. 126.

[34] Eight commodities were specified as being subject to mandatory purchase: tortoise shell, elephant tusk, rhinoceros horn, a special kind of steel known as *bintie* 鑌鐵 used for weapons, water lizard skin for making drums, coral, agate and frankincense. See Ma, *Commercial Development and Urban Change in Sung China*, pp. 37–38.

instituted between "coarse goods" (*cuse* 粗色) such as textiles and fine (*xise* 細色) goods like many of the precious commodities. Initially the coarse goods were taxed at a rate of 30 percent, but after 1136 this was changed to 15 percent.[35] Zhu Yu, describes the working of this complex taxation in early twelfth century Guangzhou:

> Using units of 10%, all fine goods such as real pearls and Borneo camphor are levied at 10%; and all coarse goods such as tortoise shells and sappan caesal pinia are levied at 30%, and there are different assessments among the market officials. After this the merchants receive back their goods. Consignments of ivory weighing 30 *jin* 斤 and of frankincense are all subject to monopoly purchase in the official market, apart from the levy, so merchants with large shipments of ivory have to divide into pieces of less than 30 *jin*, so that by the regulations they can be exempt from the official market.

Noting that the low price the government pays is aggravating to the merchants, such are the punishments for trying to cheat the system that "the merchants dare not disobey."[36]

Maritime trade was a lucrative source of income for the government. Through most of the Northern Song, the annual revenues from the trade were around half a million strings of cash, and accounted for only a small portion of overall revenues. However, maritime tariffs increased to an average of 1.1 million in the years 1102 to 1110, and then swelled to around 2 million in the mid-twelfth century, funds that were especially important for the Southern Song government, operating as it was under straitened conditions.[37]

It should be noted that, under the emperor Shenzong 神宗 (r. 1068–1085), maritime tribute missions underwent a renewed efflorescence. As shown in Table 2.1, after a mere 13 Nanhai missions in the years 1023 to 1067, there were 18 such missions in the 18 years of Shenzong's reign. Similarly, Korea ended a 38-year hiatus of missions in 1068 and sent 7 between then and 1085. Among the 18 Nanhai missions, 4 were from Champa, 3 from Arabia and 3 from Srivijaya, three states that had also been dominant in the early Song. Also of note were four missions from other states in western Asia: Zanzibar in 1071 and 1081, Muscat in 1072 and Bahrein in 1074. Following Shenzong's

---

[35] Schottenhammer, "China's Emergence as a Maritime Power," p. 468.

[36] Zhu Yu, *Pingzhou ketan* 2, p. 25.

[37] Clark, *Community, Trade, and Networks*, p. 132. In the 1130s the maritime revenues may have accounted for as much as 10 percent of all government revenues, but for the most part, it probably did not exceed 5 percent. Yoshinobu Shiba estimates that overseas trade account for 2 to 3 percent of total government revenues in the early Song. "Sung Foreign Trade: Its Scope and Organization," in Morris Rossabi, ed., *China among Equals: The Middle Kingdom and Its Neighbors, 10th–14th Centuries* (Berkeley, CA: University of California Press, 1983), p. 106.

reign, the missions continued at a reduced level – though still above that of the Renzong period – until the end of the Northern Song. The reason for the revival of these missions was clearly not economic but rather the more muscular foreign policy of the emperor Shenzong, which was subsequently echoed by his son Huizong 徽宗 (r. 1100–1126).

The more economically significant development of the late Northern Song period was the establishment of new maritime trade offices: possibly in Shanghai 上海 in 1074, in Quanzhou in 1087, in Jiaozhou 膠州 (near the modern city of Qingdao in Shandong) in 1088 and in Xiujiu 秀 州 in Liangzhe in 1113.[38] These new offices marked the end of the Song attempt to channel all maritime trade into three ports and began an era of multi-port commerce that lasted through the Southern Song, when three more offices were opened. By far the most important of these new offices was that of Quanzhou, for it allowed a port that long been thriving, legally or illegally, on the maritime trade to eclipse all other ports, including Guangzhou, by the Southern Song if not before.[39] In fact, the revenues from Quanzhou were undoubtedly a factor in the increase in maritime revenues from a half million to a million strings per year described above.

The Song policy of encouraging the trade was most famously articulated by the emperor Gaozong 高宗 (r. 1127–1162) in 1137. In the midst of his efforts to reestablish the dynasty following its loss of northern China to the Jurchen, he stated that "The profits from maritime trade are greatest. If managed properly, the income can reach millions (of cash). Is this not better than taxing the people? We should therefore pay more attention [to maritime trade] in order to relieve the tax burden

---

[38] See the very detailed treatment of Angela Schottenhammer in "China's Emergence as a Maritime Power, pp. 470–479." The Shanghai office is only mentioned in Ming dynasty sources, and therefore its existence is uncertain.

[39] Foreign traders were not barred from visiting them and trading, but by law they could only do so after stopping at Guangzhou or Mingzhou and paying their import taxes, so the question concerning pre-1087 Quanzhou is whether they followed the law, at considerable competitive disadvantage, or in fact were circumventing the law with the connivance of local officials. Billy So, in *Prosperity, Region, and Institutions*, pp. 39–40, has argued the former, particularly that the foreign trade was managed largely by Chinese merchants in Quanzhou who brought the goods in from the official ports. I have argued the contrary in "At the Intersection of Empire and World Trade: The Chinese Port City of Quanzhou (Zaitun), Eleventh–Fifteenth Centuries," in Kenneth R. Hall, ed., *Secondary Cities and Urban Networking in the Indian Ocean Realm, c. 1400–1800* (Lanham, MD: Rowman & Littlefield Publishers, 2008), pp. 103–108. In this I have followed in part the argument of Hugh Clark, "The Politics of Trade and the Establishment of the Quanzhou Trade Superintendency," in *Zhongguo yu haishang sichou zhi lu* 中国与海上丝绸之路 (*China and the Maritime Silk Route*), edited by Lianheguo jiaokewen zuzhi haishang sichou zhilu zonghe kaocha Quanzhou guoji xueshu taolunhui zuzhi weiyuanhui 联合国教科文组织海上丝绸上之路综合考察泉州国际学术讨论会组织委员会 (Fuzhou: Fujian renmin chubanshe, 1991), pp. 384–386.

on the people."[40] Nine years later, in the course of demoting an official for harming the merchants by unfairly deflating the prices of goods when serving as superintendent in Guangzhou, the emperor remarked: "The profits from maritime trade contribute much to the national income. In accordance with former regulations, the people from distant lands should be encouraged to come and trade."[41]

This encouragement was not limited to Gaozong. We saw it in the paternalistic functions of the superintendencies described earlier. It was evident in the Song policy of rewarding merchants who brought in cargoes of exceptional value with official rank, a subject to which we shall return. It was also reflected in the prohibition, enacted in 1080, on the personal participation by officials in the maritime trade, a restriction representing a dramatic contrast with the Tang, where, as we saw in Chapter 1, postings to Guangzhou were considered sure passports to wealth.[42]

For the foreign merchants, the government's welcoming attitude together with dependable-if-high tariff levels, made Chinese ports attractive places to settle and do business. Again in contrast to the Tang, those ports were no longer in frontier regions of the empire, for by the Song the southeastern coast had become fully integrated into the imperial polity, with regions like Fujian and Zhejiang emerging as among the most economically prosperous and politically successful parts of the empire. As a result, the foreign merchant communities were also more integrated into the economic mainstream than had previously been the case.

Maritime Merchant Communities

In his youthful explorations of Guangzhou, Zhu Yu was fascinated by the diversity of peoples and practices that he encountered. In addition to details about shipping and seafaring, he tells us about gambling using a variant of Chinese chess;[43] he mentions Koreans, whom he describes as "able to write" despite being barbarians;[44] he describes the black "demon slaves" (guinu 鬼奴), individuals of great strength who were commonly owned by the foreign merchants of Guangzhou;[45] and he recounts his attendance at a celebratory feast in the foreign quarter of Guangzhou at

---

[40] SHY, Zhiguan 44, pp. 20a–b. For other translations, see Gang Deng, Maritime Sector, Institutions and Sea Power, p. 120, and Kuwabara, "On P'u Shou-keng," Part 1, p. 24.

[41] SHY, Zhiguan 44, p. 24b; Kuwabara, "On P'u Shou-keng," Part 1, p. 24.

[42] Gang Deng, Maritime Sector, Institutions and Seapower, p. 120. Deng does not provide the original source.

[43] Zhu, Pingzhou ketan 2, p. 29.   [44] Zhu, Pingzhou ketan 2, p. 36.

[45] Zhu, Pingzhou ketan 2, p. 27. See Don Wyatt's comprehensive treatment of these black slaves and Zhu Yu's representation of them in The Blacks of Premodern China, pp. 48–60.

which a man from Srivijaya provided a recitation of the Buddhist *Classic of the Bright Phoenix King* (*Kong cui ming wang jing* 孔崔明王經). He is very critical of the performer for not knowing the proper readings (*zhenyan* 真言 – "true words") for the text. Rather,

The sound was truly like the pouring of boiling soup from a bottle, and moreover there was not a single sound that resembled the true recitation of the *[Bright] Phoenix* as it has been passed down through the generations. I said: "This book has been through many translations, so it is easy to have differences. However, according to prevailing customs, this book (is used to) summon the deceased, and I do not know how the Chinese spirits will understand it."[46]

Drawing on his own knowledge of Buddhism – a thoroughly Sinicized foreign religion – Zhu views southeast Asian practices as incorrect, at least in the context of Guangzhou, since the recitation would be incomprehensible to the local spirits.

As Zhu Yu's account suggests, a visitor strolling the streets of Guangzhou or one of the other Song maritime trading ports during the Song would have encountered people from every part of the known world. The Koreans mentioned by him as well as the Japanese were principally to be found in the more northerly ports of Hangzhou, Mingzhou and Quanzhou, where the lines of communication were closest. Indeed, such was the volume of commerce between China and Korea that numerous Arab merchants are recorded in Korean sources as having made their way there (via China, of course).[47] Southeast Asians were very much in evidence as key actors in the flourishing Sino-southeast Asian trade.[48] The Srivijayan Buddhists who sponsored the Buddhist recitation provide one example of that presence. Another is provided by the thirteenth-century Shi Nuowei, a Srivijayan merchant who established what was clearly a Muslim cemetery in Quanzhou. This incident, which will be discussed at length below, points to the increasingly international character of Islam in China during the Song, a development of great importance.

Our visitor would also have encountered south Asian seafarers and merchants who by Song times were active throughout maritime Asia,

---

[46] Zhu, *Pingzhou ketan*, 2, p. 29.

[47] Hee-Soo Lee, *The Advent of Islam in Korea*, pp. 55–59. See especially the table on p. 58, with statistics in 25-year intervals of Chinese ships arriving in Korea. These peaked with 35 ships in 1050–1075. See Li Yukun's 李玉昆 description of 19 recorded visits by Quanzhou merchants to Korea during the Northern Song. *Quanzhou haiwai jiaotong shilue* 泉州海外交通史略 (Xiamen: Xiamen University Press, 1995), pp. 48–50.

[48] See Heng, *Sino-Malay Trade and Diplomacy*, Chapter 4, where he argues that the Song constituted the apogee of southeast Asian merchant activity in China. For his discussion of the Buddhist recitation, see p. 118.

especially following the rise of the Chola empire. The arrival in Quanzhou during the Yongxi period (984–988) of the Buddhist monk Luohuna 囉護哪 (Rahula?) from India (Tianzhu 天竺) is not surprising, given the long history of Sino-Indian contact related to the transmission of Buddhism. But the response to his arrival was instructive; the foreign merchants (*fanshang* 番商) showered him with gifts of gold, silks and jewels, and he built a temple in the southern suburbs of the city, the Baolin Yuan 寶林院, which was still flourishing in the early thirteenth century.[49] Truly remarkable, however, was the Hindu temple dedicated to Siva that was built in Quanzhou in 1281, complete with a Tamil and Chinese inscription. Although the date and content of the inscription (which offers prayers to the great khan) place it in the early years of the Yuan dynasty, there must have been a significant Tamil-Hindu community in late Song Quanzhou for such an undertaking to have occurred just five years after the city came under Mongol control.[50]

Chinese overseas merchants and the mariners who transported them were yet another group who would not have been present in Tang ports. To give a few examples, Wang Yuanmao 王元懋 grew up in a Buddhist monastery doing odd jobs, but managed to study with monks and learn about foreign countries. Later he went on a merchant ship to Champa (Zhancheng), and because of his proficiency in writing both Chinese and foreign languages (i.e., Cham), he gained the affection of the king of Champa, married a princess, and lived there for ten years. After this he returned to Quanzhou and became an established maritime merchant.[51] Lin Zhaoqing 林昭慶 (1027–1089) was originally a monk at a the Kaiyuan Monastery 開元寺 in Zhangzhou 漳州 (Fujian), sent there as a child by his impoverished family. As a young monk he ventured into overseas commerce. With the financial support of people in his community he organized a maritime trade group (*haishang jituan* 海商集團), made a fortune

---

[49] Hirth and Rockhill, *Chao Ju-kua*, p. 111; Sen, *Buddhism, Diplomacy and Trade*, p. 181.

[50] See John Guy, "Tamil Merchant Guilds and the Quanzhou Trade," in Angela Schottenhammer, ed., *The Emporium of the World: Maritime Quanzhou, 1000–1400* (Leiden: Brill, 2001), pp. 283–309; Jan Wisseman Christie, "Javanese Markets and the Asian Sea Trade Boom," pp. 341–381; and Risha Lee, "Rethinking Community: The Indic Carvings of Quanzhou," in Hermann Kulke, K. Kesavapany, and Vijay Sakhuja, eds., *Nagapattinam to Suvarnadwipa: Reflections on the Chola Naval Expeditions to Southeast Asia* (Singapore: Institute of Southeast Asian Studies, 2010), pp. 240–270.

[51] Li Yukun, *Quanzhou haiwai jiaotong shilue*, pp. 45–46, citing Hong Mai 洪邁, *Yijian zhi* 夷堅志 (Taipei: Mingwen shuju, 1982), Part 3, 6, pp. 1344–1346. Li provides numerous examples of Chinese overseas merchants, including a number not cited here, of Chinese maritime merchants. See, also, Billy So, *Prosperity, Region, and Institutions*, passim.

during the Huangyou period (1049–1054), and returned to his monastic life, gaining fame as a Linji 臨濟 monk.[52]

As the reference to "maritime trade group" indicates, overseas ventures were costly undertakings that were often jointly underwritten by a group of investors. The traveling merchant groups were also highly organized. According to Zhu Yu,

> The large seaships have several hundred men and the smaller ones over one hundred. The major merchants serve as the captain (*gangshou* 綱首), assistant leader (*fugangshou* 副綱首), and purser (*zashi* 雜事). The superintendency provides a vermilion stamp (*zhuji* 朱記), permits the use of flogging on the crew, and requires that the assets of those who died [during the trip] be recorded.[53]

Indeed, when Lin Chong 林充 led a group of merchants from Mingzhou on a trading venture to Japan in 1102, they were organized into three groups totaling 65 men as well as a purser, an assistant and Lin.[54] This last was not an isolated venture. According to Nakamura Tsubasa, not only are there dozens of recorded commercial trips between China and Japan (mainly from Mingzhou) in the twelfth and thirteenth centuries, but they also resulted in the emergence of a substantial Chinese settlement in the port of Hakata.[55]

Foreign and Chinese merchants alike shared far-flung networks of business associates and contacts, and must have interacted with each other as rivals and partners. There was, however, an important restriction on merchants during the Song, namely an 1167 requirement that Chinese merchant vessels venturing overseas return within a year of their departure.[56] This did not prevent individual sojourners like Wang Yuanmao from extended stays abroad, nor did it prevent a lucrative trade between Chinese and southeast Asian ports, but as Derek Heng has argued, it focused the trade of Chinese ships on southeast Asia (since trips into the Indian Ocean generally required over a year) and limited the number of stops they could make while in southeast Asian waters.[57]

---

[52] Li Yukun, *Quanzhou haiwai jiaotong shilue*, pp. 45–46, citing Qin Guan, *Huaihai ji*, 3.

[53] Zhu Yu, *Pingzhou ketan* 2, p. 26.

[54] Li Yukun, *Quanzhou haiwai jiaotong shilue*, pp. 46–47. Li does not provide a source for this information. For a detailed treatment of the organization of maritime merchant groups and ship ownership, see Shiba Yoshinobu, *Commerce and Society in Sung China*, Mark Elvin, trans. (Ann Arbor: Center for Chinese Studies, University of Michigan, 1970), pp. 15–45.

[55] Nakamura Tsubasa, "The Maritime East Asian Network in the Song-Yuan Period," paper presented at the Conference on Middle Period China, 800–1400, Harvard University, June 5–7, 2014, pp. 6–10. According to a table that he provides (pp. 7–8), there were 13 recorded trips in the eleventh century and 19 in the twelfth century.

[56] SHY, *Zhiguan* 44, pp. 27a–28a.

[57] Heng, *Sino-Malay Trade and Diplomacy*, Chapter 4, especially p. 125ff. Gang Deng argues that the government imposed the 1164 restriction in order to maximize trade by

We turn finally to the Muslim visitors to and residents of the Song ports, many (but by no means all) of whom were Arabs or even west Asian. The qualification is important, for the Muslim trade diaspora had evolved dramatically from its beginnings in Tang times, and the relationship between Arab and Islamic identities had grown complex. In his periodization of the Islamization of maritime Asia, Andre Wink characterizes the eleventh to thirteenth centuries as a period in which the Middle East declined vis-à-vis Europe and China, but also one that witnessed a proliferation of ties among Muslim communities in west Asia, south India and Sri Lanka, and maritime southeast Asia. He notes further that the Malayali Muslims of southern India "made vigorous attempts to prove the pure Arab origin of their religion and thereby to enhance their status vis-à-vis other Muslim groups, particularly the descendants of the Afghan and Turkish invaders of North India."[58] The Muslim merchants who traded and settled in Song ports were participants in this rich and varied world of Islam, which included Arabs and Persians, those of Arab or Persian descent and converts from across the breadth of maritime Asia, united by their faith and the use of Arabic as a *lingua franca*. If the prominence of individuals with Arabic names in the historical evidence relating to the merchant communities of the Song Guangzhou and Quanzhou is any guide, then it would appear that those Muslim merchants were the leading, perhaps dominant group among the foreign maritime merchants. So when the sources simply refer to "foreign merchants" or the like, as is the case with some of those referenced in the following section, it is reasonable to assume that they refer to – or at least include – the Muslim merchants.

Governance, Law and Residence

The Song government viewed the foreign merchant communities as a group apart, and it was content to let them live separately and govern themselves. This is most succinctly spelled out in an oft-quoted description by Zhu Yu of the foreign community in Guangzhou in the late eleventh century:

The foreign ward (*fanfang* 蕃坊) is where those from the various countries from across the ocean congregate and live. There is a foreign headman (*fanzhang* 蕃長) who administers the public affairs of the foreign quarter and is specifically responsible for exhorting the foreign merchants to send in tribute. Foreign

increasing the turnover rate of the trading ships. *Maritime Sector, Institutions and Sea Power*, p. 121.

[58] Wink, *Al-Hind*, pp. 3, 70, 76.

officials (*fanguan* 蕃官) are used for this, and their hats, robes, shoes and tablets are like those of Chinese (*Huaren* 華人). When foreigners have a crime, they go to Guangzhou for investigation of the particulars, and then the matter is sent to the foreign quarter to dispose of it. [The guilty party] is tied up on a wooden ladder, and is beaten with a bamboo cane... In cases of serious crime the Guangzhou [government] adjudicates.[59]

Thanks, perhaps, to the vividness of this description of Guangzhou's foreign ward and the similarities between it and the quarters for foreign merchants found in many other Eurasian ports, which were often legally designated as such, the idea that foreign merchants in China resided in foreign quarters and were largely responsible for their own affairs has gained wide acceptance among historians.[60] In fact, historical records reveal a rather more complicated picture.

The several references that I have found to foreign headmen (*fanzhang*) in Song sources share certain characteristics. Except for Zhu Yu's accounts, all are mentioned in connection with tribute missions, and with just a few exceptions they involve Arab headmen in Guangzhou.[61] In Chapter 2 we learned that a letter from the headman to Pu Ximi was responsible for his tribute mission in 993. In the 1070s, during renewed encouragement of tribute missions under the emperor Shenzong, we again encounter headmen from Guangzhou.

In 1072, the Muscat envoy Xinya Tuoluo 辛押陀羅 requested that during the course of his return [to Muscat] he be given permission to examine the affairs of the headman's office in Guangzhou (fanzhang si 蕃長司), and he also offered to make a donation for the restoration of Guangzhou's city walls. His request was referred to the Guangzhou authorities for decision, while his offer was declined.[62] Most scholars in discussing this passage have focused on the city wall proposal, and we shall return to that, but his request is also revealing for its reference to the unsurprising but important fact that the headman had an administrative organization – something suggested by Zhu Yu's "foreign officials" in

---

[59] Zhu, *Pingzhou ketan* 2, p. 27.

[60] See, for example, Wheatley, "Geographical Notes," pp. 28–29; Kuwabara, "P'u Shou-keng," Part 2, p. 34; and John Guy, "Tamil Merchant Guilds," p. 287. For an excellent consideration of the evidence concerning foreign quarters, see Chen Dasheng, "Synthetical Study Program," pp. 173–174. See, too, Ma Juan's 馬娟 informative treatment of the *fanfang* and its varied functions in the Tang and Song, "Tang Song shiqi Yisilan fanfang kao唐宋時期伊斯兰蕃坊考," *Huizu yanjiu* 回族研究 1998, No. 3, pp. 31–36. However, she does not treat the question of a foreign quarter in Quanzhou, for her evidence is drawn almost exclusively from Guangzhou.

[61] There is an account from 1017 of a Jurchen headman connected to a Korean tribute mission. SHY, *Fanyi* 3, pp. 2b–3a.

[62] SHY, *Fanyi* 4, p. 84a; SS 490, p. 14121.

their robes of office – and also for suggesting an interest by the home government in the Guangzhou community.[63]

The following year the Arab headman in Guangdong, the maintaining submission commandant[64] (*baoshun langjiang* 保順郎將) Pu Tuopoli Ci 蒲陀婆離慈 (Abu Dawal?) asked to have his son Mawu 麻勿 (Abu Mahmud?) succeed him, he was turned down, though Mawu was given the lesser rank of commandant (*langjiang* 郎將). The account then provides this gloss on the headman's jurisdiction:

The countries [with merchants] subordinate [to the headman] were varied in name. Thus there was Wuxun 勿巡 (Muscat, Oman), Tuopoli 陀婆離 (?), Yuluhedi 俞盧和地 (Al-Katif, a port in Bahrain), Maluoba 麻囉拔 (Merbat), and others, but all are headed (*guan* 冠) by the Arabs.[65]

Since the Arab headman's authority was confined to west Asians, there were presumably other headmen for other groups. From 1176 we have reference to a Champa headman in Quanzhou.[66] In addition, Derek Heng has argued that Srivijayan headmen were appointed in Guangzhou in 1079, 1082, 1083 and 1156, and while the evidence for this in Song official sources is only circumstantial,[67] such a development would have been consistent with their growing presence, especially since Zhu Yu, in his account of the Srivijayan Buddhist recitation described earlier, states that it was organized by the headman, who would certainly have been Srivijayan himself. Still, the available evidence suggests that the Arab headman was the leading foreign merchant authority, at least within Song Guangzhou.

The judicial proceedings described by Zhu Yu constituted another important element in the foreign merchant presence. As we saw in Chapter 1, already in the Tang a principle of extraterritoriality had been codified into the law and its exercise by a Muslim *qadi* described by the merchant Sulayman. As Zhu indicates, this principle continued in effect during the Song, but as we shall see it was not without its critics.

---

[63] It is of course possible that Pu's request was personally motivated, but it was made in his capacity as envoy and received a positive response from the court.

[64] Charles Hucker, *A Dictionary of Official Titles in Imperial China* (Stanford, CA: Stanford University Press, 1985), p. 369 (#4496): "Sung laudatory title conferred on friendly alien military chiefs."

[65] SS 490, p. 14121.   [66] SHY, *Fanyi* 4, p. 84a.

[67] Heng, *Sino-Malay Trade and Diplomacy*, pp. 90–93, 96. Heng argues that by the 1050s the practice was established with Arab headmen that they would receive the official rank of commandant, and that the subsequent naming of Srivijayan envoys with that rank signifies that they were headmen. Because none of the sources explicitly connect the headman position to official ranks (in fact, as we saw above Pu Mawu was given the rank of commandant but his father's request to have him made headman was rejected), Heng's conclusion must be treated with caution.

The *Song History* biography of Wang Huanzhi 王渙之 (1060–1124) describes a case he dealt with while serving as prefect of Guangzhou: "Here a foreigner killed a slave. The superintendent of maritime trade, according to the judicial precedent, was for sending the offender to his [head-]master to undergo flogging. But Wang Huanzhi did not permit this, and tried him according to the regular laws."[68] In a similar vein Wang Dayou 汪大猷 (1120–1200), while serving as prefect of Quanzhou, argued for the application of Chinese laws in cases involving foreign merchants:

In the past when a foreign merchant had a dispute (*zhengdou* 爭鬥) with another person, unless it involved bodily injury, [the offence] was indemnified with payment of an ox (or oxen). Dayou said: "Why should the Middle Kingdom use the customs of the island barbarians? If they [the foreigners] are within our borders, we should use our laws."[69]

This is a curious passage, coming by itself as it does in Wang's *Song History* biography. A slightly fuller version is given in Lou Yue's biography of Wang and it provides some interesting additional details:

Foreign merchants reside amongst the people, yet according to past law, disputes with local people, unless they involve bodily injury, are indemnified with payment of an ox (or oxen). *[In cases like this] guilt is increasingly hard to determine. Dayou exclaimed to the multitude*: "Why should the Middle Kingdom use the customs of the barbarians? If they [the foreigners] have come before us, we should use our law to settle [the cases]. *Only then will they be afraid and not dare to quarrel.*"[70]

Lou's account historicizes the issue by establishing a residential context – the foreign merchants living among the Chinese – and by its assertion that the issue was becoming more problematic. We also have the curious detail of Wang addressing his question to the multitude (*hao yu zhong* 號于眾), making an oral rather than a written representation. In terms of the legal issues, however, both versions have Wang creating an opposition between Chinese law and barbarian custom, thereby delegitimizing the latter. Most important, Wang's complaint itself is evidence that "barbarian customs" were used in Southern Song Quanzhou to handle minor disputes.

We are not informed of the outcome of Wang's complaint, but it certainly did not result in a change in the law, as a remarkable case from the same period demonstrates:

---

[68] SS 347, p. 11001; following Kuwabara, "On P'u Shou-keng," Part 1, p. 47, modified. Kuwabara's translation is that Wang Huangzhi "could not bear this, and tried him according to the regular laws," thereby implying that Song punishments were less severe than those of the foreigners. In my view, however, "bear" is a mistranslation.

[69] SS 400, p. 12145; cited by Kuwabara, "On P'u Shou-keng," Part 1, p. 47.

[70] Lou Yue 樓鑰, *Gongkui ji* 攻媿集 (Sibu congkan chubian ed.) 88, p. 817.

In the second year of Chunxi (1175), a Japanese sailor called Teng Taiming 滕太明 struck to death a man by the name of Zheng Zuo 鄭作. The emperor commanded him to be put into fetters, and delivered him to the headman of the Japanese crew, and let him take the offender back to his country and punish him according to the Japanese laws.[71]

Here we have a capital case involving a Chinese victim – so we can infer from his name – and both the Tang statute and the Song practices described above would have dictated that the sailor be turned over to the local officials for trial. Why emperor Xiaozong had him remanded to Japan is not explained, but since this was an imperial decision it seems reasonable that he might have been swayed by other considerations – perhaps diplomatic – rather than by the opinions of local officials like Wang. It is also significant that the sailor was sent to Japan and not a local Japanese community, thereby limiting the precedent-value of the decision. Nevertheless, there can be no doubt that extraterritoriality was alive and well in the emperor's eyes.

These few examples admittedly give rise to far more questions than answers. How did the principle of using the laws – or customs – of a person's country of origin work for the different national and religious groups with their different headmen? What happened in disputes over commercial or civil law? How common was it for officials like Wang Huanzhi to disregard the statutes and insist that foreigners be tried according to Chinese law?

Although we have no way of answering these questions, we might gain some perspective by considering how foreign merchants might have regarded Chinese legal practices. Again we must be selective, for since we know so little about the legal practices of south and southeast Asia, it is hard to speculate about their merchant communities in China. However, the Muslims – mainly Arabs and Persians – are another matter, for not only are the legal cultures of merchants in medieval southwestern Asia quite well documented, but the well-established and far-flung trade networks of the Muslim traders made them the most important trade diaspora in the medieval maritime world, China included.

Within the southwestern Asian and Mediterranean world of Islam, minority enclaves of Jews and Christians, in particular, operating with considerable social and legal autonomy, were a well-established fact of life. Of course, they were all required to pay the personal tax or *jizya*, which was assessed only on non-Muslims, but apart from that they enjoyed considerable autonomy. According to G. F. Hourani, the Abbasid Caliphate appointed prominent Jewish leaders as Exilarchs

---

[71] SS 491, p. 14137; following Kuwabara, "On P'u Shou-keng," Part 1, p. 47.

(two in Iraq and one in Palestine) to head up the Jewish communities in the caliphate and they in turn named the local judges.[72] Describing a slightly later period in Cairo, S. D. Goitein has provided a detailed account of the functioning of *muqaddam*, appointed leaders who had both religious and judicial functions, and who in their courts ruled over a wide variety of religious, civil and commercial (though apparently not criminal) cases, ruling according to a body of law that was the same whether one was "in Granada, Spain, in Jerusalem, or in some port on the Malabar Coast of India."[73]

Similarly, Christian communities had their own leaders who, while sometimes under the overall authority of Nestorian and/or Coptic patriarchs, exercised a wide range of administrative functions. According to Hourani, "they supervised the schools and social services, and tried to prevent deviations in doctrine or liturgical practice. They also supervised the courts in which judges administered law in civil cases involving two members of the community, or reconciled disagreements." Hourani adds the important caveat that, if they wished, "Jews and Christians could take their cases to the Muslim *qadi*, and they seem to have done so frequently."[74]

Given these practices in Muslim lands, it is not surprising that Muslim merchants adapted similarly to functioning within minority enclaves elsewhere. This was especially the case along the coast of India, though Patricia Risso has made the interesting observation that Muslims there "did not have the same kind of minority concerns as did Jews and Armenians because Muslims were numerous and Islamic imperial powers ensured that the Muslim community as a whole would thrive."[75] Like the Jews and Christians mentioned earlier, the entire Muslim trade diaspora was unified by a common legal system, at least with regard to religious and commercial practices.[76] Concerning the latter, the forms of partnership and contract (especially the *commenda*) which underlay Muslim commercial activities from northern Africa to east Asia would not have been possible without such common law.[77]

---

[72] Hourani, *Arab Seafaring in the Indian Ocean*, p. 119.

[73] S. D. Goitein, *A Mediterranean Society: The Jewish Communities of the Arab World as Portrayed in the Documents of the Cairo Geniza, Vol. 2 The Community* (Berkeley, CA: University of California Press, 1971), p. 333. For the role of the *muqaddam* and the institutions and practice of law within Jewish communities, see pp. 68–75 and 311–344.

[74] Hourani, *Arab Seafaring in the Indian Ocean*, p. 119.

[75] Patricia Risso, *Merchants and Faith: Muslim Commerce and Culture in the Indian Ocean* (Boulder: Westview Press, Inc., 1995), p. 70.

[76] Risso, *Merchants and Faith*, p. 18.

[77] Udovitch, "Commercial Techniques in Early Medieval Islamic Trade," pp. 37–62.

Turning to China, despite certain surface similarities in provisions for legal autonomy and self-government, there were three important differences that made conditions there unique. First, in China the legal privileges discussed above seem to have been granted by the imperial government as a kind of "barbarian management" tool rather than pertaining to religious and communal divisions that were of great concern to the rulers, as was the case in western Asia. For that reason, I would suggest that the use of these privileges was less enshrined in law and more dependent on the judgment of local officials than was the case elsewhere in Asia.

Second, foreign merchants upon arriving in Guangzhou, Quanzhou or other port cities of Song China immediately confronted a government presence in the form of the superintendencies of maritime trade that was unlike any other in the medieval maritime world. As noted earlier, these institutions, which commanded great resources thanks to the taxes they collected, had a variety of functions that went far beyond taxation. At the same time, their location in port cities in a corner of the Song empire meant that foreign merchants lacked the kind of access to the ruler than they had in many other parts of Asia. In the early Northern Song, this was somewhat offset by frequent tribute missions to the Song court in which merchants often served as envoys, but these became relatively rare after the 1020s. Although we do not know how this more bureaucratic reality affected the foreign merchant communities, it must have created structures and dynamics very different from those found elsewhere in the maritime world.

Third, as we shall see below, despite the wishes of the government that they live in the foreign quarters, Song foreign merchants increasingly settled among the Chinese population, and indeed members of wealthy foreign merchant families began to enter the ranks of Song officialdom. Such assimilationist tendencies could well have worked to undermine extraterritorial principles and help to explain the complaints of Wang Dayou discussed above.

The foreign ward described by Zhu Yu was undoubtedly real, but many foreign merchants did not live in it. An official in 1018 described how "In Guangzhou there are many foreign and Chinese great merchants [whose homes] lack the protection of the city walls (*wu chengchi fuguo* 無城池郛郭) and proposed some military protection for the district."[78] It is conceivable that he was referring to the foreign ward, but Zheng Zai 鄭載, the former fiscal intendent of Guangdong, clearly was not, when he reported in 1036 that "Every year in Guangzhou there are many foreign

---

[78] Li Tao, *Xu zizhi tongjian changbian* 94, p. 2166.

guests (*fanke* 藩客) who take their wives and sons to reside outside of Guangzhou."[79] Then there were those who settled within the city walls. Yue Ke 岳珂 (1183–1240) recounts the case of a merchant, a "white foreigner" (*baifanren* 白番人 – a west Asian) from Champa, who had received permission from the king of that country to stay in Guangzhou, where he ran a lucrative shipping business.

> In the course of time he took a permanent residence inside the city. His house and rooms were very luxurious, even trespassing the laws. But as the object of the inspector of trading ships was to encourage the coming of foreign traders, thereby to increase the national revenue, and also as he [the merchant] was not Chinese, the authorities did not investigate the matter.[80]

In the case of Quanzhou, there is no evidence that a foreign ward even existed. It is true that in one of the few extant references to foreign residents in Quanzhou, Zhu Mu 祝穆 (d. after 1246) wrote that "There are two types of foreigners. One is white and the other black. All live in Quanzhou. The place where they are living has been called 'foreigners' lane' (*fanren xiang* 蕃人巷)."[81] Apart from its intriguing division of foreigners along racial lines – Arabs vs. south and southeast Asians? – the passage's use of "lane" suggests a rather more informal unit than "ward" (*fang*), with its connotations of a walled block. The Northern Song scholar-official Zheng Xia 鄭俠 (1044–1119) had this description of Quanzhou: "Maritime merchants crowd the place. Mixing together are Chinese and foreigners. Many find rich and powerful neighbors."[82] Although he could have been talking only about conditions in the market-place, the maritime commercial district, which lay between the city's southern wall and the river, was also the location of three of the city's mosques, strongly suggesting that the foreigners generally resided in that district (see Map 4). We also have a thirteenth-century description of Quanzhou as a place where "foreign merchants live scattered amidst the people."[83]

Of greater concern to the government than residency per se was the fear that foreign merchants might become major landowners or reside within the city walls of either port. In 1034, the emperor Renzong 仁宗 (r. 1023–1064) decreed, "The foreign merchants of Guangzhou and

---

[79] SHY, *Xingfa* 2, p. 21a.
[80] Yue Ke, *Tingshi* 11, p. 125, following Kuwabara, "On P'u Shou-keng," Pt. 1, p. 44.
[81] Zhu Mu 祝穆, *Fangyu shenglan* 方輿生覽 (Song; Taipei: Wenhai chubanshe, 1981), 11, p. 5a.
[82] Zheng Xia 鄭俠, *Xitang ji* 西塘集 (Siku quanshu edn.) 8, p. 20b.
[83] Lou Yue 樓鑰, *Houcun xiansheng da quanji* 後村先生大全集 62, cited in Chen Gaohua 陳高華, and Chen Shangsheng 陳尚耘, *Zhongguo haiwai jiaotong shi* 中國海外交通史 (Taipei: Wenjin chubanshe, 1998), p. 153.

Hainan may not possess many fields, markets or houses, or live among the Chinese."[84] The 1036 complaint by Zheng Zai of foreigners and their families residing outside of Guangzhou was undoubtedly in response to this decree. His solution was to focus on the Chinese rather than foreigners: "Hereafter we should ban [those in] Guangzhou from selling them any real estate." The matter was referred to local officials for their opinion and it is not clear whether the suggested prohibition was enacted.[85] But over a century later Yue Ke and Zhu Xi 朱熹 (1130–1200) both claimed that it was illegal for foreign merchants to reside within the walled city (of Guangzhou and Quanzhou respectively).[86]

In the face of the urban sprawl that characterized these Song port cities, residential restrictions were frequently violated, or at least ignored. In Quanzhou, the foreign merchant community was located primarily in the highly commercial area between city and river immediately south of the city wall, but over time it spread to the east and west and even into the city,[87] thanks in large part to the enormous wealth of the great foreign merchants. For example, Xinya Tuoluo 辛押陀羅, the Arab merchant and Muscat envoy whom we encountered in our discussion of headmen (he asked to investigate the Guangzhou headman's offices), had amassed a fortune of several million strings of cash by the time of his return to Muscat in 1072.[88] The seventeenth-century historian Gu Yanwu 顧炎武 provides this vivid description of wealthy foreign merchants in the Song:

In Song times, the merchant families had great wealth, in their personal adornment everything was of gold, pearls, and fine silk, and their implements were all of gold and silver. If they bullied the natives, the military officials severely punished them, and Chinese who offered their services to foreign families could be (condemned to be) executed without the possibility of pardon.[89]

These individuals were obviously not representative. The foreign merchant communities were complex, classed entities. Beyond the butchers, slaves and stone carvers for whom we have specific evidence, we can reasonably infer that they included a variety of petty merchants and occupational groups (like the butchers), restaurants, household servants, functionaries under the headman or attached to mosques, household servants and family members, and since the lifeblood of community was

---

[84] Li Tao, *Xu zizhi tongjian changbian*, 118, p. 2782.   [85] SHY, *Xingfa* 2, p. 21a.
[86] Yue Ke, *T'ing-shih* 11, p. 125; Zhu Xi 朱熹, *Zhu Wengong wenji* 朱文公文集 (Song; Siku quanshu zhenben ed.) 98, p. 1750.
[87] Huang Chunyan 黃純艶, *Songdai haiwai maoyi* 宋代海外贸易 (Beijing: Shehui kexue wenxian chubanshe, 2003), p. 120.
[88] Su Che 蘇撤, *Longchuan lüe zhi* 龍川略志 (Beijing: Zhonghua shuju, 1982), 5, pp. 28–29.
[89] Gu Yanwu 顧炎武, *Tianxia junguo libing shu* 天下郡國利病書 (Siku quanshu zhenben edn.), Guangzhou shang, p. 104a.

the maritime trade, ship captains, mates and traveling merchants (often family or kin to the resident merchants), as well as the crews and roustabouts.[90] All of them were under the general authority of the headman, for the local officials did not want to deal with them, and if we are to believe the prohibition on Chinese serving the foreigners cited by Gu Yanwu, they seem to have gone to some lengths to ensure the separation of the Chinese and foreign communities. In any case, like their Chinese counterparts, the bulk of the foreign community has been lost to the gaze of history.

The great foreign merchants were another matter; renowned for their immense wealth – as they had been in the Tang – they were individuals of consequence, not lightly to be crossed when they flouted Chinese laws. Zhu Xi 朱熹 (1130–1200), in his biography of Zhuan Zide 傅自得 (1116–1183), offers this account from Quanzhou:

There was a foreign merchant who built a multistoried house in front of the prefectural school. Scholars considered this harmful and reported it to the prefecture, but the merchant's funds were enormous, the high and low all received bribes, and no one dared challenge them until they collectively reported (this) to the authorities.

Zhuan, then serving as vice prefect of Quanzhou, was given the matter, and he declared that it was illegal for non-Chinese to live within the city walls. However, his order to mobilize military officials to deal with the matter was countermanded and nothing was done about the situation, even though, writes Zhu Xi, the correctness of Zhuan's reasoning was unquestioned.[91] Within the urban landscape of Song China, government schools had an almost hallowed place, representing as they did the culture of learning central to the Confucian state and the pathway to office for the literati. One would imagine that a foreign merchant having built a residence across from the prefectural school, and a multistoried building at that, would have elicited protests not only from the local literati but also from Zhu Xi himself, the greatest Confucian scholar of the age and an examination graduate himself.[92] So it is striking that Zhu does not voice

---

[90] Concerning the stone carvers, see Chen Dasheng 陳達生, "Chinese Islamic Influence on Archaeological Finds in South Asia," in *South East Asia & China: Art, Interaction & Commerce*, ed. by Rosemary Scott and John Guy, *Colloquies on Art & Archaeology in Asia*, No. 17 (London: University of London Percival David Foundation of Chinese Art, 1995), pp. 60–62, where he argues that a Muslim gravestone in Brunei dated 1301 must have come from Quanzhou and been carved by stone carvers who produced gravestones for the Muslim community there.

[91] Zhu Xi, *Zhu Wengong wenji*, 98, p. 1750.

[92] It should be noted that, as we can see in Table 4, the prefectural school was located within the city walls but near the south gate, and so, very close to the commercial district which also contained the mosques.

outrage in his account. Indeed, the focus of his account is less on the building itself rather than the corruption of the officials, bought off by the merchant's wealth.

Zhu Xi mentions foreign merchants in yet another biography, that of Fan Rugui 范如圭 (1102–1160), who late in his life served as the prefect of Quanzhou:

> (At Quanzhou) there was the South Branch of the Imperial Clan Court. The officials of it, relying on their court influence, committed unlawful acts, but former governors did not dare to interfere with them. They, therefore, went so far as to rob the sea-faring ships belonging to foreigners, whereupon the foreigners appealed to the prefecture and superintendency of maritime trade, but (the authorities) would not come to any decision for three years. They employed several hundred soldiers of the Imperial guard for their private business, and they further stole the proceeds from the salt extracted from sea-water, ignoring the regulations of the salt-monopoly of the government. They have become a nuisance to the people in general.[93]

In this case, the villains were not the foreign merchants but rather officials of the imperial clan offices, which had been established in Quanzhou in the early Southern Song and which made Quanzhou the leading center for imperial clan members for the remainder of the dynasty.[94] Indeed, the foreign merchants are here an injured party, unsuccessfully entreating the local authorities for redress of their grievances.

I would suggest that these two passages are remarkable precisely because of the unremarkable way in which the foreign merchants are portrayed by Zhu Xi. They are familiar actors in the urban landscape, villains in one case and victims in the other, but in neither case does Zhu exoticize them. As a corollary to that familiarity, most of what we know about the social, cultural and political characteristics of the foreign merchant community in general, and of the Muslim merchants in particular, in fact pertains to this sub-class of wealthy merchants, and so it is to them and their lives that we will now turn.

The Foreign Merchant Elite

Let us begin with Pu, the Arab from Champa, who as we learned earlier was of such importance as a merchant that local officials looked the other

---

[93] Zhu Xi, *Zhu Wengong wenji*, 89, p. 1583. The translation, with changes, is from Kuwabara, "On P'u Shou-keng," Pt. 2, p. 64.

[94] See John Chaffee, *Branches of Heaven: A History of the Imperial Clan of Sung China* (Cambridge, MA: Harvard University Asia Center, 1999), Chapter 9, for a treatment of the imperial clan in Quanzhou. Unfortunately, I was not aware of this passage when I wrote the book.

way when he built his mansion within the city walls of Guangzhou ("singularly magnificent, extensive and large, the premier [mansion] of the day"). Like Zhu Yu a century earlier, in 1192 Yue Ke (1183–1240) accompanied his father, an official, to a posting in Guangzhou, and much later described Pu and the Guangzhou Muslims in an essay entitled "The Sea Barbarians of Fanyu [county]" 番禺海獠, which is the most detailed account that we have of the lives of wealthy Muslim merchants in the Song.[95] For example, Yue provides this description of their breakfast:

In the morning they gather to eat; oblivious to spoons and chopsticks, they use large vessels of gold and silver, combine roasted *gui* 鮭 (salmon or globefish) and millet-seed together, sprinkle with rosewater, and scatter borneol (*bingnao* 冰腦).

This culinary combination may have been unusual, but it is the luxuriousness of the breakfast, with fine fish on gold and silver plates, that particularly seems to have impressed Yue, that and the fact that they ate with their hands, as was common of south and west Asians.

What most interests Yue, however, are their religious practices and buildings:

The nature of the barbarians (*lao* 獠) is to honor god(s) and love purity, and they do so all day long, together prostrating themselves in prayers for happiness. They have a hall in which they worship a named [one], like the Buddhists in the Central Kingdom, but in fact they have no images, and one cannot know what it is that they chant, or who their god is. In the hall there is a stele several tens of feet (*shu zhang* 數丈) in height and breadth, and on it is extraordinary carved writing, like seal characters.

That there was Muslim worship in twelfth-century Guangzhou is not in itself surprising; by the Southern Song we know there were Muslims in Guangzhou, Quanzhou and Hangzhou, so Muslim observances would not have been unfamiliar to residents of those cities.[96] What makes Yue Ke's account noteworthy is its eyewitness character. He describes what he saw (the hall, people prostrated in prayer "all day long," the lack of images, and the stele) and heard (the chants). He also confesses that he does not know what it all means, even though the modern reader can readily supply the details of Islam: the worship of Allah, the five daily prayers, and the inscriptions in Arabic.[97] Perhaps most remarkable is the

---

[95] Yue Ke, *Tingshi*, "Fanyu hailao" (The sea-barbarians of Fanyu), 11, pp. 125–127. *Tingshi* is dated 1214, which was 22 years after Yue's time in Guangzhou. Since he was only nine (or ten, Chinese style) in 1192, the remarkable detail of his descriptions suggest that his memories were enhanced by those of his father.

[96] Leslie, *Islam in Traditional China*, pp. 40–44.

[97] Wu Youxiong 吳幼雄, *Quanzhou zongjiao wenhua* 泉州宗教文化 (Xiamen: Lujiang chubanshe, 1963), p. 184, describes how a Japanese monk obtained a sample of Arabic writing while passing through Quanzhou in 1217 and took it back to Japan.

fact that Yue Ke, the adult writing this essay, presents the religious practices of these non-Chinese "barbarians" respectfully and by including the stele in his description, points out their literacy. In other words, he is portraying a civilized people.

Although Yue does not name this as a mosque – which it surely is – simply calling it a "hall," he is clearly describing the Huaishengsi ("cherishing the saints mosque") 懷聖寺, commemorating the supposed coming to Guangzhou of Sahaba Saad Wakkas and his fellow missionaries in the early seventh century, which we discussed in Chapter 1. The most striking feature of the contemporary Huaisheng Mosque in downtown Guangzhou is the Guangta 光塔 (tower of light), a round tower or minaret which rises 36.3 meters (119 feet) in the southeastern corner of the mosque grounds (see Figure 3.2). Whether this is the Song tower cannot be verified,[98] but Yue Ke describes a remarkably similar structure:

To the rear, there is a stupa (*sudupo* 窣堵坡) that reaches into the heavens. Its form is different from other pagodas (*ta* 塔). From a circular brick foundation it rises tier on tier to a great height, and the outside is coated over with mortar. It looks like silver brush. At the base there is a door through which one ascends on spiral steps, which cannot be seen from the outside. At every score of steps there is an opening to a window.

There are some puzzles in this account. Yue himself seems unclear of his terminology, first using "stupa" (a Buddhist reliquary in Indian Buddhism which in south and southeast Asia took the form of a towering solid structure) and then "*ta*" or "pagoda", which itself had its origins as an East Asian adaptation of the stupa.[99] There is also a question of location. Kuwabara Jitsuzō interpreted it to mean to the rear of the Pu mansion, but the problem with that interpretation is that the Huaisheng Mosque stands within what used to be the foreign quarter (*fanfang*), whereas the Pu mansion was notoriously located within the city walls.[100] Since the Guangta is to the left of the entryway into the mosque, it is unclear what Yue means by "to the rear" (*hou* 後).

[98] Nancy Shatzman Steinhardt, "China's Earliest Mosques," *Journal of the Society of Architectural Historians* 67.3 (September 2008), pp. 336–339. For a full treatment of the mosque and its history, see *Haishang sichou zhi lu – Guangzhou wenhua yichan: Dishang shiji juan* 海上丝绸之路–广州文化遗产：地上史迹卷 (*Maritime Silk Road – Cultural Heritage in Guangzhou: Historical Sites*) (Guangzhou: Wenwu chubanshe, 2008), pp. 88–105.

[99] To complicate things further, Yue elsewhere in the essay describes a "tower" (*lou* 樓) of over one hundred feet (*chi* 尺) in height, but since his description of it differs from the minaret, I believe that he is describing a tower on the grounds of the Pu estate and not the minaret.

[100] Kuwabara, "On P'u Shou-keng," Pt. 2, p. 29.

Figure 3.2 The Guangta at the Huaisheng Mosque in Guangzhou

Whatever the precise location of the Guangta, it played a signal role in the life of the maritime merchants, as the following makes clear:

Every year in the fourth and fifth months when the [merchant] ships will be arriving, a crowd of foreigners enter the pagoda, and from the windows come calls like the twittering of birds, with which they pray for the south wind, and the prayer is always effective. On the top of the pagoda, there is a gold cock, very large in diameter, which stands for the nine-wheels at the top of a Buddhist stupa. One of the legs of the cock is now lost.[101]

[101] Yue Ke, *Tingshi* 11, p. 126.

This practice, which is corroborated by a briefer account by Fang Xinru, underlines the critical importance of the summer monsoon in bringing the season's ships in from the south.[102] Given the Muslim setting in Guangzhou and the statement that it was the "barbarians" who went up the minaret, it seems likely that the "twittering of birds" was Arabic prayer. It has also been suggested by modern scholars that the golden cock – now lost – was a weathervane, which helped provide guidance to mariners about the winds.[103]

One of the striking features of Yue Ke's account of the mosque and minaret is the sense of community that it reflects. These imposing structures together with the large stele and the worshiping congregation testify to both rootedness and the wealth provided by merchants like Pu. The same can be said of the Shengyousi 聖友寺 or Ashab Mosque (Masjid al-Ashab) in Quanzhou, which was built in the A. H. year 400 (1009–1010 CE).[104] The date is significant in that it was 77 years prior to the opening of a maritime trade office or superintendency in that city, an indication of the vital role played by Quanzhou in maritime commerce even without the benefits conferred by an office. The roofless but still intact and majestic brick and stone remains of the mosque in contemporary Quanzhou (see Figure 3.3) – located just to the south of the Song city wall – date to a mid-fourteenth century renovation, but they give us a good sense of the Song mosque, which according to Nancy Steinhardt was modeled upon Abbasid-period "hypostyle mosques such as the Samarra mosque or the Great Mosque in Qayrawan in northwestern Tunesia," thus pointing to close ties with the Muslim heartland.[105] As Steinhardt further notes, both the Shengyousi and the Guangta in Guangzhou "proclaimed the presence of Islam" in the streets of their respective cities, a testimonial both to the self-confidence of the Muslim communities and to the tolerance of the

---

[102] In an essay on the "foreign pagoda" (*fan ta* 番塔), which Fang says was built in Tang times and which he says was topped by a golden cock, he writes that in the fifth and sixth months each year, foreigners would collectively climb to the top of the pagoda and invoke the Buddha to influence the wind's direction. He then mentions that there was a worship hall (*libaitang* 禮拜堂) at the base of the pagoda. The Buddhist reference indicates that Fang was not familiar with Islam – or its differences with Buddhism. Fang Xinru 方信孺, *Nanhai bai yong* 南海百詠 (Shanghai: Jiangsu guji chubanshe, 1988), p. 20.

[103] *Haishang sichou zhi lu – Guangzhou wenhua yichan*, pp. 102 and 142, citing a poem and account of the minaret, both by Fang Xinru, describing the golden cock as swiveling.

[104] Chen Dasheng, *Quanzhou Yisilan jiao shike*, p. 4. The source for this is an Arabic inscription on one of the north wall of the Ashab Mosque in Quanzhou. The building dates to the middle of the fourteenth century.

[105] Steinhardt, "China's Earliest Mosques," p. 340. The Shengyousi is treated on pp. 339–341.

Figure 3.3 Ashab Mosque, Quanzhou, and mosque façade

Chinese authorities in permitting such structures, who in Quanzhou permitted two more mosques to be built. One of them, the Qingjing Mosque 清淨寺, was financed by a merchant from Siraf in 1131. The account of its establishment in an inscription marking its 1351 renovation, speaks to the sense of community among the Quanzhou Muslims:

In the first year of the Shaoxing reign [1131], one Najib Muzhir al-Din came to Quanzhou via trading ship from Siraf [Chinese: Sanawei]. He built this mosque in the southern suburbs of Quanzhou. He installed silver lamps and incense burners to worship Heaven, and he bought land and built houses for his followers.[106]

Like mosques, cemeteries were essential elements in the religious and social fabric of the Muslim maritime communities, and both Song Guangzhou and Quanzhou had Muslim cemeteries as well. Fang Xinru describes a cemetery for several thousand foreigners ten *li* west of Guangzhou in which the deceased were buried with their heads to the south but facing west.[107] For Song Quanzhou, there is a wonderfully detailed account by Lin Zhiqi 林之奇 (1112–1176) of the creation of a cemetery by a Srivijayan merchant:

There are scores of rich merchants from Srivijaya who are living or were born in Quanzhou. Among them is a man called Shi Nuowei 施郎幃. Shi is famous for his generosity among his fellow foreign residents in Quanzhou. The building of a cemetery is but one of his many generous deeds. This cemetery project was first proposed by another foreigner named Pu Xiaxin 蒲霞辛 [who did not see it through]. The idea has been carried out and accomplished by Shi. The location of this cemetery is on the hillside to the east of the city. After the wild weeds and rubble were cleared, many graves have been built. The cemetery is covered with a roof, enclosed by a wall, and safely locked. All foreign merchants who die in Quanzhou are to be buried there. Construction started in 1162 and was finished a year later. Such a benevolent deed releases all foreigners in this land from worry [concerning their own graves after death] and enables the dead to be free of regrets. Such kindness will certainly promote overseas trade and encourage foreigners to come. It is much appreciated that Shi has carried it out. Therefore, I write this essay to commemorate the event so that [news of it] will be widely circulated overseas.[108]

Many scholars have argued from a slightly later account of this cemetery in Zhao Rukua's 趙汝适 *Zhufan zhi* 諸蕃志 that Shi was an Arab from Siraf.[109]

---

[106] Hugh Clark, "Muslims and Hindus in the Culture and Morphology of Quanzhou," p. 60. See too Chen Dasheng's translation and discussion of the mosque and the inscription in *Quanzhou Yisilan jiao shike*, pp. 13–19. The third Song mosque was one built by a Yemeni merchant. The memorial stele containing this information is undated but has tentatively been ascribed to the Song on the basis of where it was excavated. See Clark, "Muslims and Hindus," p. 61.

[107] Fang Xinru, *Nanhai bai yong*, cited in Leslie (1984), 43.

[108] So, *Prosperity, Region and Institutions*, pp. 53–54, from Lin Zhiqi 林之奇, *Zhuozhai wenji* 拙齋文集 (Siku quanshu edn.) 15, pp. 1b–2a.

[109] Hirth and Rockhill, *Chao Ju-kua*, p. 111. See Clark, "Muslims and Hindus," pp. 59–60, who argues that *Shinawei* is in fact a transliteration for the Arabic *shilavi*, meaning "man of Siraf."

Billy So has shown conclusively how Lin's account, with its description of Shi as a Srivijayan, is the earlier and more reliable.[110] However, I would suggest that the early role of Pu Xiaxin – presumably an Arab – in proposing the cemetery and the reiterated statement that it was for "all foreign merchants" suggests that Shi was a Muslim and that the cemetery was intended for the use of the Muslim community, given the preeminent role played by the Muslims among the foreigners in Quanzhou.[111] Whether or not this cemetery is the same as the ancient Muslim cemetery that is well maintained in Quanzhou today (see Figure 3.4), the anecdote provides evidence for the increasingly multi-national character of the Muslim trade diaspora during Song times.

At the end of his essay on Pu and the Guangzhou Muslims, Yue Ke relates that he had recently been informed that the Pus had lost their fortune and their mansion lay in ruins. His informant also told him about one Shiluowei 尸羅圍, a foreign maritime merchant in Quanzhou with a fortune second only to that of Pu (possibly Shi Nuowei, the patron of the Muslim cemetery in Quanzhou described above), whose fortune had likewise been lost and his family scattered.[112] These examples offer a sobering reminder of the transience and insecurity that faced even the wealthiest of the foreign merchant families, but they should not be taken as the norm, for the greater body of our evidence points to successful and long-term settlement by the wealthy maritime merchants, who benefited from forces that fostered their integration into the local societies of the port cities.

There was, for one, considerable official toleration and even, at times, encouragement of expanding foreign activities in Song life, especially during the reigns of Shenzong and Huizong when the reform party was in power. In 1104 permission was given for foreign merchants and "locally born foreign guests" to travel to other prefectures and even Kaifeng, so long as they had first procured a certificate from the superintendent of maritime trade. This was done at the suggestion of the Guangzhou superintendent, who stated that foreign guests from Arabia and other countries had recently requested permission to do so.[113]

Even more striking was the government's support of study by foreign boys to study in Chinese schools. The biography of Cheng Shimeng

---

[110] So, *Prosperity, Region and Institutions*, pp. 54–55.
[111] In further support of this argument is the fact that the major Muslim cemetery in Quanzhou, dating to Song-Yuan times and existing to this day, is found to the east of the city.
[112] Yue Ke, *Tingshi* 11, p. 127.
[113] SHY, Zhiguan 44, pp. 8b–9a; *Song huiyao jigao bubian* 宋會要輯稿補編 (Beijing: Quanguo tushuguan wenxian shuwei fuhi zhongxin chuban, 1988), p. 642.

Figure 3.4 Quanzhou Muslim cemetery

程師孟 describes his educational activities while serving as of Guangzhou during the Xining era (1068–1077): "[He performed] a major restoration of the [prefectural] school, and daily led the students in their instruction, so that those who arrived with their books on their backs came one after the other. The sons of foreigners all desired admission to the school."[114] Cai Tao 蔡條 (d. after 1147) describes how, during the Daguan (1107–1010) and Zhenghe (1111–1117) eras, the prefectures of Guangzhou and Quanzhou asked to establish foreign schools (*fanxue* 蕃學).[115] The *Song huiyao* provides an account of the appointment of a preceptor for the Guangzhou foreign school. This was done in 1108 at the suggestion of Zeng Tingdan 曾鼎旦, the former preceptor of the Jiazhou 賀州 prefectural school in Guangdong, who received the appointment. In his memorial Zeng stated:

I have observed that the school for foreigners in Guangzhou has gradually become well ordered, and I would like to request that the court select someone of talent from the southern prefectures who would work [on reforming] the local customs, committed to the task of instruction, and to working for months and even years. I anticipate that among the sons sent by foreigners [to the school], those who receive the pleasure of education will have mutual regard [with the educated] of the southern provinces.[116]

Not only does Zeng report that the Guangzhou school is functioning successfully, but he also seems to be arguing for a unitary concept of "local customs," and the possibility that, through education, the foreign and native scholars can achieve mutual regard. These are clearly idealized aspirations rather than a reflection of social realities. It nevertheless reflects a remarkably positive view of the foreign merchant families by a member of the local elite.

I would suggest that this liberal attitude reflected an emerging social reality. By the late Northern Song, the maritime communities had flourished in Guangzhou for close to two hundred years and elsewhere for at least several generations. Although there must have been a constant coming-and-going of merchants from abroad, there were core communities which, through intermarriage, had settled and established families, taking on more and more of a settler identity. This is reflected in an edict from 1114 which decreed that families among the "foreign guests from various countries" (*zhuguo fanke* 諸國蕃客) who had lived in China for

---

[114] Gong Mingzhi 龔明之, *Zhongwu jiwen* 中吳紀聞, (Shanghai: Shanghai guji chubanshe, 1986) 3, p. 55.

[115] Cai Tao 蔡條, *Tieweishan congtan* 鐵圍山叢談, 2; cited by Kuwabara, 59. Cai went on to describe how Huizong personally examined Korean students who had been studying at the Imperial University. It should also be noted that the Song government also opened *fanxue* in border regions to the north and northwest during the late eleventh and early twelfth centuries serving the children of Khitans and other non-Han peoples. See Li Tao, *Xu zizhi tongjian changbian* 120, 248, 261, 270.

[116] SHY, *Chongru* 2, p. 12a.

five generations were to be treated according to the Chinese laws when the family head died without heirs, and that this be administered by the maritime trade offices.[117]

We know little about the wives whom the foreign merchants married and where they came from, but what we have is instructive. Writing in the seventeenth century, Gu Yanwu broadly asserted that the Song foreign merchants "gradually merged with Chinese (*Huaren*) through marriage."[118] However, specific Song examples of foreign merchant–Chinese intermarriage almost all involve objections it. In 1137, a complaint was lodged against a military official for having married his younger sister to a "great merchant" by the name of Pu Yali 蒲亞里 (a two-time envoy from Arabia) "in order to profit from his [Pu's] wealth." The emperor's response was interesting; he directed the complainant – the Guangzhou prefect – to "urge" Pu to return to his own country.[119] More remarkably, during the Yuanyou era (1086–1093), the court discovered to its alarm that a man surnamed Liu 劉 from the foreign quarter of Guangzhou had married an imperial clanswoman, and forbade any repetition.[120] We do not know whether or not the injunction was consistently followed, but according to the Fujianese Liu Kezhuang 劉克莊 (1187–1269), "the foreign merchant family of Pu [in Quanzhou] sought marriage with the imperial house."[121]

This fragmentary evidence is important in light of the critical role played by marriage in the creation of social and political networks among the Chinese elites. Wealth, status and personal connections were among the most important factors behind marriages, which were as a rule arranged, and as Dieter Kuhn has noted, wealth was a far more important factor in Song elite weddings than it had been in the Tang.[122] The port cities of Song China were host to an unprecedented mix of elite social groups. The Chinese maritime merchants were a new and prosperous group during the Song, including not only those who dealt in maritime

---

[117] According to an edict in SHY, *Zhiguan* 44, pp. 9b–10a (also in *Song huiyao jigao bubian*, p. 642), dated 1114, maritime foreigners from the various countries had lived in China for five generations (*wushi* 五世).

[118] Cited by Huang Chunyan, *Songdai haiwai maoyi*, p. 122.

[119] SHY, *Zhiguan* 44, pp. 20a–b. Pu had been a tribute envoy from Arabia in 1131 and again, in 1134, when his ship was attacked by pirates off the coast of Champa, losing four men and his goods and suffering injury. SHY, *Fanyi* 4, pp. 93–94.

[120] Zhu Yu, *Pingzhou ketan* 2, pp. 31–32. See Chaffee, *Branches of Heaven*, pp. 92–93, and Heng, *Sino-Malay Trade and Diplomacy*, pp. 115–116.

[121] Huang Chunyan, *Songdai haiwai maoyi*, p. 122, citing Liu Kezhuang 劉克莊, *Houcun xiansheng da quan ji* 後村先生大全集, 155.

[122] Dieter Kuhn, *The Age of Confucian Rule: The Song Transformation of China* (Cambridge, MA: Belnap Press of Harvard University Press, 2009), p. 140.

commerce from the safety of Chinese ports, but who also went abroad in large numbers, making their own impact in turn on port cities of south and southeast Asia.[123] In light of the large overlap in their economic interests and activities, and most likely of marriage ties, Billy So has argued that the foreign and Chinese merchants of Quanzhou collectively constituted a "South Fukien merchant group."[124] Although I have some reservations about such a formulation, given the continuing differences in ethnicity and religion, the trend during the Song was clearly towards increasing integration between the foreign and Chinese merchant communities. A second group, the Song imperial clan, attained exceptional prominence and power in Southern Song Quanzhou, which in the years following the fall of northern China and the capital of Kaifeng became home to the Southern Office of the clan. For the remainder of the dynasty hundreds of clan members, many of them officials, were supported in clan residences with stipends from the government.[125] Not surprisingly, clansmen participated in the overseas trade and, as noted earlier, may have been the owners of the large junk that sank, its southeast Asian cargo intact, in the environs of Quanzhou in the 1270s. Given that activity, the desire by the Quanzhou Pus to intermarry with the imperial clan suggests that they had the requisite connections and wealth for that to be a realistic possibility. The third discernable elite group consisted of the literati who dominated the civil service examinations and, as scholar-officials, the government. Quanzhou was outstanding in this regard, with a total of 926 Song *jinshi* (the highest-level examination degree), making it one of the six most productive prefectures in the empire, but all of the southeastern port cities were well represented.[126] In sharp contrast to Tang Guangzhou, which was really a colonial outpost, the southeastern ports were fully incorporated into the imperial polity and well represented politically. Although there is no evidence of foreign merchant intermarriages with literati and scholar-official families during the Song, we can be sure that the interactions among them were numerous.

---

[123] Li Yukun, *Quanzhou haiwai jiaotong shilue*, pp. 45–67.

[124] So, *Prosperity, Region, and Institutions*, pp. 205–210.

[125] See John Chaffee, "The Impact of the Song Imperial Clan," pp. 13–46, and *Branches of Heaven*, pp. 227–246. The Southern Office was originally a satellite complex of the imperial clan established during the late Northern Song in the southern capital of Yingtianfu 應天府. Because the Southern Office clan members were able to make their way south in much greater numbers than those in Kaifeng or Luoyang (home to the Western Office center), they comprised the largest imperial clan group in the Southern Song.

[126] John Chaffee, *The Thorny Gates of Learning in Sung China: A Social History of Examinations*, New Edition (Albany, NY: State University of New York Press, 1995), Appendix 3. For comparison, Guangzhou produced 134 *jinshi*, Mingzhou 873, and Hangzhou 658.

A number of foreigners, most of them with Arab names, were given official rank during the course of the Song. Zhu Yu's description of the Guangzhou headman describes him as a "foreign official" with the appurtenances of a regular official, and in fact we know that some of the headmen, at least, were granted official rank, as were many of the tribute envoys. In 1136, the cash-strapped Song court rewarded the Arab merchant Pu Luoxin 蒲囉辛 with the official title of *chengxinlang* 承信郎 (Gentleman of Trust – a prestige title for officials which had the rank of 9B) for importing a cargo of frankincense valued at 300,000 strings.[127] Although such honors may well have had the primary effect of setting such individuals above their fellow merchants, and may in fact have been provided routinely to foreign headmen, I would suggest that the sartorial and ritual privileges that accompanied official rank would also have given them respectability and entrée into local elite society. It is noteworthy that in the Southern Song we find cases of foreigners contributing to public works, a typically elite activity. Although Xinya Tuoluo's offer of funds to rebuild the Guangzhou city walls was turned down in 1072, as noted above, in 1211 the foreign merchant Pulu 簿錄, was publicly acknowledged for his contributions to the rebuilding of the Quanzhou walls.[128] Foreign merchant contributions also underwrote the coast guard ships in the Quanzhou region in the late twelfth century.[129]

During the last years of the Song, the Pu family of Quanzhou achieved a far more substantial measure of political success. The family had come to China from Arabia via time spent in the Nanhai – probably a southeast Asian kingdom, and may in fact have been the wealthy Pu family of Guangzhou described earlier. Pu Kaizong 蒲開宗 migrated from Guangzhou to Quanzhou, and was able to obtain official rank, most likely due to the value of the goods he imported, and established his family. He had two – perhaps three – sons, one of whom, Pu Shoucheng 蒲壽宬, was a civil official who served with distinction as the prefect of Meizhou 梅州 (in Guangdong) and was a prolific poet whose poems were described as "belonging to an undefiled school breathing an authentic old spirit,"[130]

---

[127] SS 185, pp. 4537–4538; SHY, *Fanyi* 7, p. 46a. The motivation behind this was clearly to encourage the maritime trade so as to raised revenue for the cash-strapped government. In addition to Pu, a Chinese merchant named Cai Jingfang was similarly rewarded for a cargo worth 980,000 strings. The edict further stated that maritime affairs officials in Guangzhou and Fujian would be promoted one rank when cargoes of 120,000 ounces of silver.

[128] Kuwabara, "On P'u Shou-keng," Pt. 1, p. 52, citing *Quanzhou fuzhi* 泉州府志, zh. 4.

[129] Kuwabara, "On P'u Shou-keng," Pt. 1, p. 52. Jung-pang Lo in *China as a Sea Power*, p. 196, notes that a portion of the Song maritime tax was earmarked for military expenses.

[130] Cited by Kuwabara, "On P'u Shou-keng," Part 2, p. 89.

an illustration of the remarkable degree to which the family had been able to join literati society. The most famous son, however, was Pu Shougeng 蒲壽庚 (d. 1296), who in the mid-1270s was serving concurrently as superintendent of maritime trade and *zhaofushi* 招撫使 or "master of pacification," a term used for local military commanders.[131] According to the *Book of Min*, although Shougeng was "wild and unreliable when young" (*shao haoxia wu lai* 少豪俠無賴), late in the Xianchun period (1265–1274), his success in the pacification of sea-pirates resulted in his official appointments.[132]

The naval power implied by this success is consonant with other expressions of Pu's maritime dominance. The *Song History* states that, by 1276, Shougeng had "controlled foreign shipping profits for thirty years,"[133] while the *Book of Min* states that he "managed the commerce of all the foreigners."[134] We are also told that Shougeng erected a Sea

---

[131] The literature on Pu Shougeng is large, and complicated, for elements of his biography and genealogy are disputed. The three principle sources which provide markedly different accounts of his origins are the late Ming Muslim scholar He Qiaoyuan's 何喬袁, *Min shu* 閩書, 5 vols. (late Ming; Fuzhou: Fujian renmin chubanshe, 1995); Ding Guoyong 丁國勇, *Nanhai Ganqiao Pu shi jiapu* 南海甘蕉蒲氏家譜, in *Zhongguo huizu guji congshu* 中國回族古籍叢書 (Tianjin: Tianjin guji chubanshe, 1987) from Guangzhou, and the *Family Genealogy of Pu Shougeng* 蒲壽庚家 from Dehua county in Quanzhou, which is treated in Luo Xianglin 羅香林 [Lo Hsiang-lin], *Pu Shougeng yanjiu* 蒲壽庚研究. (Hong Kong: Zhongguo xueshe, 1959). I have dealt at length with this question in "Pu Shougeng Reconsidered: Pu, His Family, and their Role in the Maritime Trade of Quanzhou," *Beyond the Silk Road: New Approaches to Asian Maritime History* (Wiesbaden: Harrassowitz Verlag, 2018). My favoring of the *Minshu* account owes much to Billy So, *Prosperity, Region and Institutions*, pp. 107–110, and Appendix B (pp. 301–305), and also (as Su Jilang 蘇基朗), in *Tang Song Minnan Quanzhou shidi lungao* 唐宋時代閩南泉州史地論稿 (Taipei: Taiwan Shangwu yinshuguan, 1992), pp. 1–35. However, I have also made extensive use of Kuwabara, "On Pu Shougeng," Part 2, and especially Luo Xianglin, *Pu Shougeng yanjiu*.

[132] He Qiaoyuan, *Minshu* 152, p. 4496. According to the Ming writer Cao Xuequan's 曹學佺 *Da Ming yudi mingsheng zhi* 大明輿地名勝志, Shoucheng was also involved in the pirate suppression effort and was offered the prefectship of Jizhou 吉州 (Jiangnanxi) as a reward, though he did not take it. Cited in Luo, *Pu Shougeng yanjiu*, p. 11.

[133] SS 47, p. 942. This phrase follows one identifying Shougeng as the Superintendent for Maritime Trade, and has been taken by some scholars to mean that he held the post of superintendent for 30 years. However, as Billy So has shown, such an interpretation of the passage is untenable. So, *Prosperity, Region, and Institutions*, pp. 302–305.

[134] He Qiaoyuan, *Minshu* 152, p. 4496. Zhuang Weiji 庄為璣 has argued that the late Song shipwreck with a complete cargo from overseas which was excavated at Houzhu 后渚 on the outskirts of Quanzhou was owned by the Pus. "Quanzhou Qingjingsi de lishi wenti 泉州清净寺的历史问题," in *Quanzhou Yisilanjiao yanjiu lunwenxuan* 泉州伊斯兰教研究论文选 (Fuzhou: Renmin chubanshe, 1983), pp. 65–82. The case that he makes, however, is largely circumstantial. Following Fu Zongwen, I have argued that the ship was owned by the Song imperial clan, for a number of goods are identified either by clan individuals or as coming from the "Southern Family" 南家, which I take to refer to the Southern Office of the Imperial Clan 南外宗政司, which was located in Quanzhou throughout the Southern Song. Chaffee, *The Branches of Heaven*, pp. 236–238; Fu Zongwen, "Houzhu

Transport Tower (*haiyunlou* 海運樓) in the northeast of Quanzhou, from which one could view the approach of sea-ships.[135] This tower, reminiscent of the Guangta in Guangzhou which served a similar purpose, is curious in that invocations and sacrifices to the gods of the sea had long been held at Nine-Day Mountain (Jiurishan 九日山) to the west of the city.[136] But while it is possible that the tower had ceremonial functions, it is more likely that its purpose was utilitarian: keeping track of the shipping in what was probably the busiest harbor in the world, especially because much of that shipping belonged to the Pus.

There is also an intriguing incident recounted by Zhou Mi 周密 (1232–1308) about how Shougeng purchased a large and highly valued replica of an ancient stele commemorating a literary party that had been held in Zhejiang in the year 353, during the Eastern Jin dynasty (317–420). Shougeng presumably purchased the stele after the fall of the chief councilor Jia Sidao 賈似道 (1213–1275), who had originally commissioned it. The stele never made it to Quanzhou, for it was lost at sea while being shipped there, but the very fact that he purchased it in the first place reflects the wealth and connections that Shougeng commanded.[137]

Such anecdotes pale in comparison to the act for which Shougeng is best known, one which propelled him into a position of power and influence in Yuan Quanzhou. Late in 1276, as the Song war against the Mongols had entered its final chapter, a remnant of the Song court with a child emperor made its way down the southeastern coast. After relations with Zhang Shijie 張世傑, the commander of the Song fleet, turned hostile, Shougeng surrendered Quanzhou to the Mongols, in the process massacring some 3000 imperial clan members living in the city. He was almost certainly not acting alone. His brother Shoucheng was said to have played a significant role in the intrigue leading up to the surrender of Quanzhou in 1276, in one Ming account actually being the mastermind behind Shougeng's plot.[138] But more important is the support that he must have had, not only from the prefect Tian Zhenzi 田真子, but also

---

guchuan," pp. 77–83. If in fact the ship was owned by the Pus, then clearly the imperial clansmen was among their chief customers.

[135] Huang Zhongzhao 黃仲昭, *Ba Min tongzhi* 八閩通志, 73, cited by Kuwabara, "On P'u Shou-keng," Part 2, p. 56.

[136] Chaffee, *Branches of Heaven*, p. 240.

[137] Zhou Mi 周密, *Zhiyatang za chao* 志雅堂雜鈔, last chapter, cited by Kuwabara, "On P'u Shou-keng," Part 2, pp. 88–89.

[138] Ch'en Yüan, in *Western and Central Asians in China under the Mongols: Their Transformation into Chinese* (Los Angeles, CA: Monumenta Serica at the University of California, 1966), p. 14, cites a claim in the *Ba Min tongzhi* that the plot to deny entry to Zhang Shijie and the imperial princes was Shoucheng's idea.

from significant portions of the city's elite, as Billy So has demonstrated.[139] This also did not end Song resistance; the court made its way to Guangdong, where it held out until early 1279, when the destruction of the Song fleet at the battle of Yaishan brought a final end to the dynasty. For many later Chinese, Shougeng's surrender marked him as a traitor. In the short run, however, it brought him and his family power and prestige in Yuan dynasty Quanzhou, as we shall see in Chapter 4.

The Thirteenth-Century World and the Muslim Trade Diaspora

By the early years of the thirteenth century the Song maritime trading system based upon key ports and trade offices or superintendencies had been in existence for close to two centuries, and for some three-quarters of a century maritime trade had gained even greater importance in the truncated empire of the Southern Song. In west Asia, Abbasid hegemony had given way to competing groups in the western Indian Ocean, just as the decline of Srivijaya in southeast Asia had led to a growth in states involved in maritime commerce. Perhaps most important, the multimodal and segmented trade that was just emerging in the tenth century was fully developed, and it was peopled by a variety of groups, including Chinese merchants who were active throughout east and southeast Asian waters.

For the Chinese, the thirteenth century – or late Southern Song – witnessed problems with this well-established overseas trade. Well before the Mongols began to cause military and economic strains in eastern Asia and elsewhere, an enormous demand for metals from China was causing the Song government concern. These included tin, lead, silver, gold and iron – the last in the form of iron implements and a testament to the sophistication of the Chinese iron industry. But most important was the outflow of copper and bronze, the primary metals of Chinese coinage, which were in high demand throughout maritime Asia, both as a medium of exchange (as coins) but also for their religious and social uses. This outflow, which first became noticeable in the late twelfth century, led to

---

[139] Su Jilang, *Tang Song Minnan Quanzhou shidi lungao*, pp. 1–35. For more general accounts of Shougeng's role in the Quanzhou surrender, see Chaffee, *Branches of Heaven*, pp. 254–245; Richard Davis, "The Reign of Tu-tsung (1264–1274) and His Successors to 1279," in *The Cambridge History of China*, vol. 5, part 1: *The Sung Dynasties and Its Precursors, 907–1279*, Denis Twitchett and Paul Jakov Smith, eds. (Cambridge: Cambridge University Press, 2009), pp. 950–951.

prohibitions on the export of metals and attempts to curb smuggling, but to little avail.[140]

The early thirteenth century also witnessed a decline in the commercial fortunes of Quanzhou. In 1231, Zhen Dexiu 真德修 (1178–1235), then serving as prefect of Quanzhou, described the faltering foreign trade in that city and the corresponding decline in the fortunes of the prefecture at large. The primary cause, in his view, was the burden of providing support to the imperial clan members, who at that time numbered 2300, a cost that was borne by Quanzhou, two neighboring prefectures, and the Quanzhou superintendency of maritime trade.[141] In making a persuasive case for Quanzhou's thirteenth-century decline, Billy So discounts the cost of the imperial clan as a factor and ascribes primary responsibility to the shortage of copper coins caused by the copper drain.[142] This decline must be put in perspective; several thirteenth-century Quanzhou officials were credited with improving conditions for trade and thereby increasing the numbers of ships coming to that port,[143] though one could argue that the recurring theme of local officials bringing about reform points to the continued need for improvement itself points to chronic problems that we never satisfactorily addressed.

If we accept that there was a decline in the commerce of thirteenth century Quanzhou, that raises the further question of whether the decline was unique to that city or reflected a regional decline in maritime trade. Given the scarcity of records, no definitive answer is possible, but the mixed evidence as assembled by Billy So suggests that there was no discernable regional decline. Koryo's problems with the Mongols reduced their trade with the Song beginning in the mid-1220s (but Song-Japanese trade continued to develop), while Champa was under the control of the Khmer empire in the early thirteenth century – thereby damaging their maritime activities – but that in fact ended in the 1220s.[144] However, there is indirect evidence that Guangzhou was flourishing in the early thirteenth century, at least in part at the expense of

---

[140] This is explored in depth in Angela Schottenhammer, "The Role of Metals and the Impact of the Introduction of Huizi Paper Notes in Quanzhou on the Development of Maritime Trade in the Song Period," in Angela Schottenhammer, ed., *The Emporium of the World: Maritime Quanzhou, 1000–1400* (Leiden: Brill, 2001), pp. 95–176.

[141] Zhen Dexiu 真德秀, *Zhen wenzhong gong wenji* 真文忠公文集 (Sibu conkan edn.) 15, pp. 12b–15a; 17, pp. 19a–b.

[142] Billy Kee Long So, "Financial Crisis and Local Economy: Ch'üan-chou in the Thirteenth Century," *T'oung Pao* 77 (1991), pp. 119–137. See especially pp. 124–129 on the decline of overseas trade.

[143] For three such examples, all of them imperial clansmen serving as officials in Quanzhou, see Chaffee, "Impact of the Song Imperial Clan," pp. 36–37.

[144] So, "Financial Crisis and Local Economy," pp. 127–128.

Quanzhou.[145] And while we can assume that the protracted war with the Mongols, which waxed and waned from the 1230s to the demise of the Song in the 1270s, must have been damaging to the Song appetite for foreign goods, there is no evidence to suggest a collapse or severe decline in maritime trade.

The Muslim trade diaspora of the thirteenth century world had evolved considerably from that of the early Song. In fact, when speaking of the Asian maritime world as a whole, "diaspora" would apply most appropriately to the Muslim merchants, for at the least their network in eastern Asia was distinct from that in the west. In part this was the result of the continued expansion of Islam, especially on the Indian subcontinent, and the enormous ethnic variety of Muslims. But it also reflected the segmentation of the long-distance trade described in Chapter 2. The Muslim trade diaspora linking coastal cities in western India with Aden that has been meticulously mapped by Elizabeth Lambourn did not extend east of Malabar (Ma'bar), and while its dating is to the 1290s and was thus during the Mongol period (and the subject of Chapter 4), such a clear-cut geographical pattern surely extended well before that.[146]

For the Muslim traders in China, this sharp segmentation meant that they were effectively cut off from western Asia. The only tribute mission from that region during the Southern Song came from Arabia in 1165, and it was a disaster. When stopping in a Champa harbor en route to China, the Arab ship was attacked by a group of Chams, Chinese (*Tangren* 唐人) and foreigners under the direction of the Champa *fanshou* 蕃首 ("foreign head"), which made off with many of its tribute goods, leaving only aromatics and ivory. To add insult to injury, when a Champa tribute mission arrived in 1168, the Arab ambassador Wushidian 烏師點 (still in China) brought suit, claiming that some of its tribute goods had in fact been stolen from the Arab mission. In fact, even though the term "*fanshou*" might suggest that the raid was run by foreigners, the 1168 Champa mission was sent by the Champa *fanshou* Zou Yana 鄒亞娜, that is King Jaya Indravarman IV. The court agreed with the Arab protest and refused to accept the goods as tribute.[147]

Whether because of this incident or for other reasons, this was the last of the missions and therefore the end of any formal ties between the Muslim merchants and their original homelands in the far west. Long-distance trade and communication undoubtedly continued, but the movement of merchants between east and west Asia appears to have

---

[145] So, "Financial Crisis and Local Economy," p. 124.
[146] Elizabeth Lambourn, "India from Aden," pp. 55–98. The article is based upon a group of documents from the customs house at Aden under the Rasulid Sultans.
[147] SHY, Fanyi 4, p. 82a; 7, pp. 50b–51a; SS 489, p. 14086.

been curtailed. Arabic travel accounts and geographical treatments of China and southeast Asia based upon first-hand knowledge almost disappear after the early eleventh century.[148] It is also noteworthy that the two most prominent merchants in Southern Song Guangzhou and Quanzhou were the merchant Pu and Shi Nuowei, who had come to China from Champa and Srivijaya, respectively.

In an article on the maritime role of Ly dynasty Dai Viet (1009–1225), Li Tana has pointed to the importance of networks of Muslim merchants around the South China Sea. Noting the critical role played by Hainan in trade between Champa and the ports of southeastern China – especially Quanzhou – and the flourishing Muslim communities in all of those places, Li argues that:

> ... merchants from Champa, operating out of Hainan or regularly calling there, had some influence in mainland China's trading ports and that these groups were in close touch with, competed against or cooperated with other Islamic communities and the Fujianese.[149]

I would suggest that the network Li is describing constituted the core of the east Asian Muslim trade diaspora. It was not in any way a closed group; like all merchants, the Muslim merchants interacted and did business with people of diverse languages, religions and geographical backgrounds, and it is quite possible that common residence in Quanzhou served as a networking focus for Muslims and Chinese merchants from that city. Nevertheless, shared faith, a common knowledge of at least some Arabic and shared (for the most part) cultural origins offered a kind of cohesion that went beyond networking based purely on personal ties. It is likely that they made use of Muslim merchant practices such as *commenda* contracts, but the sources shed no light on this point. Writing from the perspective of the Vietnamese coast, Li Tana emphasizes the role of the Champa Muslims. That group was clearly important, especially since the diaspora would have encompassed the Muslim communities in southeast Asian ports (and also the small Muslim community in Korea), thus increasing Champa's centrality. But Quanzhou and, secondarily, Guangzhou were more likely to have constituted the diasporic anchors, where Muslims congregated in greatest numbers and where the wealthiest merchants chose to settle. As the portals to the China

---

[148] G. R. Tibbetts ascribes this "falling off of source material" to a decline in trade and to a diminution in the intellectual activity of Arab geographers. *A Study of the Arabic Texts*, p. 10. I would question his trade hypothesis and suggest that a decline in the numbers of people like Buzurg the ship captain who were constantly traveling across the breadth of maritime Asia is a more persuasive explanation.

[149] Li Tana, "A View from the Sea: Perspectives on the Northern and Central Vietnamese Coast," *Journal of Southeast Asian Studies*, 37.1 (2006), pp. 93–94.

market, their economic importance dwarfed that of other ports, as did the Muslim cultural amenities that they offered, such as mosques and cemeteries. Above all they provided stability and even security in the maritime trade superintendencies. This is not to say that merchants did not suffer from time from official corruption or the arbitrary exactions, but they were generally well treated by superintendency officials and did not have to fear the kind of plunder suffered by the Arab mission in Champa in 1165.

To a large extent, the activities of this trade diaspora were beyond the reach of historical documents to document. However, there is an intriguing Chinese stone inscription from a Muslim cemetery in Borneo for a Mr. Pu 蒲 ("Abu"), supervisor (*panyuan* 判院) from Quanzhou, dated 1264, which suggests a uniquely Sino-Muslim merchant activity.[150] Kenneth Hall argues quite plausibly that Pu was a member of the Muslim Pu clan of Pu Shougeng. He also points to another tombstone from 1301, possibly that of the first Brunei sultan, as further evidence of Sino-Muslims from Quanzhou, for it "is similar to contemporary Quanzhou tombstones, and seems to have been shipped to Brunei from China."[151] In a study of Muslim grave memorials in southeast Asia (including the 1273 stele), Elizabeth Lambourn has argued for Quanzhou a likely source of the gravestones, which were individually commissioned.[152] Chen Dasheng has conclusively demonstrated that one of those stones – from Brunei, inscribed in Arabic and dated 1301 – was produced in Quanzhou, suggesting that Quanzhou had become a primary producer of Muslim stone inscriptions in eastern Asia; even today the quarries of Quanzhou's eastern

---

[150] Wolfgang Franke and Tieh Fan Chen, "A Chinese Tomb Inscription of A.D. 1264, discovered recently in Brunei," *Brunei Museum Journal* 3 (1973), pp. 91–99; and Wolfgang Franke, "China's Overseas Communications with Southeast Asia as Reflected in Chinese Epigraphic Materials, 1264–1800," in *Zhongguo yu haishang sichou zhi lu* 海上丝绸之路-广州文化遗产：地上史迹卷 (*China and the Maritime Silk Route*), edited by Lianheguo jiaokewen zuzhi haishang sichou zhilu zonghe kaocha Quanzhou guoji xueshu taolunhui zuzhi weiyuanhui 联合国教科文组织海上丝绸上之路综合考察泉州国际学术讨论会组织委员会 (Fuzhou: Fujian renmin chubanshe, 1991), pp. 309–322.

[151] Kenneth R. Hall, "Coastal Cities in an Age of Transition: Upstream-Downstream Networking and Societal Development in Fifteenth- and Sixteenth-Century Maritime Southeast Asia," in Kenneth Hall, ed., *Secondary Cities and Urban Networking in the Indian Ocean Region, c. 1400–1800* (Lanham, MD: Rowman and Littlefield, 2008), p. 186.

[152] Elizabeth Lambourn, "Carving and Communities: Marble Carving for Muslim Communities at Khambhat and Around the Indian Ocean Rim (late 13th to mid-15th centuries CE)," *Ars Orientalis*. Fiftieth Anniversary Volume on Communities and Commodities: Western India and the Indian Ocean, eleventh to fifteenth centuries, pp. 99–133.

county of Chongwu 崇武 make it an important center for stone carving and sculpture.[153,154]

Although this evidence takes us into the post-Song era, it demonstrates activities of the Muslim trade diaspora that had to have begun during the Song. By 1301, however, the Muslim communities in Quanzhou and other cities on the Chinese coast had come under Mongol rule and had undergone radical transformations, which are the subject of Chapter 4.

---

[153] Chen Dasheng, "A Brunei Sultan of the Early Fourteenth Century," in Vadime Elisseeff, ed., *The Silk Roads: Highways of Culture and Commerce* (New York, NY, and Oxford: UNESCO Publishing, Berghahn Books, 1999), pp. 145–151. His reasons are that the gravestone is made from diabase, not found in Brunei but used in a majority of Quanzhou tombstones; the dimensions of the gravestone match those in Quanzhou precisely; that the Arabic calligraphy matches that of gravestones in Quanzhou; and finally that the gravestone is entirely in Arabic, unlike other Brunei tombstones (pp. 149–151).

[154] See Chen Dasheng 陳達生, *Quanzhou Yisilan jiao shike* 泉州伊斯兰教石刻 (Islamic Inscriptions in Quanzhou (Zaitun)). (Fuzhou: Ningxia renmin chubanshe, Fujian renmin chubanshe, 1984), with its detailed analysis of three Southern Song and thirty-nine Yuan Muslim stone inscriptions from Quanzhou. In all, Chen presents 204 carved stone pieces from the Muslim community of Song-Yuan Quanzhou.

4   The Mongols and Merchant Power

Let us begin with a paradox: of all Chinese dynasties, the Yuan, ruled by the nomadic Mongols who created the world's greatest land-based empire, was the most engaged with the sea. Although our concern in this chapter is the Mongols' encouragement of – as well as restrictions on – maritime trade, we must recognize that their engagement was first and foremost a matter of military and political expansion.

Their conquest of the Southern Song was in large part a naval undertaking. Their victory in 1273 in the seven-year battle for Xiangyang on the Han River and their final defeat of Song forces in the 1279 battle of Yaishan on the Guangdong coast both involved massive navies created – on the Mongols' side – with the aid of northern Chinese and other defeated peoples. Even as the Song campaign was progressing, the great Khan Khubilai, also known as the Yuan emperor Shizu 世祖, was looking abroad for further conquests to further the world conquering goals that had begun with his grandfather. He sent envoys throughout maritime Asia demanding that states submit to the Mongol Khanate, and when these failed (as most did), naval forces followed. His ill-fated invasion of Japan in 1274 was followed by a much larger expedition in 1281 using ships requisitioned from up and down the coast of China and Korea, including Quanzhou, and similarly failed. Through much of the 1280s his attention was focused upon Vietnam, with major naval expeditions launched against Champa in 1283 and Annam in 1285 and 1287, all of them repulsed. Finally, in 1292 a fleet was sent to Java to avenge poor treatment of a Yuan envoy, and while the Yuan forces made landfall successfully early in the year, after just two months they departed with little if anything to show for it.[1]

Khubilai's approach to south Asia was different. Although he initially harbored thoughts of invasion, he decided instead on diplomacy, and between 1280 and 1296 sent thirteen missions to Ma'bar (Malabar) and Kollam, the two most important states in southern India, receiving in turn

---

[1] These events are well covered in Lo, *China as a Sea Power*.

a comparable number of missions from them.[2] An important reason for this more peaceful approach – apart from the fact that the other maritime ventures were tying up much of the Yuan's naval resources – had to do with the need for a secure route to the Il-khanate in Persia.

The Il-khanate was not one of the four great khanates established after the death of Chingghis. It stemmed, rather, from a decision by Mönke to send Hülegü to Persia in 1251, and it was Hülegü who, following the sacking of Baghdad in 1256, established the Il-khanate as one of the wealthiest khanates in the empire, but one that answered to the Toluids. Following Mönke's death in 1259 and the ensuing Toluid civil war of 1260–1264 over succession to the grand khanate, Hülegü supported Khubilai over Arike Böke, thereby cementing the vassalage of the Il-khans to Khubilai.[3] In the 1280s and 1290s, when the Mongol empire was buffeted by internecine warfare involving the Golden Horde, the forces of Ögödei's son Khaidu (d. 1301), ruler of Transoxiana, and the Yuan forces of Khubilai, the support of the Il-khanate, particularly of the Il-khan Arghun (r. 1284–1291), was critical, and it made the sea route more important than ever.[4] This resulted in an unprecedented movement of goods, people and knowledge between Persia and China, a development to which we shall return.[5]

It is of course the movement of goods and the merchants who managed those that moved goods via trade that primarily concern us, and on this score the Yuan government's encouragement of maritime trade was remarkable. It set the basic import taxes at a modest 10 percent for fine goods and 6.5 percent for coarse goods, even lower than those that pertained in the Song, and although there were some adjustments upward thereafter, they still remained extremely low.[6] In the view of Derek Heng, "the fiscal regime of the Yuan period was more favorable for those engaged in China's import trade of foreign products than the regime imposed during the Song."[7] But lest we imagine the Mongols to be precursors to Adam Smith, we should remember that they were warriors and empire-builders first and foremost, who over the course of their

---

[2] Tansen Sen, "South Asia and the Mongol Empire," in Michal Biran and Kim Hodong, eds., *The Cambridge History of the Mongol Empire, Vol. 1* (Cambridge: Cambridge University Press, forthcoming).

[3] Thomas Allsen, *Culture and Conquest in Mongol Eurasia* (Cambridge: Cambridge University Press, 2001), pp. 20–23.

[4] Morris Rossabi, *Khubilai Khan: His Life and Times* (Berkeley, CA: University of California Press, 1988), pp. 221–224.

[5] Thomas T. Allsen, *Culture and Conquest in Mongol Eurasia*.

[6] Song Lian 宋濂, *Yuan shi* 遠史 (Beijing: Zhonghua shuju, 1976) 94, p. 2401. This will hereafter be cited as YS.

[7] Heng, *Malay Trade and Diplomacy*, p. 67.

conquests had developed a particular approach to trade and traders that differed dramatically from that of previous dynasties. As we will also see, that approach led to a remaking of the Muslim diaspora that was radical in both its nature and scope.

The Mongols' Management of Trade

From the very beginning of the Mongol Empire, merchants occupied a privileged position – understandably so, since it was they who had the ability to turn war booty and gifts from emissaries into usable commodities. In 1215, Chinggis addressed an envoy from the Khwarazm Empire:

I am the ruler of the East and thou the ruler of the West. Between us let there be a firm treaty of friendship, amity, and peace, and from both sides let merchants (*tujar*) and caravans come and go and let the fineries and wares of my lands be brought to thou and let those of thy lands likewise be directed [to mine].[8]

According to Thomas Allsen, the importance that Chinggis placed upon the merchants was such that his conquest of the Khwarazm empire in 1219 was motivated not by the goal of world conquest, as has often been argued, but rather as retribution for the destruction by a Khwarazm governor of a large caravan led by four Muslim merchants that had been dispatched by Chinggis, thus violating the trade agreement that had been concluded in 1215.[9]

The merchants who served the Mongols were known as *ortoy*, or "partners" (from the Turkish *ortaq*; in Chinese *wotuo* 斡脱). They were provided with capital – or loans – by the khans, princes or court nobles, and upon their successful return they provided their benefactors with the bulk of the profits while keeping the remainder themselves, an arrangement that proved very lucrative for them. According to Allsen, the majority of the *ortoy* through much of the thirteenth century were Turkestani Muslims and Uighurs, but also included Persians, Armenians, Jews and Syriac Christians. As a group that was wealthy, literate, and necessarily multilingual, with extensive networks and trusted by their Mongol overlords, the *ortoy* came to perform additional functions: they acted as commercial agents and tax farmers in northern China, diplomats and even spies. All of this proved extremely lucrative to the *ortoy*, so it is not surprising that over the course of time the Mongol rulers became increasingly indebted to them.[10]

---

[8] Thomas T. Allsen, "Mongolian Princes and Their Merchant Partners, 1200–1260," *Asia Major*, Third Series, 2.2 (1989): p. 88, quoting Juvani.

[9] Allsen, "Mongolian Princes and Their Merchant Partners," pp. 90–92.

[10] This information is all taken from Allsen, "Mongolian Princes and Their Merchant Partners," especially pp. 118, 121 and 124.

As the new Yuan dynasty developed institutionally, there was a bureaucratization of *ortoy* activities. In 1268 the Wotuo zongguanfu 斡脫總管府 (general administration for the supervision of the *ortoy*) was established, to be followed in 1272 with the wotuosuo 斡脫所 (regional offices for the supervision of the *ortoy*).[11] In 1280, the Wotuo zongguanfu was replaced by the ortoy affairs office (Quanfusi 泉府司, lit. "supervising money office"), which was charged with managing the affairs relating to the incomes and expenditures of the emperor, empresses and imperial princes, and overseeing the activities of the *ortoy*.[12]

In 1280, with the Southern Song having been defeated and the Mongols turning their attention to the sea for war and trade, the center of the *ortoy's* activities moved to the southeastern coast of China, where they encountered long-standing practices of maritime trade. What ensued was a lengthy period in which both institutions and regulations underwent frequent and often-confusing change.

At the heart of these changes were two competing models for the conduct of maritime commerce: the Song model of relatively open trade supervised by maritime trade offices (shibosi 市舶司) and the *ortoy* form of imperially capitalized trade. In 1277, a maritime trade office was established in Quanzhou, which, thanks to Pu Shougeng, had just been surrendered into Yuan hands, and shortly thereafter maritime trade offices were created in Qingyuan 慶元 (modern Ningbo), Shanghai 上海 and Ganpu 澉浦, all under the direction of the pacification commissioner Yang Fa 楊發 in Fujian. According to the *Yuan History*,

Every year the maritime merchants (*boshang* 舶商) were assembled [to go] to foreign lands and trade for pearls, kingfisher (feathers), aromatics, and the like. The next year upon their return, in accordance with regulations they paid a percentage levy [to the government] and thereafter they were permitted to sell their goods.[13]

The percentage levy (*choujie* 抽解, or, more commonly, *choufen* 抽分) was the basic import tax on foreign goods, consisting of 1 part in 10 (10 percent) for fine goods and 1 part in 15 (6.5 percent) for coarse goods, a rate of taxation that compared favorably with the Song. In 1192 a small additional tax of one-twenty-fifth for fine goods and one-thirtieth for coarse goods was levied on goods that had already paid the percentage

---

[11] YS, 6, p. 117 and 7, p. 142; Elizabeth Endicott-West, "Merchant Associations in Yuan China: The *Ortoy*," *Asia Major*, Third Series, 2.2 (1989), p. 133.

[12] YS 10, p. 227.

[13] YS 43 p. 2401; Franz Schurmann, *Economic Structure of the Yuan Dynasty* (Cambridge, MA: Harvard-Yenching Institute, 1956), p. 231.

levy in Quanzhou but were taken to another city with a maritime trade office.[14]

What did change in 1284 was the right of merchants in China to engage in trade abroad. In the ninth month of 1284, a new office entitled the Maritime Trade and Salt Administration Office (shibo du zhuanyun si 市舶都轉運司) was established in Hangzhou and Quanzhou, with wide-ranging powers:

Officials are to provide the ships and capital and select the people to go abroad to trade in all kinds of goods. As to the profits, officials took 7 parts out 10 and the traders 易人 received 3. Rich and powerful families are all prohibited from using their own money to go abroad and trade. Those who disobey will be punished: half of their family property is to be confiscated. The foreign guests traveling on the government ships to come and trade are subject to the percentage levy.[15]

Neither the *ortoy* nor any *ortoy* institution is mentioned in this description, but the procedure described for conducting trade corresponds closely to *ortoy* practices. How this relates to the institutional role of the *ortoy* is not entirely clear. But as Elizabeth Endicott-West has shown, the lucrative nature of maritime trade made the *ortoy* role in it a concern and controversy at the highest levels of the court. As a result, the *ortoy* affairs office was abolished in 1284, only to be resurrected the next year, even as the maritime trade offices were entirely subsumed by the salt administration office. But then in 1286, the *ortoy* affairs office was given jurisdiction over the maritime trade offices, and thus over the revenues of all foreign trade.[16] From 1288 there is reference to a provincial *ortoy* affairs office (xing-quanfusi 行泉府司). It was charged with managing naval relay stations between Quanzhou and Hangzhou, which would assist in

---

[14] YS 43, 2402; merchants paying this second tax were exempted from any further taxes. In 1314 there was an announced percentage levy of 2/10 for fine goods and 2/15 for coarse goods to be collected from government ships returning from abroad (this in a period when private trade was prohibited), but whether these rates were subsequently applied to private shipping or foreign ships arriving from abroad is unclear. It should be noted that Marco Polo describes much higher rates of taxation on imports, while insisting that despite those rates the trade was still lucrative for the merchants: "I can tell you further that the revenue accruing to the Great Khan from this city and port is something colossal, because I would have you know that all the ships coming from India pay a 10 per cent duty on all their wares, including gems and pearls, that is to say a tithe of everything. Payment for the hire of ships, that is for freight, is reckoned at the rate of 30 per cent on small wares, 44 per cent on pepper, and 40 per cent on aloes and sandalwood and all bulky wares. So that, what with freight and the imperial tithe, the merchants pay half the value of what they import. And yet from the half that falls to their share they make such a profit that they ask nothing better than to return with another cargo." Marco Polo, *The Travels of Marco Polo*, p. 237.

[15] YS 13, p. 269 and 43, p. 2402. See Schurmann, *Economic Structure*, p. 231. Presumably this division was made after the initial capital had been returned.

[16] YS 14, p. 292.

transporting tribute goods and rare commercial items to the capital, but presumably it was the functional arm of the capital-based *ortoy* affairs office, as it oversaw maritime trade more broadly.[17]

According to the *Yuan History*'s brief account of the maritime trade offices, the ban on private maritime trade was lifted in 1294 by order of the new emperor Chengzong 成宗 (Temür Khan, r. 1294–1307); then, for some reason it was lifted again in 1298, reinstated in 1314, lifted in 1320, reinstated in 1322, and lifted permanently in 1323.[18] This period also witnessed a number of related institutional changes. The provincial *ortoy* affairs office was abolished in 1297, though in 1308 a Quanfuyuan 泉府院 (supervising money bureau) was established with authority over the maritime trade offices. The next year, the bureau was abolished, with maritime affairs being put under a maritime trade superintendency (shibo tijusi 市舶提舉司), which itself was abolished in 1311, then reestablished in 1314 even as the ban on private trade was reinstated.[19] What are we to make of these often-contradictory actions? Their very number suggests that maritime trade policy was unsettled and highly contested, a point to which we will return. It should also come as no surprise that some of the specifics concerning trade during this 40-year period at times seem to be at odds with the timeline sketched out above.

An important case in point is a 22-article set of rules and regulations for maritime trade preserved in the *Institutes of the Yuan* (*Yuan dianzhang* 元典章).[20] Dated 1292–1293, when the ban on private trade was theoretically in effect, it offers an invaluable portrait of the official treatment of maritime commerce. The regulations begin by stating that the percentage levy (*choufen*) was the basic tax (one-tenth for fine goods, one-fifteenth for coarse goods plus a surtax of one-thirtieth) and warning that if the local officials in the provincial administration, *ortoy* affairs office and maritime trade offices and "rich and powerful households" did not pay them they would be punished (article 1). Those same groups were also warned against using their own funds to finance the purchases by merchants abroad and then avoiding the basic tax (article 2). These regulations describe the mechanisms for private trade in the first instance and a prohibition against *ortoy*-style trade by the local officials in the second. The private trade, however, was highly regulated. Merchants had to register their ships at the maritime trade office, which also exempted

---

[17] YS 15, p. 320.   [18] YS 94, pp. 2401–2403.

[19] YS 94, pp. 2402–2403; Schurmann, *Economic Structure*, p. 233.

[20] *Yuan dianzhang* 元典章 (Beijing: Zhongguo shudian, 1990) 22, pp. 71a–78b. See Schurmann's useful summary of each article in *Economic Structure*, pp. 226–227. The basic document was dated Zhiyuan 29 (1292), but the includes additions from the following year.

those ships from being drafted for service (article 15). Prior to any trip abroad, the merchants had to submit forms (*gongyan* 公驗) specifying their destination abroad; this was to be their only stop for trading purposes, after which they were required to return to the same port (article 6). Ship owners had to provide the names of two guarantors who assumed responsibility in case the merchants broke the law (article 7) and report the names of all of their crew (article 11), and on the day of departure their ship had to be inspected by officials (article 21). Upon their return, elaborate procedures were spelled out to ensure that there was no smuggling or other wrong-doing, which included the sealing of the cargo upon the ship's arrival at the dock until it had been properly inventoried and taxed (article 20) and their original *gongyan* forms had been checked to make sure that they were in order (article 12). If a ship had suffered a disaster and returned without being able to carry out its intended trading, an investigation was required before the original *gongyan* could be voided (article 8). These provisions applied specifically to merchants from China; foreign merchants were simply required to declare all of their goods and pay the basic tax, while goods brought by tribute missions simply had to be reported to the maritime trade office prior to being transported to the capital (article 4).[21]

This plethora of regulations illustrates the government's acute concern with managing maritime trade, and it is noteworthy that a number of the details are confirmed by the Moroccan Muslim traveler Ibn Battuta, who visited China ca. 1349. He describes the care taken by authorities to verify that all crew members who had departed with the ship had also returned, with proof of their death or escape being presented by the ship's owner if they had not, and also the great care taken by the authorities to inventory the complete cargo of a ship upon arrival, even to the point of confiscating any undeclared merchandise.[22] But one can also see these regulations as

---

[21] In addition to the measures described, others include a requirement that Buddhist, Daoist, Nestorian and Muslim clergy pay the tax on goods that they bring in unless specifically exempted by imperial decree (article 5); permission for merchants to carry weapons on their voyages, though these had to be turned over upon their arrival in China (article 10); punishments for foreign merchants who concealed portions of their cargoes from the authorities (article 13); a prohibition of smuggling metals or males and females (slaves) abroad (article 14); provisions for sending goods collected by the maritime trade offices on to Hangzhou, except for the fine goods sent directly to the capital (article 16); and to address additional issues, a directive that officials from the provincial administration, the provincial Quanfusi and the maritime trade office consult together to draw up additional regulations (article 22).

[22] Ibn Battuta, *The Travels of Ibn Battuta*, vol. 4, pp. 892–893. The question of whether Ibn Battuta actually went to China has engendered a lively debate, with detractors pointing to the many geographical inconsistencies (particularly concerning his visit to Kan Balik, the capital), problems of chronology and, at times, factual errors in his account of China (and also southeast Asia). But as Ross Dunn notes, the *Travels* "is still a story of countries and

reflecting a sense that the whole system was threatening to become unmanageable thanks to the burgeoning trade. A provision rewarding those who reported merchants who lacked the proper forms (article 9) and another offering *corvée* exemptions for merchants and crewmembers who helped the authorities collect the maritime tax (article 18) point to the inability of the officials to adequately control the trade. Such a conclusion is supported by a 1295 requirement that officials meet incoming ships on the open sea and examine them, because of the many ships that were smuggling goods into the country.[23]

To return to the role of the *ortoy*, the access to the maritime trade that followed from the conquest of the Southern Song provided an enormous opportunity, but also a challenge, since operating in the maritime world required kinds of expertise, knowledge and contacts that were foreign to these merchants of the *khan*, whose previous activities had been overwhelmingly land based. Thus it not surprising that they partnered with leading local merchants who had the requisite knowledge and experience. This has been persuasively argued by Yasuhiro Yokkoichi 四日市康博, who identifies several hierarchical patronage networks operating that extended from powerful local merchants (often merchant-officials) up through provincial financial officials, to Mongol princes in the court.[24]

We will revisit these networks and some of the individuals involved in them when we treat the merchant communities, but here it should be noted that the Mongol approach to trade – particularly maritime trade – elevated and politicized the merchants in ways that were unprecedented in Chinese history. This is most evident in the very existence of the *ortoy*, merchants who conducted business on the authority and using the capital of the emperor and princes, and often held important official positions. More generally, there was a perception of the great merchants as constituting a privileged group apart. Elizabeth Endicott-West provides this fascinating account ca. 1290 of merchant-spies:

cities visited, events experienced, people talked to, and aspects of everyday life observed," and these include details verified by Chinese sources, as in this case. I am persuaded that, however many mistakes crept into his account upon composing it in Africa some years after his visit, he in fact went to China, at least to its southeastern cities. Ross E. Dunn, *The Adventures of Ibn Battuta: A Muslim Traveler of the 14th Century*, Revised edition with a new preface (Berkeley, CA: University of California Press, 2005), pp. 253 and 263, n. 20.

[23] YS 43, p. 2402.

[24] Yasuhiro Yokkaichi, "The Structure of Political Power and the *Nanhai* Trade: From the Perspective of Local Elites in Zhejiang in the Yuan Period," paper presented to the annual meetings of the Association for Asian Studies, San Francisco, March 2006, and "Gencho kyūtei ni okeru kōeki to teishin shūdan' 元朝宮廷における交易と廷臣集団 *Bulletin of the Graduate Division of Literature of Waseda University* 早稲田大學大學院文學研究科紀要 45.4 (2000), pp. 3–15.

As for the Ch'üan-fu (Quanfu), at the beginning of the dynasty it disbursed from and took into the [imperial] treasury valuables. The great merchants traded among the people [within China] as well as among overseas peoples. They made use of dynastic documents in order to travel without interruption far and wide. No one dared to impede them. For they used this as a pretext to penetrate remote and dangerous areas to spy. It was not really for profit.[25]

The following complaint from a minister in the central secretariat in 1309 is also revealing:

Muslim merchants (*Huihui shangren* 回回商人) carry imperial letters, wear the tiger tokens of authority (*hufu* 虎服), ride government post horses, and even present a panther (*bao* 豹) to the court and request gifts in return, and many other such things. The ministers have discussed this. The tiger tokens are veritable symbols of the state and post horses are necessities for officials. To now confer them on all of the merchants is truly unbeneficial, so I request they all be rescinded.[26]

The response to this request is reported as a tepid acquiescence (*zhike* 制可), and we don't know if it was acted upon, but the complaint clearly demonstrates a sense of consternation among civil officials at the lavish treatment of merchants.

Patterns of Commerce

A prime reason for the lavish treatment of merchants was the surfeit of goods flowing into and out of the ports of China. *The Record of the Southern Sea*, a Yuan-era gazetteer from Guangzhou, provides a vivid contemporary reflection on that trade:

The Yuan dynasty covers the ends of the fours seas [all over the world] where the sun and the moon rise and set, and no one dares not to bring tribute, kowtow, and call themselves vassals. Therefore the strangeness of seas and mountains, and humans and beasts, and the diversity of pearls and rhinoceroses are always stored in the internal [governmental] storages ... the prosperity of the precious goods is now twice than that written in previous gazetteers.[27]

---

[25] Yu Ji 虞集 (1272–1348), *Daoyuan lei gao* 道園類稿, in *Yuanren wenji zhenben congkan* 元人文集珍本叢刊 (Taipei: Xinwenfeng chuban, 1985), 42, p. 30a (*Yuanren wenji congkan*), cited by Endicott-West, "Merchant Associations in Yuan China," pp. 134–135. The translation is adapted from hers. Yu Ji was describing the activities of the Tangut official Lizhiliwei 立只理威, a Tangut official who supervised the *ortoy* affairs office. The point of the account was that, although the *ortoy* affairs office officials had been ordered not to examine its financial accounts too closely because of the spying activities, Lizhiliwei would have none of this and examined them carefully.
[26] YS 22, p. 505; Endicott-West, "Merchant Associations," p. 142.
[27] Chen Dazhen 陳大震, *Dade Nanhai zhi canben* 大德南海志殘本 (Guangzhou: Guangzhou shi difang zhi yanjiusuo, 1986), 8, p. 36, cited in Park, *Mapping the Chinese and Islamic Worlds*, p. 114.

To a large extent, this commerce continued the exchanges of the pre-Mongol period. The Chinese demand for incense, aromatics, spices, perfumes, ivory, rhinoceros horn and even slaves continued unabated. Some new commodities were introduced: horses from India, as we will see in the case of Jamal al-Din, and grape wine from central Asia, introduced by the Mongols, though it probably entered predominantly through the land route.[28] To southeast Asia went textiles of many sorts, manufactured goods (including low-value metal objects like cauldrons), ceramics, metals and foodstuffs, much as had been the case during the Song.[29] In western Asia, the Il-khanate imported spices, copper, sandalwood, pearls and jewels, as well as textiles, ceramics (especially porcelain) and silver.[30]

Although it constituted only a portion of the ceramics that were traded, the role played by porcelain, which was to dominate in Ming times, was a truly cross-cultural phenomenon. This is because of the Yuan-era development of blue-and-white porcelain, which involves the use of cobalt as an underglaze blue colorant. Employing cobalt that was most likely shipped from Persia, Chinese craftsmen often used Islamic motifs to create products that were in high demand in the Il-khanate. Morris Rossabi has noted that these developments were important, "not only because they indicate that there was also a west-east avenue for the transmission of artistic ideas and techniques, but also because they demonstrate a shared artistic vocabulary."[31]

In a very different way, the Chinese export of silver was important and historically consequential. We saw in Chapter 3 that copper exports were a problem in the Song, something that the government had tried unsuccessfully to ban. Specie was also an issue in the Yuan when large quantities of silver flowed out of China, though as ingots rather than coins. As Robert Blake first noted in 1937, during the Mongol period large quantities of Chinese silver made their way to western Asia and Europe. The result was the easing of what had been a chronic silver shortage in the Muslim economic sphere and a significant increase in the minting of silver in Europe in the thirteenth to fourteenth centuries. Yasuhiro Yokkaichi,

---

[28] Liu Yingsheng 劉迎勝, "Muslim Merchants in Mongol Yuan China," in Angela Schottenhammer, ed., *The East Asian "Mediterranean": Maritime Crossroads of Culture, Commerce and Human Migration* (Wiesbaden: Harrasowitz Verlag, 2008), pp. 140–142.

[29] Heng, *Sino-Malay Trade and Diplomacy*, Chapter 5.

[30] Allsen, *Culture and Conquest in Mongol Eurasia*, pp. 42–43.

[31] Morris Rossabi, "The Mongols and Their Legacy," in Linda Komaroff and Stefano Carboni, eds., *The Legacy of Genghis Khan: Courtly Art and Culture in Western Asia, 1256–1353* (New York, NY, New Haven, CT, and London: The Metropolitan Museum of Art and Yale University Press, 2002), p. 186, n. 193.

drawing on extensive Japanese scholarship, has argued that the mechanism for this outflow was the capital in the form of silver that the Mongol princes provided to *ortoy* merchants, who then used much of it in the purchase of goods abroad.[32]

This example of the particular role of the *ortoy* in maritime trade is indicative of another characteristic of that trade in the Yuan period, namely that it gave rise to great merchants who stood out because of their wealth and the scope of their operations, which was arguably unique in the history of pre-modern maritime Asia. We are fortunate to have the well-documented cases of three such merchants, non-Chinese but very involved in the China trade.

The first is Sayyid Bin Abu Ali (1251–1299), a thirteenth-century Arab recently studied by Liu Yingsheng. At some earlier time, Sayyid's family had moved from Qalhat in the Persian Gulf and settled in Ma'bar, where they engaged in trade. When Sayyid and other Muslim merchants in south India learned of the Mongol conquest of south China and their subsequent engagement in overseas activities, they seized the opportunity and sent ships to Quanzhou, the first arriving before 1281, where they were well received. Despite the growing opposition of the King of Ma'bar, Sayyid regularly sent ships and envoys to China as well as to Persia, and provided assistance and provisions to Mongol envoys who stopped in Ma'bar on their way to Persia. In 1291, however, after having been warned that Sayyid's life was in danger from the King, Khubilai sent a merchant-envoy (one Li Bie or Ali Beg) to invite Sayyid to come to China. This he did, abandoning his family and estate in Ma'bar (taking a mere hundred servants), and living out his life in Daidu, the Mongol capital, where wives, wealth and titles were showered upon him by the throne.[33]

Sayyid's biography sheds light on a number of important aspects of maritime intercourse and trade in the late thirteenth century. We see the

---

[32] Robert P. Blake, "The Circulation of Silver in the Moslem East Down to the Mongol Epoch," *Harvard Journal of Asiatic Studies* 2.3/4 (1937), pp. 291–328, especially 326–328; Yasuhiro Yokkaichi, "The Eurasian Empire or Chinese Empire? The Mongol Impact and the Chinese Centripetal System," in *Asian Empires and Maritime Contracts before the Age of Commerce II*, Empires, Systems, and Maritime Networks: Reconstructing Supra-regional Histories in Pre-19th Century Asia, Working Paper Series 03 (Osaka: KSI, Inc., 2011), pp. 24–26. Yokkaichi further theorizes that the *ortoy* most involved with this silver export were directly under the Mongol princes and outside the control of the Quanfusi (*ortoy* affairs office), for the Quanfusi from 1291 required that *ortoy* under their jurisdiction conduct their business with paper money.

[33] Liu Yingsheng, "An Inscription in Memory of Sayyid Bin Abu Ali: A Study of Relations between China and Oman from the Eleventh to the Fifteenth Century," in Vadime Elisseeff, ed., *The Silk Roads: Highways of Culture and Commerce* (New York, NY, and Oxford: UNESCO Publishing, Berghahn Books, 1999), pp. 124–125.

critical role played by the Muslim merchants like him in southern India in both initiating Yuan-era maritime trade and serving as middlemen between China and Persia. The fact that his initial ship(s) arrived in Quanzhou in 1281, when there was a ban on private trade, seems to have mattered not at all, since this involved foreign merchants coming to China rather than China-based merchants going abroad, but also because the lines between public and private were constantly blurred. Sayyid the merchant was able to send envoys east and west, even in the face of his king's growing displeasure, and when he abandoned his holdings in Ma'bar he was amply rewarded by the Yuan emperor.

As significant as Sayyid's activities may have been, they came to be overshadowed by those of Jamal al-Din Ibrahim (d. 1306). The head of the al-Tibi family and Lord of Kish, Jamal al-Din is credited with dominating the Persian Gulf as early as 1281, and he was named governor of Fars province by the west Asian Il-Khanate in 1291 and was granted the title of Malik al-Islam.[34] From his center at Kish (a thriving island city located west of Hormuz), Jamal al-Din oversaw a trading empire, which is described by the historian Wassaf Taqqi al-Din, a contemporary of his: "He enriched himself on trade with China, which he himself had visited and controlled in an exclusive manner the trade from India to the oceans and seas of the Far East ... He had almost a hundred boats always in motion."[35] Wassaf vividly depicts that control in his description of the arrival in Kish of merchandise from China and India:

When the merchandise arrives from the Far East and from India, officials and agents prevent all trading, and keep back for him (Djamal al-Din) anything which is of interest. This they send to Qais in their own ships, and there too no one may trade until after the agents of Malik al-Islam (Djamal al-Din) have made their choice, particularly in stuffs. Afterwards they authorize other merchants to purchase.[36]

The al-Tibi ties to China were further strengthened in 1297, when Jamal's son, Fakhr al-Din Ahmad, was sent as an envoy to China in 1297 by the Il-khan, Ghazan (1271–1304), with authority over commercial transactions, which he pursued vigorously during his stay there.[37]

Even more consequential than the formal ties that Jamal al-Din and his family maintained with China was the role that they played in Ma'bar,

---

[34] Ralph Kauz, "The Maritime Trade of Kish during the Mongol Period," in Linda Komaroff, ed., *Beyond the Legacy of Genghis Khan, Islamic History and Civilization, Studies and Texts 64* (Leiden and Boston, MA: Brill, 2006), p. 58.

[35] Tampoe, *Maritime Trade between China and the West*, pp. 124–125; Kervran, "Famous Merchants of the Arabian Gulf," p. 22.

[36] Kervran, "Famous Merchants of the Arabian Gulf," p. 23.

[37] Yokkaichi, "Chinese and Muslim Diasporas," pp. 77–78.

where his brother Malik Taqi al-Din served as vizier under the Pandiyah Dynasty on the eastern coast of India, in charge of the management of three ports.[38] Ma'bar was both "the major link between Kish and China and as an immense market in itself."[39] It was also a major purchaser of west Asian horses, a fact that proved of great benefit to Jamal al-Din, for the rulers of Ma'bar assigned him a yearly quota of 1600 horses at a fixed price of 220 golden *dinars* each, payable even if the horse died in transit![40] This arrangement allowed the al-Tibi family a leading role in the sale in south Asia of west Asian horses, which were traded against Chinese silver.[41] It is noteworthy that this arrangement and, more generally, the al-Tibi family's powerful position in Ma'bar materialized less than a decade following Sayyid's 1291 flight to China, thus underlining the importance of coastal India as a transshipment zone for the long-distance east-west trade, and the particular role of the Muslim merchants there.

To the accounts of Sayyid Abu Ali and Jamal al-Din we can add two brief references to ship owners of great wealth. Ibn Battuta encountered one in Calicut: "In this town too lives the famous shipowner Mithqal, who possesses vast wealth and many ships for his trade with India, China, al-Yaman [Yemen], and Fars."[42] Then from China this description the Yuan writer Zhou Mi 周密 described the Bahrain merchant Fo Lian:

In Quanzhou there was a great merchant, the Muslim Fo Lian 佛蓮, who was the son-in-law 婿 of the Pu 蒲 family. His family was extremely wealthy, owning 80 seagoing ships. When he died in the Guiyi 癸巳 year (1293), he had young daughter(s) but no sons, officials impounded his estate, which included some 130 *shi* 石 of pearls 珍珠 as well as other goods.[43]

Despite its brevity, this passage provides three important facts. First, Fo Lian was what we would today call a shipping magnate, for his fleet of 80 ships put him in the same class as Jamal al-Din. Second, as the son-in-law of Pu Shougeng, another of the great merchants, he was related to the most powerful and prestigious Sino-Muslim family in the southeast, one

---

[38] The ports controlled by Malik Taqi al-din were Fatan, Malifatan and Qail. Following his death, his son, and later his grandson, succeeded to his position. Merhdad Shokoohy, *Muslim Architecture of South India: The Sultanate of Ma'bar and the Traditions of the Maritime Settlers on the Malabar and Coromandel Coasts (Tamil Nadu, Kerala and Goa)* (London: Routledge Curzon, 2003), p. 24.

[39] Kauz, "The Maritime Trade of Kish," p. 65.

[40] Shokoohy, *Muslim Architecture of South India*, p. 25; Kauz, "The Maritime Trade of Kish," p. 66.

[41] Yokkaichi, "Chinese and Muslim Diasporas," p. 77.

[42] Ibn Battuta, *Travels of Ibn Battuta*, vol. 4, p. 813.

[43] Zhou Mi 周密, *Guixin zashi, xuji* 癸辛雜識 (Beijing: Zhonghua shuju, 1988), p. 193. According to Jituzo Kuwabara, "On P'u Shou-keng", Pt. 2, p. 95, 130 *shi* was the equivalent of 15,600 catties.

that we shall be examining later in depth. Although Zhou Mi does not mention the *ortoy* merchants, Fo Lian must have been one of them, since he was operating his fleet during the period of monopoly trade. Finally, it is noteworthy that, despite his great wealth and marriage tie to the Pus, Fo Lian was liable to Chinese inheritance laws and unable to pass his estate on to his daughter(s).

The cases of Sayyid Bin Abu Ali, Jamal al-Din and Fo Lian point to a combination of wealth and economic power by a small group of merchants that was unique in the history of pre-modern maritime Asia. The broad geographical scope of their activity also points to a commercial development: although the segmented trade that was largely characteristic of the Song undoubtedly continued, we see a resurgence of long-distance trade connecting east and west Asia, a development encouraged by the political alliance between the Yuan and Il-khanate. We also have evidence of Chinese merchants active throughout southeast and south Asia. The traveler Wang Dayuan 王大淵 describes how, in Champa, Chinese merchants (*Tangren* 唐人) often took local Cham women as wives and how, in Longyamen 龍牙門 (near modern Singapore), Chinese (*Zhongguoren* 中國人) were living among the local population.[44] Even further afield, Ibn Battuta describes large numbers of Chinese ships and merchants congregating in various cities of coastal India, among them Calicut and Kollam [Quilon].[45] As we will see in Chapter 5, by the early fifteenth century there were communities of Chinese in various southeast Asian locales, and their beginnings were most likely during the Yuan.

It should be noted that most of the trade-related evidence described above comes from the late thirteenth and early fourteenth centuries, with the last half-century of the Yuan little represented. This is a general reflection of the historical record and resulting historiography; for example, the evidence relating to the supervision of trade described above is concentrated in the earlier period. Accounts of the later Yuan focus upon political intrigues, an overstaffed bureaucracy, major revenue shortfalls on the part of the government, the silting of the Grand Canal resulting in sea-borne shipments of goods and revenue from the south to the capital, and chronic piracy.[46] These problems presumably hurt maritime trade in Quanzhou and elsewhere, though in the absence of evidence we can only

---

[44] Wang Dayuan 王大源 (1311–1350), *Daoyi zhilüe xiaoshi* 島夷誌略校釋 (Beijing: Zhonghua shuju, 1981) 55, p. 213; cited by Heng, *Sino-Malay Trade and Diplomacy*, p. 133. Wang traveled across the breadth of maritime Asia in two trips in the 1330s.

[45] Ibn Battuta, *Travels of Ibn Battuta*, vol. 4, pp. 812–813.

[46] See, for example, Ch'i-ch'ing Hsiao, "Mid-Yuan politics," in Herbert Franke and Denis Twitchett, eds., *The Cambridge History of China: Volume 6: Alien Regimes and Border States* (Cambridge: Cambridge University Press, 1994), pp. 490–560.

speculate. However, in light of the account of Ibn Battuta that will be treated in the next section, an impressive level of foreign commerce continued in the mid-fourteenth century.

The Yuan Maritime Emporia

Maritime trade during the Yuan benefited a host of cities along the coast. Although the number of maritime trade offices varied over time, in 1293 they numbered seven. From north to south, they were Shanghai and Ganpu in the Yangzi Delta; Hangzhou, Qingyuan (Ningbo) and Wenzhou in Zhejiang; Quanzhou in Fujian; and Guangzhou in Guangdong.[47] Of these, several were particularly important for the Nanhai trade and hosted communities of foreign merchants, especially Guangzhou, the historic gateway from the south into China; Hangzhou, the former capital and largest metropolis of the south; and Quanzhou. Marco Polo (1254–1324) and Ibn Battuta (1304–1369), the two great foreign travelers of the age, both spoke admiringly of Quanzhou, while Ibn Battuta also praised Guangzhou (Polo did not travel there).

Guangzhou, or Sin Kalan, impressed Ibn Battuta for the international character of its ships and goods. He described it as "one of the biggest cities and the finest in respect of its bazaars. Among the largest of the bazaars is that of the potters, whose wares are exported to other provinces of China and to India and al-Yaman."[48] He was especially impressed by its Muslim community, to which we will return soon.

Both travelers were greatly impressed by Hangzhou – Kinsai (Polo) or Khansa (Ibn Battuta). Polo commented in detail on its enormous size and urban organization; Ibn Battuta, on the lavish Muslim quarter. However, neither talks about its sea trade, suggesting that its presence did not loom large in the vast city.

Quanzhou, by contrast, was the port emporium par excellence. With its deep-water anchorage and well-developed hinterland,[49] it had emerged in the Song as the premier port for maritime commerce, and continued as such in the Yuan. Known to both Polo and Ibn Battuta as Zaitun (the Arabic word for olive), Polo writes of the city:

At the end of the five days' journey lies the splendid city of Zaiton, at which is the port for all the ships that arrive from India laden with costly wares and precious stones of great price and big pearls of fine quality. It is also a port for the merchants of Manzi, that is, of all the surrounding territory, so that the total amount of traffic in gems and other merchandise entering and leaving this port is a marvel to

---

[47] YS 94, p. 2402.   [48] Ibn Battuta, *The Travels of Ibn Battuta*, vol. 4, pp. 895–896.
[49] So, *Prosperity, Region and Institutions*, pp. 134–135.

behold. From this city and its port goods are exported to the whole province of Manzi. And I assure you that for one spice ship that goes to Alexandria or elsewhere to pick up pepper for export to Christendom, Zaiton is visited by a hundred. For you must know that it is one of the two ports in the world with the biggest flow of merchandise.[50]

Ibn Battuta's description is even more effusive concerning the city's size and the volume of its shipping:

It is a huge and important city in which are manufactured the fabrics of velvet, damask and satin which are known by its name and which are superior to those of Khansa [Hangzhou] and Khan Baliq [Daidu, the capital]. Its harbor is among the biggest in the world, or rather is the biggest; I have seen about a hundred big junks there and innumerable little ones.[51]

But perhaps the most informative description of Yuan Quanzhou came from the scholar-official Wu Cheng 吳澄 (1249–1333):

Quanzhou is the capital of the seven prefectures of Min (Fujian). It is a depot for foreign goods, items from afar, extraordinary valuables, and exotic trinkets. It is where wealthy merchants and great traders gathered from foreign lands and other regions live. It is called the greatest [emporium] in the world. Its people are ingenious and profit-seeking. Those who understand morality are few and in recent years it has become even worse. Yet it has not always been thus.[52]

Quanzhou was indeed the capital of Yuan Fujian; more to the point, it was the designated center for maritime trade, the site of China's largest and most prominent foreign merchant community, as Wu's quotation suggests, and quite possibly the largest port in the world.[53] But what is most noteworthy here is the disapproving tone of Wu, who was a famous Neo-Confucian scholar as well as an official.[54] He is writing to send off his colleague Jiang Manqing 姜曼卿 to serve as an official in Quanzhou, and he continues with an historical account of the prefecture, how over the course of the Tang and Song it developed culturally and educationally so that, thanks in large part to its successes in the examinations, "by the late Song the Confucian culture (rufeng 儒風) of Fujian was supreme throughout the southeast." It is his hope that Jiang Manqing, the official to whom Wu's essay is addressed, who is going to serve as prefect of Quanzhou, will

---

[50] Polo, *The Travels of Marco Polo*, p. 237.

[51] Ibn Battuta, *The Travels of Ibn Battuta*, vol. 4, p. 894.

[52] Wu Cheng 吳澄, *Wu Wenzheng ji* 吳文正集 (Yuanren wenji zhenben congkan 元人文集珍本叢刊 edn.), vol. 3, 16, pp. 10b–12a. See Endicott-West, "Merchant Associations in Yuan China," pp. 139–140, for a slightly different translation.

[53] Note on the secondary literature on Yuan Quanzhou.

[54] See David Gedalecia, "Wu Ch'eng and the Perpetuation of the Classical Heritage in the Yuan," in John D. Langlois, Jr., ed., *China under Mongol Rule* (Princeton, NJ: Princeton University Press, 1981), pp. 186–211.

be able to reform the local customs. Wu's hopes were almost certainly not realized. The Yuan social and political order, with its reliance on foreigners, brought dramatic changes to many cities, but to none more than Quanzhou. A great influx of foreigners – merchants, officials and soldiers – allowed them to dominate the social and economic landscape. By contrast, the literati families, which, as we saw in Chapter 3, had been spectacularly successful in the Song examinations and government, largely faded into the background. It is to those foreigners, especially the Muslims who were the most prominent among them, that we shall now turn.

Muslim Communities

In contrast to the Song, where as we observed in Chapter 3, ethnic and religious identities within the foreign merchant communities are often hard to determine based on the contemporary sources, which typically refer to the *fan* 蕃 (foreign) merchants, ships and the like, for the Yuan we have indisputable evidence for specific foreign groups, most particularly Muslims, towards whom the term *huihui* 回回 was commonly used. There were good reasons for this change. The Mongols' famous four-class hierarchy for the selection of officials of Mongols, non-Mongol foreigners (*semu* 色目), northern Chinese (*Hanren* 漢人) and southern Chinese (*Nanren* 南人) was indicative of the privileges they accorded foreigners from across Eurasia, and the numerous references to officials with Uighur, Arabic, Persian and other central Asian names bears this out.

It is important to recognize that the foreigners employed by the Mongols or otherwise present in Yuan China were hardly limited to Muslims. The full spectrum of Eurasian religions could be found across China, and particularly in Quanzhou. Hindus, Manichaeans and Christians all left their imprints; among the last, the Roman Catholics had a bishopric in Quanzhou during the first half of the fourteenth century. Nevertheless, in terms of numbers and importance – both political and economic – the Muslims predominated.[55]

The primary evidence for the Yuan Muslim communities is of three sorts. The first is statistical. Scattered throughout Yuan records are references to officials with Islamic (i.e., Arabic or Persian) names. Mukai Masaki has combed through the Ming provincial gazetteer for Fujian, the *Bamin tongzhi* 八閩通志, for those with such names (excluding

[55] See John Guy, "Quanzhou: Cosmopolitan City of Faiths," in James C. Y. Watt, ed., *The World of Khubilai Khan: Chinese Art in the Yuan Dynasty* (New York, NY: Metropolitan Museum of Art, 2010), pp. 150–178. A memorial stele for Andrew of Perugia, the third bishop of Quanzhou, is preserved in the Quanzhou Maritime Museum.

clerks) and has found that these individuals constituted 19 percent of Quanzhou prefectural officials (23 out of 119), 25 percent of maritime trade office officials (17 out of 67) and 17 percent (17 out of 100) and 16 percent (9 out of 55) of the Quanzhou counties of Jinjiang 晉江 and Dehua 德化, respectively.[56] These are remarkable percentages for what was, after all, the premier port for Yuan foreign trade, and point to the remarkable political presence of Muslims in Fujian.

Second is the invaluable testimony of the Arab traveler Ibn Battuta, who describes separate settlements of Muslims in the four southeastern cities that he treats at length. He speaks of a "separate city" for the Muslims in Zaitun (Quanzhou), of their living "within the third wall" in Qanjanfu (Fuzhou?[57]), of their occupying the third of six "cities" in Khansa (Hangzhou) and of a "town of the Muslims" in Sin al-Sin (Guangzhou). Concerning the last, he states that it contained a congregational mosque, hospice and bazaar, as well as a *qadi* and a *sheikh*, and he continues: "In every town in China there is a Shaikh al-Islam [in effect, a headman] to whom all the affairs of the Muslims are referred."[58] Ibn Battuta was of course writing for a Muslim audience, so a desire to paint as positive as possible a picture of the Muslim presence in China may well have resulted in a degree of exaggeration. Nevertheless, his general portrait of thriving Muslim communities in a number of cities operating with a degree of self-governance (something that we encountered in earlier eras as well) is persuasive.[59]

The third kind of evidence is physical, that obtained from mosques, cemeteries and stelae, particularly tombstones with inscribed surnames indicating their places of origin (*nisbas*). Numerous locales have yielded such finds: Yangzhou and Zhenjiang on the Yangzi River, Hangzhou, Guangzhou, and Lingshui County in Hainan Island.[60] But whereas the findings in each of these locales are in the teens or less, 201 Muslim

---

[56] Mukai Masaki 向正樹, "The Interests of the Rulers, Agents and Merchants Behind the Southward Expansion of the Yuan Dynasty," *Journal of the Turfan Studies: Essays on the Third International Conference on Turfan Studies: The Origins and Migrations of Eurasian Nomadic Peoples* (Shanghai: Shanghai Guji, 2010), p. 440.

[57] The identity of Qanjanfu is unclear. Zhenjiangfu has been suggested because of the linguistic similarity between the two names, but its location on the Yangzi makes no sense in terms of Ibn Battuta's travel narrative, whereas Fuzhou in Fujian makes the most sense geographically. Gibbs' conclusion is that Fuzhou "is the most natural identification." Ibn Battuta, *The Travels of Ibn Battuta*, vol. 4, p. 899.

[58] Ibn Battuta, *The Travels of Ibn Battuta*, vol. 4, pp. 894, 899, 901 and 896, respectively.

[59] This conclusion is strongly supported by Morris Rossabi, who describes the Muslim community of Quanzhou, in particular, as "virtually self-governing," with its own bazaars, hospitals and mosque(s). "The Muslims in Early Yüan Dynasty," in *China under Mongol Rule*, ed., John D. Langlois, Jr. (Princeton, NJ: Princeton University Press, 1981), p. 275.

[60] Chen Dasheng, "Synthetical Study Program on the Islamic Inscriptions," pp. 163–165.

tombstones with Persian and Arabic inscriptions have been found in Quanzhou.[61] In his 1984 compilation of Quanzhou inscriptions, Chen Dasheng provides forty-two gravestone inscriptions in Arabic or Arabic and Persian (three contain Chinese as well) and all but three were of Yuan origin (the three being Southern Song). Of these, seven were for women and three are recorded as having performed the Haj, or pilgrimage to Mecca. Twenty-five of the entries provide *nisbas*, and the distribution is striking. Three were from Arabic locales (two from Siraf and one from Yemen), two from central Asia (Bukhara, Armenia and Turkestan), and the remaining nineteen from Persia or cities in Persia. Of the three inscriptions that use Chinese, two provide no place of origin, while the third, for a Persian, suggests that his mother or wife was Chinese.[62] The inscriptions also employ a variety of titles: *shaykh, amir, sayyed* (descendant of the Prophet) and the Persian *esfahsalar* (general).[63] These inscriptions are remarkable for apparently reflecting a community of new immigrants in constant contact with the Muslim world of western Asia, with uncertain ties to the pre-Mongol Muslim diaspora that had been characteristic of the Quanzhou Muslims. There is little evidence of sinicization, and much to suggest that the deceased were recent arrivals.

Returning to Ibn Battuta, after describing the procedures for handling incoming ships, he goes on to recount how individual merchants then proceeded:

> When a Muslim merchant arrives in a Chinese town he chooses whether to stay with one of the Muslim merchants designated among those domiciled there, or in the *funduq* [hostelry]. If he prefers to stay with the merchant his money is impounded, the merchant with whom he is to reside takes charge of it, and spends from it on his behalf honestly. When he wishes to leave his money is examined and if any of it is missing the merchant with whom he has stayed and to whom it was entrusted makes it good.[64]

Although these arrangements are not corroborated by any Chinese documents, the provision of housing is fully consonant with the attention to merchant welfare that had begun with the Song maritime trade offices and continued in the Yuan. The monetary arrangements for merchants

---

[61] Chen Dasheng, and Ludvik Kalus, *Corpus d'Inscriptions Arabes et Persanes*. See also Chen Dasheng, *Quanzhou Yisilan jiao shike*.

[62] Chen Dasheng *Quanzhou Yisilan jiao shike*. The last-mentioned inscription is No. 46, for one Ahmad bin Khawaja Kakyin Alad, and the Arabic/Persian part of the inscription states that "he died in Zaytun, the town where the mother of the Ahmad family lives" (pp. 38–39).

[63] Chen Dasheng, "Persian Settlements in Southeastern China during the T'ang, Sung and Yuan Dynasties," in *Encyclopedia Iranica*, Eshan Yarshater, ed. (Costa Mesa, CA: Mazda Publishers, 1992), vol. 5, p. 445.

[64] Ibn Battuta, *The Travels of Ibn Battuta*, vol. 4, p. 893.

staying with a Muslim merchant host are striking and certainly unusual in the Chinese context, but in fact conform quite closely with the Muslim practice of *ibda* or *bida* within the *commenda* system, whereby a merchant acted for free on behalf of another who for some reason could not undertake his business, a situation that could well describe a merchant newly arrived in China.[65] They also underline the importance of the Muslim merchants resident in China and their role in the processes of long-distance commerce.

These resident merchants come into particular focus when Ibn Battuta describes his arrival in Zaitun. He first encounters an envoy from India with whom Ibn Battuta had previously traveled, who notified the Chinese authorities of his arrival and arranged lodgings for him. Ibn Battuta then received visits from various local notables, all Persians: the *qadi* (judge) Taj al-Din of Ardabil, the Shaikh al-Islam Kamal al-Din 'Abdallah from Isfahan and important merchants, including Sharaf al-Din from Tabriz, whom he had known and borrowed money from when in India. He also mentions Shaikh Burhan al-Din of Kazurun, who ran a religious establishment outside of Quanzhou.[66] Ibn Battuta comments:

As these merchants live in infidel country they are delighted when a Muslim arrives among them. They say: "He has come from the land of Islam", and give him the legal alms due on their property so that he becomes as rich as one of them.[67]

Ibn Battuta was no ordinary traveler. Born in Morocco and trained as a jurist in Cairo, he had traveled through most of the known world and, among other things, served as a *qadi* in Delhi and other Indian principalities. He was a notable, so it is not surprising that he attracted leading members of the Muslim community upon his arrival in Quanzhou. That said, this passage is noteworthy on two counts. It illustrates the role of Islam as a glue binding strangers together, especially when they encountered each other beyond the Dar al Islam. Moreover, the role of legal alms – defined by H. A. Gibb as a Qur'anic injunction to give alms to

---

[65] "This was a form of quasi-agency. It involved a merchant who, unable personally to attend to a business affair, hands over some of his property to another party for the latter to take care of for him. Upon completion of his task, the outside party, without receiving any commission, profit or compensation in any other form, returns the proceeds of the transaction to the merchant whose bidding he has done." Udovitch, "Commercial Techniques in Early Medieval Islamic Trade," pp. 59–60.

[66] Gibb uses the term "hospice," but Chen Dasheng explains: "When Ebn Battuta met him he was shaikh of a*zāwīa* (retreat) outside the city and responsible for collecting the pious offerings from travelers on behalf of his order." Chen, "Persian Settlements in Southeastern China."

[67] Ibn Battuta, *The Travels of Ibn Battuta*, vol. 4, pp. 894–895.

"parents, kindred, orphans, the poor, and the wayfarer"[68] – along with the *commenda*, provided some amelioration of the risks inherent in long-distance trade. Together, these can be seen as factors essential to the functioning of the Muslim trade diaspora.

Before turning to the broader Muslim community in Quanzhou, a distinction should be made between the Muslim trade diaspora and the general Muslim diaspora. In contrast to pre-Mongol times, when virtually all Muslims in the port cities of China were there because of trade (merchants and sailors), the Yuan witnessed an influx of foreigners from abroad, many though not all of them Muslim, and Quanzhou as the center of maritime trade was a particular magnet. Many of those who came had no connection to commerce, but rather were in government service or the military, and they came from many parts of Asia, especially central Asia. The Muslims collectively can be considered a diasporic community with a shared interest in the practice of Islam, but only a subset of them were part of the Muslim trade diaspora, with its transregional identity and activities spanning the breadth of maritime Asia. And because of its deep roots in China, the trade diaspora in Quanzhou in particular was increasingly Sino-Muslim in character, a development that had important consequences in the post-Yuan period, as we will see in Chapter 5.

Mosques stood at the heart of the Muslim communities, and according to one Yuan inscription Quanzhou had six to seven mosques in that period, roughly double the three that we know existed in the Song.[69] Of these, it is only the two most famous of the Song mosques that we know about in any detail. The Shengyousi 聖友寺 or Ashab Mosque is a graceful granite structure (minus its roof) that is one of the historical jewels of contemporary Quanzhou. As we noted in Chapter 3, it was first built in 1009–1010 (A. H. 400), but its rebuilding in 1310 produced the mosque as we know it today.[70] This is described in an Arabic inscription on the north wall of the mosque:

This is the first mosque in this land [probably a reference to the region rather than to China]. It is both antique and ancient, named the Great Mosque, known by locals as Masjid al-Ashab. It was built in the year 400 AH (1009–10). Some three hundred years later it was restored, at which time the tall arcade, high portico, venerable entry, and new windows were made and installed. The year was 710 AH (1310–11). May it please God most high, by Ahmad b. Muhammad al-Qudsi

---

[68] Ibn Battuta, *Travels in Asia and Africa*, p. 370, n. 12.
[69] Chen Dasheng *Quanzhou Yisilan jiao shike*, p. 15. The extant stele is actually a copy of the 1349 original that was made in 1507.
[70] Nancy Steinhardt, *China's Early Mosques*. Edinburgh Studies in Islamic Art (Edinburgh: Edinburgh University Press, 2016), Chapter 2.

al-hajji [who has made the *hajj*] al-Shirazi [a man or family from Shiraz]. May Allah forgive him and his family.[71]

The second is the Qingjing Mosque, whose origins in 1131 were also described in Chapter 3. We know about it thanks to an inscription found at the Ashab Mosque, dated 1507, which is a copy of an original stele from 1349 by Wu Jian 吳鑒. Wu describes the restoration process for the Qingjing Mosque, which had been badly damaged in the early Zhizheng reign period (1341–1370):

In the ninth year of the Zhizheng era (1349), H. E. Hedar, a high official in Minhai Province, was stationed at Quanzhou for some time. He gave the people a degree of peace and liberty thus winning their confidence and respect. Meanwhile, Shaikh al-Islam Burhan al-Din (Shesilian Buluhanding 攝思廉不魯罕丁) ordered Sharif al-Din Hatib (Shelafuding Hetibu 舍剌甫丁哈悌卜) to lead the followers in lodging a lawsuit, whereupon, the said official made a thorough investigation of the case and held His Excellency Xie Yuli 偰玉立, the prefect of Quanzhou, responsible for restoring the mosque and its property. This was to the great satisfaction of everyone. Fully supporting this action, a native by the name of Jin Ali 金阿里 financed the renovation of the mosque. He asked me to write an account of it.[72]

This undertaking, like many through the course of Chinese history, was the result of collaboration between local officials and the local elites, but this account reveals some interesting complexities. The initial proposal for the restoration as well as what was probably a petition requesting it came from foreign Muslims: Shaikh al-Islam Burhan al-Din and Sharif al-Din Hatib, both of whom Ibn Battuta encountered when visiting Quanzhou that same year, though it should be noted that Burhan al-Din was a long-term resident of Quanzhou; a Persian, he first came to the city in 1312–1313, when he was imam of the Qingjing Mosque.[73] The project was then authorized by the prefect Qu Yuli, a Uighur Muslim, and financed by Jin Ali, to whom we shall return.

A genealogy of the Pu family, which claimed descent from Pu Shougeng and his brother Shoucheng, adds further details to the Qingjinsi restoration with an entry dating to the Ming:

---

[71] Nancy Steinhardt, *China's Early Mosques*, Chapter 2. For other recent translations, see Chen Dasheng and Ludvik Kalus, *Corpus d'Inscriptions Arabes et Persanes en Chine*, p. 64, and Chen Dasheng, *Quanzhou Yisilan jiao shike*, p. 4.

[72] "Quanzhou Qingjingsi bei ji" 泉州清净寺碑记, in Chen Dasheng, *Quanzhou Yisilan jiao shike*, 15. The translation, with modifications, is by Chen Dasheng. See, too, Hyunhee Park's treatment of the stele in *Mapping the Chinese and Islamic Worlds*, pp. 119–121. For a thorough analysis of the textual problems related to this inscription, see Maejima Shinji, "The Muslims in Ch'üan-chou at the End of the Yuan Dynasty, Part 1, *Memoirs of the Research Department of the Tōyō Bunko* 31 (1973), pp. 35–51; this passage is analyzed on pp. 43–45.

[73] Chen Dasheng, "Persian Settlements in Southeastern China."

[Pu] Rihe 日和, style Guifu 貴甫, was the second son of Pu Shoucheng. He was a Muslim believer, prudent in his speech and cautious in his actions. He regularly attended daily prayers. During the Zhizheng reign period (1341–1370) of Yuan dynasty, the mosque was damaged with no means of repair. Together with Jin Ali from his hometown, they attended to this matter and restored the building. Throughout they used big slabs of stone for the construction and the outcome was most magnificent. An inscription, with his name, on a board to the right of the building's entrance, exists till this day.[74]

Although this could be a false genealogical claim, since Pu Rihe is not mentioned in Wu Jian's inscription, I am convinced that it is accurate and have so argued elsewhere.[75] Taken together, these sources point to religious leadership by west Asians supported politically by Muslim local officials and financially by prominent Sino-Muslims from Quanzhou. It is to this last group – families of the foreign Muslims who settled in Quanzhou – that we will now turn.

In contrast to the Song and earlier periods, in the Yuan period – specifically in Yuan Quanzhou – a number of Muslim individuals and families come into view. This is partly due to the increased political importance of the Muslims and other of the *semu* people who, as we will see, played significant roles in Yuan politics, and whose representation in Quanzhou governance we saw in the statistics of Mukai Masaki above, but also important are the genealogies of five Quanzhou lineages that trace their origins to Muslims in the Yuan. They must be used with care, for they were subject to false claims, but for the most part the genealogies present credible Ming prefaces and genealogical entries. As we shall see, the Muslim diaspora of Yuan Quanzhou expanded beyond the confines of a trade diaspora, for people came as officials and soldiers as well as merchants.

We begin with the Pu family, whose power and wealth made them a dominant force in Quanzhou's Muslim community. This was especially true in the early Yuan, when Pu Shougeng and his family were important players in the city's governance. From the start, Shougeng was rewarded handsomely for his role in bringing about Quanzhou's surrender. As a sign of imperial favor, when confronted in 1277 with a report that the Yuan admiral Dong Wenbing 董文炳 had given Pu

---

[74] Luo Xianglin 羅香林 [Lo Hsiang-lin], *Pu Shougeng yanjiu* 蒲壽庚研究 (Hong Kong: Zhongguo xueshe, 1959), p. 12; Oded Abt, "Locking and Unlocking the City Gates: Muslim Memories of Song-Yuan-Ming Transition in Southeast China," Harvard Middle Period Conference, June 2014, pp. 22–25. The translation follows Abt, with minor changes.

[75] John W. Chaffee, "Pu Shougeng Reconsidered: Pu, His Family, and Their Role in the Maritime Trade of Quanzhou," in Robert J. Antony and Angela Schottenhammer, eds., *Beyond the Silk Road: New Discoursses on China's Role in East Asian Maritime History* (Wiesbaden: Harrassowitz Verlag, 2018), pp. 72–73.

a gold tiger badge (*jinhufu* 金虎符) that Khubilai had personally given him, the emperor was first angry, but after hearing about Pu's role in guarding the city against "pirates" (the Song forces?) and bringing all of the foreign merchants under submission with the Yuan, he was delighted and ordered the formal conferral of the badge on Pu.[76] In 1278, Pu was appointed deputy governor of Fujian province (Fujian sheng zuocheng 福建省左丞), and in 1284 deputy governor of Jiang-Huai, then briefly governor of Quanzhou (Quanzhou xingsheng pingzhang zhengshi 泉州行省平章政事).[77]

Pu's recorded activities are virtually all related to maritime activities. In 1278/8, he and the Fujian pacification commissioner, Soyudu (Soudu 唆都, d. 1285), submitted a memorial asking that foreign merchants be invited to come and trade:

The foreign states live scattered among the islands of the southeast, and all have a desire to emulate the good. We request an imperial statement saying that who can sincerely come will be esteemed and respected, and that those who come and go for trading will be able to follow their desires.

Khubilai's response was ambiguous. He talked generally about the need for good governance and then promoted both Soyudu and Pu to the office of deputy governor and Dong Wenbing – not named in the memorial – to governor. However, a year later, in 1279/5, the emperor denied a request by Pu to invite the foreigners from overseas (to come and trade).[78] These actions must be viewed in the context of Khubilai's continued military campaigns, which we discussed earlier. In 1279, with the victory over the Southern Song virtually complete, Khubilai was preparing for a new invasion of Japan, since the first had failed in 1274. In fact, in 1279/2 Yangzhou 揚州, Hunan 湖南, Ganzhou 贛州 and Quanzhou 泉州 had been tasked with providing 600 warships for that invasion, of which 200 were to come from Quanzhou. Here we see Pu again, in this case successfully requesting that the Quanzhou quota be reduced to the fifty ships that had been built, on the grounds that this demand was a hardship for the people.[79]

Pu was operating within the complex and fluid political landscape of post-conquest southern China. In the hierarchical patronage networks that operated through the *ortoy* structure, which were previously

---

[76] YS 156, p. 2673; Lo, *China as a Seapower*, p. 231.

[77] Wu Youxiong 吳幼雄, "Yuandai Quanzhou ba ci she sheng yu Pu Shougeng Ren Quanzhou xingsheng pingzhang zhengshi kao" 元代泉州八次设省與蒲壽庚任泉州行省平章政事考, *Fujian difangshi yanjiu* 福建地方史研究 No. 2 (1988), pp. 43–46. The different province names were the result of multiple reorganizations of the provinces in the last decades of the thirteenth century. These are detailed by Wu.

[78] YS 10, p. 204 and 10, p. 211.   [79] YS 10, p. 209 and 11, p. 230.

described, power was held first and foremost by Yuan generals and high – usually Mongol – officials, who answered to their imperial patrons. Beneath them were local individuals from the world of shipping and maritime commerce such as the former pirate Zhu Qing 朱清 and the salt merchant Zhang Xuan 張瑄 – who had had no official standing in the Song but had given timely support to the Yuan cause – as well as Pu Shougeng. Pu was closely connected to two of the leading generals from the conquest – Soyudu prior to his departure to Champa in 1281, and Möngtei (Mangwudai 忙兀歹, d. 1297) in the 1280s – and above them to Shihab al-Din (Shafuding 沙福丁), a high official with close ties to the court. To quote Yokkaichi Yasuhiro, "Pu Shougeng was a somewhat Sinicized Muslim and had the nature of Chinese local elite, being versed in the local Chinese merchants and markets."[80] Thus Pu managed the actual trade and the traders while Soyudu and Möngtei fulfilled the *ortoy* role of securing the capital from the imperial family, and since this was underway even before Soyudu's departure for Champa in 1281, it is clear that there was an active maritime trade even during these early years.

That Pu Shougeng loomed large in Quanzhou society is indicated by descriptions of him in two separate funeral inscriptions for the admiral Dong Wenbing:

Pu Shougeng was originally a Uighur whose occupation was maritime shipping 以海舶為業. His family fortune was estimated to be many tens of thousands (of strings). Among the Nanhai foreigners of many states, all submitted to him in fear.

The prefect of Quanzhou Pu Shougeng was originally a man of the Western Regions. Being good at commerce, he came and went to sea, accumulating a fortune of many tens of thousands (of strings), with several thousand menservants. Following the surrender, he, his sons and kinsmen worked sincerely to protect the southeastern corner (of the empire) . . . Their protection was certainly without mishap.[81]

Although these passages do not agree on Pu's origins (except insofar as they were foreign), when taken together a picture emerges of a man who made his fortune through maritime commerce (even going abroad himself), became enormously wealthy and was powerful, even feared. Reinforcing this connection between wealth, power and maritime commerce is the Sea Transport Tower (*Haiyunlou* 海運樓) that Shougeng built in the thirty-sixth district in northeastern Quanzhou, from which he

---

[80] Yokkaichi Yasuhiro 四日市康博, "The Structure of Political Power and the *Nanhai* Trade," p. 14.

[81] Wu Youxiong, *Quanzhou zongjiao wenhua*, p. 221. Wu's source for both inscriptions is the Jiaqing (1522–1566) *Gaocheng County Gazetteer* 藁城縣志: 董文炳神道碑 in zh. 9 for the former and 藁城令董文炳遺受碑 in zh. 8 for the latter.

could view the ships arriving and departing.[82] As Mukai Masaki has shown, the large Pu estate spread across much of the commercial district to the south of the Quanzhou city wall (see Map 4), thus further attesting to the importance of the Pus.[83]

The mention in Dong Wenbing's inscription about Shougeng's sons and kinsmen protecting the entire southeast points to the role of his family in the maintenance of political and commercial power, something that we will see with other prominent merchant-officials. For the Pus, the role played by his eldest son, Shiwen 師文 (d. 1292), was particularly important. In 1281, he was made the Fujian maritime trade superintendent, and he also had the titles of pacification commissioner (xuanweishi 宣慰使) and right vice-commander-in-chief of the Chief Military Command (youfudu yuanshuai 右副都元帥), and he eventually achieved the position of assistant administrator of the Fujian Branch Secretariat (Fujian xing zhongshusheng canzhi zhengshi 福建行中書省 參知政事). At the time of the Java invasion, Shiwen, then designated as the "pacification commissioner for overseas foreigners," was commanded along with Sun Shengfu 孫勝夫 and You Yongxian 尤永賢 to keep the routes to foreign countries open and manage the affairs of foreigners 通道外國, 宣撫諸夷.[84]

After the mid-1280s, neither Shougeng nor Shiwen (nor any other Pus) are explicitly linked to maritime trade or other activities, and it may be, as Mukai Masaki has suggested, that this was a reflection of Shougeng's loss of Mongol patronage.[85] The Pu family, however, produced a remarkable record of success in Yuan officialdom. Shougeng's second and third sons, Shisi 師斯 and Yunwen 允文, served, respectively, in the prestigious Hanlin Astrological Commission (Hanlin taishiyuan guan 翰林太史院官) and as advisor to the Heir Apparent (You yude 右諭德) and, concurrently, Secretariat drafter (Zhongshusheng zhizhi 中書省知制). Shisi's oldest

---

[82] Kuwabara, "On P'u Shou-keng," Pt. 2, p. 59, citing *Pa Min tongzhi*, 73.

[83] Mukai Masaki, "Regenerating Trade Diaspora: Supra-Regional Contacts and the Role of "Hybrid Muslims" in the South China Sea since the late 10th to mid-13th Century," in *Exploring Global Linkages between Asian Maritime World and Trans-Atlantic World*, Global History and Maritime Asia Working and Discussion Paper Series, No. 19 (Osaka: Osaka University, 2010), pp. 72–73. He maps out the rough dimensions of the Pu estate through the analysis of place names in contemporary Quanzhou that echo descriptions of the estate in earlier sources.

[84] Luo, *Pu Shougeng yanjiu*, pp. 71–72. The anecdote concerning Java is from Wu Jian 吳鑒. *Daoyi zhi lue xiao shi* 島夷誌畧校釋 (Beijing: Zhonghua shuju, 2000), p. 5.

[85] Mukai Masaaki, "The Interests of the Rulers, Agents and Merchants behind the Southward Expansion of the Yuan Dynasty," *Journal of the Turfan Studies: Essays on the Third International Conference on Turfan Studies, The Origins and Migrations of Eurasian Nomadic Peoples*, (Shanghai: Shanghai Guji, 2010), p. 439. Mukai speculates, however, that Shougeng may well have intentionally quit his political activities in order to advance his commercial interests in southeast Asia at the time of the Java invasion.

son, Chongmo 蒲崇謨 (d. 1334), served as manager of governmental affairs (rank 1B), the second-highest position in the Secretariat. In addition, two of Shougeng's nephews (sons of Shoucheng) held minor posts in Fujian.[86]

Underlying this array of accomplishments was an extraordinary accumulation of wealth, the source of which was maritime trade, though obviously aided by the Pu's political connections. The "tens of thousands (of strings), with several thousand men-servants" attributed to Pu Shougeng in the funeral inscription to Dong Wenbing cited earlier may have been an exaggeration, but it bespeaks a kind of ostentatious luxury that was evident in the Sea Transport Tower that he built in the late Southern Song, which we encountered in Chapter 3. There are also intriguing suggestions from the archaeological record. Chen Dasheng, when describing a stone carving that was part of a large structure in Yunlu Village to the east of Quanzhou city, elaborated:

Yunlu Village was inhabited by Arab Muslim communities in the Yuan Dynasty and was renowned for growing spice plants... It is also the place where the family of the wealthy Arab merchant Pu Shougeng lived, and where many legends of him were handed down. On the east side of the spot where the tablet was unearthed, there was the Anneli Temple, which is in ruins. At the foot of the hill, there used to be a vast burial ground which was destroyed in the fifties. According to the peasants, there were stone tablets, altars, balustrade and carved lions on the ground, which were probably relics of the Ming Dynasty. About a dozen meters down the hill from the grave, there is the "ku cha" (or ko chat in south Fujian dialect), which is said to be the back garden of Pu Shougeng's. There was a well in the garden called Anan well, which was filled up with dirt in the fifties.[87]

However great the power and influence of Pu Shougeng and his family, it did not begin to match that of Shihab al-Din, a Muslim from Kunduz in the Kharazum region of central Asia. We encountered him earlier as a patron of Pu and Möngtei in the early 1280s.[88] Through much of the 1280s he was associated with the notorious minister Sangha (Sangge 桑哥), who dominated Khubilai's government from 1282 to 1291. Sangha, a Buddhist of either Uighur or Tibetan origins, was much hated by much of Chinese officialdom, perhaps in part because of his active support of foreigners, especially Muslims. To that end, he was instrumental in halting a short-lived campaign against Muslims in the

---

[86] See my book chapter, "Pu Shougeng Reconsidered: Pu, His Family, and Their Role in the Maritime Trade of Quanzhou," *Beyond the Silk Road: New Approaches to Asian Maritime History* (Wiesbaden: Harrassowitz Verlag, 2018), for a more detailed account of the careers of these Pu offspring.

[87] Chen Dasheng, 陳達生, *Quanzhou Yisilan jiao shike*, pp. 94–95.

[88] My account of Shihab al-Din relies heavily on Yokkaichi's extensive treatment of him in "The Structure of Political Power and the *Nanhai* Trade," pp. 5–8.

early 1280s and he sponsored the founding of a National College for the Study of Muslim Script in 1289.[89]

In 1287, Sangha appointed Shihab al-Din and 'Umar, another Muslim official, as financial officials with control over the provincial *ortoy* affairs office (xing-quanfusi) in Hangzhou, which controlled both the maritime trade offices and maritime transport within the empire.[90] Shihab had a long-standing rivalry with the pirates-turned-maritime officials Zhang Xuan and Zhu Qing, who wielded great power over maritime transport (the shipping of goods to the capital) and who, as Yokkaichi has shown, operated in a competing patronage network. In 1289, he successfully obtained the emperor's support for the transfer of a group of northern soldiers and their families to serve as mariners and sailors, with the result that Zhang and Zhu's southern followers were supplanted and expelled.[91]

Two years later, Shihab's fortunes turned when his patron Sangha was tried for a host of crimes and subsequently executed. Many of Sangha's protégés, particularly Muslims, likewise lost their lives, and Shihab might well have suffered the same fate had it not been for an administrator in the Jianghuai branch secretariat who successfully argued for his importance to maritime trade:

If the state makes an investment in the maritime merchants' trading in the Nanhai, it will achieve great wealth. If Shafuding were to be punished, a lot of maritime merchants would escape and hide themselves from the public. I am afraid that it will cripple the state's finances.[92]

Shihab was saved by this intervention, but his troubles continued into the 1290s. In the preface to the previously discussed 22-article

---

[89] Morris Rossabi, *Khubilai Khan: His Life and Times* (Berkeley, CA: University of California Press, 1988), pp. 192–199, and "The Muslims in Early Yüan Dynasty," in Herbert Franke and Denis Twitchett, eds., *The Cambridge History of China, Volume 6. Alien Regimes and Border States, 907–1368* (Cambridge: Cambridge University Press, 1994), pp. 478–479.

[90] Yokkaichi, "The Structure of Political Power and the *Nanhai* Trade," especially pp. 2–3; Herbert Franke, "Sangha," in *In the Service of the Khan: Eminent Personalities of the Early Mongol-Yuan Period (1200–1300)*, edited by Igor de Rachewiltz, Hok-lam Chan, Hsiao Ch'i-ch'ing and Peter W. Geier (Wiesbaden: Harrassowitz Verlag, 1993), p. 564.

[91] YS 15, p. 322, cited by Yokkaichi, "The Structure of Political Power and the *Nanhai* Trade," p. 8. The northerners in this case had been soldiers in the service of Nayan, a Mongol prince and Nestorian who had led an unsuccessful rebellion in Manchuria against Khubilai in 1287. The reason given for the move was to relieve the northern officials of the cost of providing support to them and their families, but Shihab's motive for requesting the transfer was clearly to bolster his power vis-à-vis Zhang and Zhu.

[92] Yokkaichi, "The Structure of Political Power and the *Nanhai* Trade," pp. 2–3, citing the epitaph of Dong Shixuan 董士選 in Wu Dengzhuan 吳澄撰, *Wu wenzhenggong ji* 吳文正公集 64.

regulations on maritime trade of 1293, the assistant grand councilor Yan Gongnan 燕公楠 (1241–1302) produced a scathing critique of Shihab and Möngtei:

Recently, Mangwutai (Möngtei) and Shabuding (Shihāb al-Dīn) for their own profits ordered the army to supervise and guard all ships coming in, blocked them and took away valuable and expensive goods. Under such circumstances, their ships seldom come in and our ships seldom depart for there. Consequently, official business in the *shibosi* has been neglected.[93]

The fact that Yan Gongnan was an opponent of Sangha's who subsequently rose to high office helps to explain his charges against Shihab and Möngtei. In the wake of Sangha's death Shihab's fortunes underwent a decline, and he was forced from office by Zhu Qing and Zhang Xuan.[94] However it was Shihab who ultimately prospered. In 1303 Zhu and Zhang were the targets of a massive corruption investigation that resulted, among other things, in their execution and the conviction of over eighteen thousand officials and clerks.[95] Eight years later, control over the vast maritime transport system was given, on the recommendation of Shihab, to his brothers Habash (Hebashi 合八失) and Muhammad Andi (Mahemoudande 馬合謀但的). The rationale for this was that they "own ships and have a full knowledge of maritime transport." Moreover, Muhammad Andi was given the post of pacification commissioner for overseas countries (haiwaizhufan xuanweishi 海外諸蕃宣慰使), further cementing the enormous power over maritime shipping and commerce enjoyed by Shihab's family.[96]

In this history of the Muslims involved in the high-level politics surrounding maritime affairs, mention must also be made of the family of Sayyid 'Ajall Shams al-Din (1211–1279). Sayyid 'Ajall, born in Bukhara, was renowned as the Sinicizing governor of the newly conquered Yunnan in the 1270s.[97] One of his sons, known in Chinese genealogical sources as Ding Jin 丁謹 (1251–1298) – or Master Jiezhai 節齋公 – was considered

---

[93] *Yuan dianzhang* 22, p. 71b, cited by Yokkaichi, "The Structure of Political Power and the *Nanhai* Trade," pp. 11–12. This criticism is also mentioned by Mukai, "The Interests of the Rulers, Agents and Merchants," p. 438.

[94] Yokkaichi, "The Structure of Political Power and the *Nanhai* Trade," p. 6.

[95] Ch'i-ch'ing Hsiao, "Mid-Yuan Politics," in Herbert Franke and Denis Twitchett, eds., *The Cambridge History of China, Volume 6. Alien Regimes and Border States, 907–1368* (Cambridge: Cambridge University Press, 1994), p. 499.

[96] YS 22, pp. 528–529; Yokkaichi, "The Structure of Political Power and the *Nanhai* Trade," pp. 6–7.

[97] Ding Shouzhen 丁壽真, ed., *Ding Xieyuan jiapu* 丁協源家譜 (Taipei: Chongsi zhiye youxian gongsi, 1997), p. 128, Ding Kunjian 丁崑健, "Yuan Ming shidai Jinjiang diqu Huiyi Chenjiang Ding xing zuren de Hanhua" 元明時代晉江地區回族陳江丁氏族人的漢化, in Ding Shouzhen, *Ding Xieyuan jiapu*, pp. 281–283. For an account of the governorship of Sayyid Ajall Shams al-Din and two of his sons who succeeded him as

to be the founder of the Dings of Chenjiang 陳江丁氏, a prominent Quanzhou Muslim lineage in Ming and Qing times. He is identified as having been a merchant, though that may be best understood as an *ortoy* merchant; is credited with serving an assistant director (*zuocheng* 左丞) in the Quanzhou (Wotuo) zongguanfu, which prior to 1280 administered the *ortoy*; and is credited with then serving in the maritime trade office and in the Fujian branch secretariat government.[98] This career path strongly suggests an involvement as *ortoy* in maritime trade, though beyond these tantalizing facts we have only the names, dates and places of burial for Jiezhai's offspring.

One of Ding Jin's brothers, Nasir al-Din Abu Bakr, had twelve children, among whom was Bayan (Boyan 伯顏), who in 1293 achieved the exalted rank of *pingzhang zhengshi* 平章政事 (director of political affairs) in the central government, a position just below that of grand councilor, and continued to hold high office at court through the next decade. Like his uncle Ding Jin, he was involved in maritime activities. In the *Yuan History*'s brief entry on the Philippines (Sanyu 三嶼), Bayan is seen persuading Khubilai not to send a diplomatic mission there. Citing a "knowledgeable person" (*shizhe* 識者), he describes the state as having fewer than 200 households. He goes on to discourage a similar mission to the Ryukyus (Liuqiu 琉球), based on information that he had from a merchant in Quanzhou.[99] Persian sources identify him as having served as magistrate (hakem) of Quanzhou, but more important was his close association with Zhu Qing and Zhang Xuan, and by extension his enmity with Shihab al-Din. His rise to power at court followed the execution of Sangha, when Zhu and Zhang's fortunes – and their enormous influence over maritime shipping and trade – dramatically improved, and in 1303 during the investigation that resulted in Zhu and Zhang's execution, Bayan was among those accused of complicity with them.[100] This connection was not limited to Bayan. His brother Bayanchar had connections with Zhu and Zhang in their maritime transport operation in Jiangnan, while another brother 'Omar was also identified in Persian sources as a magistrate of Quanzhou.[101]

The Li family of Rongshan (Rongshan Lishi 榮山李氏) represents a much humbler example of Muslim maritime enterprise in Yuan Quanzhou. They took as their founding ancestor one Li Lü 李閭

---

governor (Nasir al-Din and Mas'ud), see Morris Rossabi, "The Muslims in Early Yüan Dynasty," pp. 287–291.

[98] Ding Shouzhen, *Ding Xieyuan jiapu*, p. 128.   [99] YS 210, p. 4668.

[100] Yokkaichi, "The Structure of Political Power and the *Nanhai* Trade," pp. 8–9, 15–16.

[101] Yokkaichi, "The Structure of Political Power and the *Nanhai* Trade," p. 9.

(1328–1376), styled Master Muzhai 睦齋公, a wealthy commoner who was involved in maritime trade. According to the Li genealogy,

He was honest and generous to people, a man of few words, though good at making similes. He was content with simplicity and loved the old. He inherited a considerable estate from his father, and he frequently sent family retainers abroad to overseas countries 常俵家客 航泛海外諸國.[102]

Although Li is not a surname commonly associated with the Muslims, the genealogy makes it clear that the Lis were both foreign (semu) and Muslim. However, despite their foreign identity and merchant activities, even in the Yuan the family culture resembled that of the literati in various ways. Muzhai's son Li Duan 李端 (styled Master Zhizhai 直齋公), is praised for his intelligence, philanthropy, horticulture, study of the *Classics of Poetry* and *Documents* and love of simplicity, all of this despite "living by the market-place" (*zhu yu shichan* 居於市廛).[103] More remarkably, Muzhai's wife, Lady Qian 錢氏, whose father was an official originally from Zhejiang, is described as building a Buddhist hall, presumably on Muzhai's estate, and giving a gold-plated statue to the Kaiyuan Temple.[104] In short, the Rongshan Lis displayed a level of cultural ambivalence remarkable for a Muslim family. We will return to them when discussing the last years of the Yuan and the early Ming, for they more than any of the Quanzhou Muslim families demonstrate the competing pulls of their Muslim heritage and the surrounding Chinese culture.

The Su family of Yanzhi 燕支蘇氏 was, if anything, even more remarkable in its circumstances. The later lineage took as its founder Su Tangshe 蘇唐舍 (1271–1352), who adopted the Arabic name Ahemo 阿合抹, for he was a convert to Islam. His had been a wealthy and respected Quanzhou family that had come to grief in the early thirteenth century. In 1303, the Su family was charged by the local government with delivering that year's head tax revenues – some 5,180 *taels* – to the capital. Unfortunately, those undertaking the mission were robbed en route, and because all were killed, the Sus still in Quanzhou knew nothing about this – that is, until 1311, when officials arrived to investigate the non-delivery of the taxes. When family members resisted and harmed the county sheriff, a number of the Su men were imprisoned and the family's

[102] "Li shi shixi tu" 李氏世系圖, *Rongshan Lishi zupu* 榮山李氏族譜, in *Quanzhou Huizu pudie ziliao xuanbian* 泉州回族譜牒資料选编, edited by Quanzhou shi Quanzhou lishi yanjiuhui 泉州市泉州历史研究会 (Quanzhou, 1980), p. 78b.

[103] "Ershi shi Zhizhai gong kuangzhi" 二十世直齋公壙誌, *Quanzhou Huizu pudie ziliao xuanbian*, in *Quanzhou Huizu pudie ziliao xuanbian*, p. 78a.

[104] "Li shi shixi tu," *Rongshan Lishi zupu*, 78a.

lands and buildings were confiscated. Those who survived this dispersed to different locales, with Tangshe going to Yanzhi Lane 燕支巷 in Jinjiang 晉江 county, where he settled.[105]

In Tangshe's genealogical biography there is no mention of the family's difficulties, but the Qing author quotes the description of Zhu Jian 朱鑑, a Yuan court official: "He moved from Yintong to live in Yanzhi. He studied the pure teaching of the western lands (*xiyu jingjiao* 西域淨教 – i.e., Islam) and took the name Ahemo." The biography also details Tangshe's assets at the time of his death in 1352: 900 *mou* of paddy land, 5 fields of lichees and an unspecified amount of cash.[106] This was an impressive fortune for someone whose family had been disgraced and bankrupted when he was already in his 40s. How did he achieve this? We know almost nothing about his immediate offspring beyond their dates, but we are told that his son and two grandsons all married Pus. This, combined with Tangshe's conversion to Islam, points to maritime commerce under the patronage of the Pus as the source of his fortune, as Billy So has proposed. For their part, the Pus were establishing marriage ties with a venerable literati family.[107]

The Jins of Qingyuan 清源金氏 provide a very different example of a Quanzhou Muslim family, for theirs was a Xiongnu military family that traced its origins back to the Han, and they had been ready supporters of the Yuan cause.[108] The move to Quanzhou occurred during the reign of Wenzong (Tugh Temur; r. 1330–1332), when Jin Ji 金吉, a general who had been serving in the secondary capital of Shangdu, was posted there. Ji's main claim to fame concerned his actions during the Ispah Disturbance at the end of the Yuan, a subject to which we shall return. He was also the father of Jin Ali, described by the genealogists as being "martial and grand in character" and a student of Sun Zi. Ali is also described as a key benefactor for the restoration of the Qingjing Mosque in 1349, which was discussed earlier. According to his biography,

---

[105] "Zhida zhi bian taocuan shimo" 至大之變逃竄始末, in *Yanzhi Sushi zupu* 燕支蘇氏族譜, in *Quanzhou Huizu pudie ziliao xuanbian*, pp. 89b–90a. See Billy So's excellent account of these events in *Prosperity, Region and Institutions*, pp. 116–117. So claims that Tangshe's family was descended from the famous Quanzhou scholar-official Su Song 蘇頌 (1020–1101), but I have been unable to verify this. According the genealogy's 1502 preface, the family was originally from Gushi 固始 county in Guangzhou 光州 (Huainan).

[106] *Yanzhi Sushi zupu*, pp. 90b–91a.

[107] Billy So, *Prosperity, Region and Institutions*, p. 117.

[108] *Qingyuan Jin shi zupu* 清源李氏族譜, in Quanzhoushi Quanzhou lishi yanjiuhui 泉州市泉州历史研究会, ed., *Quanzhou Huizu pudie ziliao xuanbian* 泉州回族谱牒资料选编, (Quanzhou, 1980), pp. 81b–86b; *Quanzhou lichen xingshi* 泉州鲤城姓氏, Pt. 3 (http://blog.sina.com.cn/s/blog_657ba18501014rur.html).

He looked lightly upon wealth and enjoyed leisure, he was compassionate and widely charitable, and he esteemed Islam. The Muslims in Quanzhou had long had the Qingzhen Mosque, but its arch had long ago fallen into disrepair. He contributed (lit. used) wood and stone to renovate it, spending untold amounts of money. The building is strong and spacious and can be seen even today.[109]

As attractive as this account may be, there is a serious question as to whether the Jin Ali who funded the renovation of the mosque was in fact the son of Jin Ji. Chen Dasheng 陳達生, the preeminent authority on Muslim Quanzhou, has argued that Jin Ji's son, who is named in the genealogy as Heli 阿里, not Ali 阿里, could not have been the benefactor of the renovation. Apart from the implausibility of a military family like the Jins having the resources to fund a mosque renovation, Chen's analysis of the ages of Jin Ji and his offspring, as presented in the genealogy, concludes that Heli would have been a teenager (14–19 years old) in 1349. He speculates that the Ali of the renovation might have been a foreign merchant residing in Quanzhou ("Ali" being a common Chinese name used by west Asian Muslims), but is firm in his conclusion that it was not Jin Heli.[110] If Chen is right, a position strongly supported by Odet Abt, it is hardly surprising that the Ming Jin genealogists claimed the connection to the renovation, since that represented a key cultural achievement of the Muslim community in Yuan Quanzhou.[111] Also, if we are correct in our conclusion that Pu Rihe was also involved in the renovation of the mosque, his omission in the Jin account is noteworthy but not surprising, for as we shall see when discussing the events at the end of the Yuan, the Jins and Pus became bitter enemies. Indeed, if Jin Heli and Pu Rihe were not cooperating in the renovation, then it is possible that the enmity evident at the dynasty's end was also present well before that.[112]

Before leaving the subject of the Muslim communities, two points are worth noting. First, with the important exception of the Pu family, all of the Muslim individuals and families that we have discussed came from beyond Fujian – and largely from outside of China – during the Yuan,

---

[109] *Qingyuan Jin shi zupu*, p. 86b.

[110] Chen Dasheng, "Jin Ali yu Qingjingsi 金阿里与清净寺," in *Quanzhou Yisilanjiao yanjiu lunwenxuan* 泉州伊斯兰教研究论文选 (Fuzhou: Renmin chubanshe, 1983), pp. 126–130.

[111] Abt, "Locking and Unlocking the City Gates," pp. 24–29.

[112] There is also a question as to whether Jin Heli was involved in the Ispah fighting treated later in this chapter, for there are references to a Jin Ali 金阿里 as well as a Yu Ali 余阿里 playing a role. This is persuasively refuted by Abt, who considers the issue at length and rejects the identification. If it were true, it would have placed Heli with the very Ispah forces that Jin Ji is celebrated for helping to defeat. Abt, "Locking and Unlocking the City Gates," pp. 29–32. See, too, Maejima, "The Muslims of Ch'üan-chou," pp. 64–65.

though once in the southeast – and in Quanzhou, particularly – they all gravitated towards maritime trade. Second, as much as we have talked about individuals, their successes quickly spread to their kinsmen, making their engagement in maritime trade (and related political activities) family undertakings.

Dynasty's End

It was probably inevitable that high-profile power and wealth in the Muslim community – like that of the Mongols and *semu* population generally – would elicit a Chinese counter-reaction, and it came violently at the dynasty's end. But well before this, the Yuan government had begun eliminating – or at least circumscribing – privileges that the Muslims had until then enjoyed. This included limiting the powers of the Muslim head-men (*qadi*) in 1311 and abolishing the position altogether in 1328; elim-inating tax exemptions for Muslim (and other foreign) holy men in 1329; and prescribing marriage regulations in accordance with Confucian prin-ciples in 1340.[113] Indeed, such was the Muslim dissatisfaction with these changes that not a few joined the ranks of rebels and others opposing the Mongols in the mid-fourteenth century.

In Quanzhou these anti-government activities took a unique form, namely a breakaway Muslim regime known as the Ispah (*Yisibaxi* 亦思 巴奚, also called the Persian Garrison), which ruled Quanzhou and other parts of southern Fujian from 1357 to 1367. The rebellion – or regime – began in 1357 when the Persian military officials Saifuding 賽甫丁 (Saif un-Din) and Amiliding 阿迷里丁 (Amid un-Din) seized the city of Quanzhou. For five years, they and their troops, known as the Yisibaxi or Ispah (Persian for "army"), engaged in convoluted and often indeter-minate battles for control of Xinghua 興化 and even Fuzhou福州 to the north of Quanzhou.[114] In 1362, Nawuna 那巫納, another west Asian official, killed first Amiliding and subsequently Saifuding, thereby con-trolling the Ispah troops and for the next five years governing Quanzhou.[115] The Quanzhou forces attempted to extend their sway

---

[113] Leslie, *Islam in Traditional China*, pp. 89–90.
[114] Maejima Shinji, "The Muslims in Ch'üan-chou," Pt. 2, pp. 49–60. My account of the Ispah Rebellion relies heavily on Maejima's detailed account. Chang Hsing-lang, "The Rebellion of the Persian Garrison in Ch'üan-chou (1357–1366)," *Monumenta Serica* 3 (1938), pp. 611–627, has also treated the rebellion at length, but his account is largely superseded by that of Maejima. I am also following Maejima (50) in taking Yisibaxi (or Ispah) as "army" which seems more plausible than its referring to the Persian city of Isfahan (Ispahan), as Chang suggested.
[115] Some contemporary accounts use the name Awuna 阿巫那, which is almost certainly a variant of Nawuna.

north and had some success in neighboring Xinghua, but were twice rebuffed at the provincial capital of Fuzhou. Their eventual defeat came in 1367, not at the hands of Ming forces, which were not yet in the area, but to a provincial force deployed from Fuzhou. In fact, the defeat of Nawuna, which occurred with little fighting, was widely credited to the last-minute change of sides by one of Nawuna's officers, none other than the Qunzhou military official Jin Ji 金吉.[116]

Ming historians from Fujian were unanimous in their condemnation of Nawuna's regime in Quanzhou. Very similar examples of their judgments collected by Maejima Shinji include the following:

At that time Na-wu-na of the Western Frontiers and others unlawfully occupied Ch'üan-chou and slaughtered many people cruelly.

Na-wu-na of the Western Frontiers and others occupied Ch'üan-chou and oppressed the people of that locality. They robbed their fortunes. They were apt to murder the citizens, when they could not get money and property.

At that time, Na-wu-na of the Western Frontier origin occupied Ch'üan-chou, maltreated many people of the province, and murdered them with cruelty.[117]

It is impossible to know the extent to which these condemnations were colored by Nawuna's being identified by Ming writers as the chief villain in a shameful episode in Fujianese history. However, we can qualify the implication that this five-year period was one of unremitting oppression. The court continued to appoint officials to Quanzhou, the most prominent being Guansun 觀孫, a vice minister (zuocheng 左丞) who was sent in 1264 to administer Quanzhou and Xinghua. While he proved unable to control Nawuna and the Ispah forces, Nawuna gave at least limited recognition of his authority, as well as the authority of De'an, who was later appointed with a similar charge.[118] In fact, the impression given by the sources of the Ispah disturbances is military and political fluidity as well as intrigue and brutality on all sides.

Chen Dasheng has made the intriguing argument that Sunni-Shiite sectarian differences were behind much of the intrigue and violence of the Persian Garrison period. He argues that Saifuding and Amiliding, backed by the Persian troops that had been brought to Quanzhou from central China and who were Shiite, represented a Shiite reaction to the long-term Sunni domination of the Pu family. Nawuna, a Pu in-law, led the Sunni counter-reaction, while the final "treachery" of Jin Ji can be understood in

---

[116] So, *Prosperity, Region, and Institutions*, pp. 122–125.

[117] Maejima, "The Muslims in Ch'üan-chou," p. 56, quoting from the biography of Gong Mingan in *Wuwei zhi* 武衛志 13.

[118] Maejima, "The Muslims in Ch'üan-chou," pp. 60–61.

light of his sympathy with the Shiite cause.[119] Chen's theory explains a great deal about this period, but perhaps the broader point to be made is that throughout the decade-long Ispah period, the political struggles involved mainly Muslim actors in a very divided Muslim community.

There are, in fact, some non-religious dimensions to the struggles in this period suggested by the sources. Not only was Nawuna related to the Pus by marriage, he was also "in charge of merchant ships" (*zhu shibo* 主市舶) – presumably as director of the maritime trade office – at the time that he killed Amiliding. Then in 1264, when the newly arrived Guansun sent Ren Li 任立, a subordinate, to seal the customs warehouses, Nawuna emptied the warehouses prior to Ren's arrival and hindered Ren's inspection of them.[120] These connections between Nawuna and maritime trade suggest a division within Quanzhou's Muslim community between the maritime merchants represented by Nawuna and the Pus, and others drawn from officialdom and the military, such as the Jins. This division may well have corresponded largely with the religious divide, but if so it suggests that there were more factors than one dividing the Muslim community.

The Ming genealogists of the Jin lineage dramatically reflect the division between the Jins and the Pus. A good portion of the biography of Jin Ji is devoted to a scathing account of the Pus, beginning with Pu Shougeng, whose surrender of Quanzhou to the Yuan is described as an act of treachery, accompanied by the slaughter of Song imperial clan members. It continues:

> He [Shougeng] was ennobled and this enabled him to control the prefectural government. [Pu] fathers and sons through the generations counted on special favors to monopolize regulations, making use of harsh punishments to control taxation. The people suffered and were burned by the flames, this for some 90 years.

When describing the Ispah events, the account goes on to claim that it was only after the death of "bandit Pu" 蒲賊 that his nephew Nawuna established himself.[121] Although the identity of "bandit Pu" is not provided, the attempt to associate Nawuna with the Pus could not be clearer, and I would suggest that it reflects a division between the merchant, largely

---

[119] Chen Dasheng, "Quanzhou Yisilan jiaopai yu Yuanmo Yisibaxi zhanluan xingdun shitan 泉州伊斯蘭教派与元末亦思巴奚战乱性质试探," in *Quanzhou Yisilanjiao yanjiu lunwenxuan* 泉州伊斯兰教研究论文选 (Fuzhou: Renmin chubanshe, 1983), pp. 53–64.

[120] Maejima, "The Muslims in Ch'üan-chou," pp. 55 and 60, both citing the *Fujian tongzhi* 福建通志 266.

[121] *Qingyuan Jin shi zupu*, pp. 83b–84a. Jin Ji's biography has a named author but no date. However, the following biography of his son Jin Heli is dated 1502 (Hongzhi 15), though with a different author.

Sunni, community in Quanzhou, and the military, largely Shiite, community represented by the Jins.

The collapse of the Ispah forces and the quickly ensuing arrival of forces representing the new Ming government marked the end of the Muslim trade diaspora in Quanzhou, though not of Muslims in that prefecture. The historian Wu Youxiong 吳幼雄 describes the choices made by different families in 1367–1368:

In Quanzhou many of the Arabs and Persians who had been merchants or missionaries left by boat. One group that had participated in the Persian Garrison was killed. Another group, by virtue of its long residence in China, had gradually absorbed Han culture and had a relatively broad social base, but they were driven out to coastal areas (Chendi, Baiqi, etc.), into the mountains (Yongchun 永春, Dehua 德化), or even further afield into the coastal regions of Zhangpu or Lufu, or coastal areas of Zhejiang.[122]

A third group, he also notes, had such an exemplary reputation that they were able to take shelter at mosques in the city and weather the hard times that occurred.

Our accounts of those hard times come primarily from the Muslim genealogies. The most dramatic – and chilling – is from the Jin genealogy, which describes how, after the fall of Nawuna, the city reacted in a paroxysm of violence directed against the Muslims generally and the Pu family in particular:

All of the Western peoples were annihilated, with a number of foreigners with large noses mistakenly killed while for three days the gates were closed and the executions were carried out. The corpses of the Pus were all stripped naked, their faces to the west ... They were all judged according to the "five mutilating punishments" and then executed with their carcasses throwing into pig troughs. This was in revenge for their murder and rebellion in the Song.[123]

This passage stands out not only for its violence but also for its anti-Muslim references: the west-facing burials (towards Mecca, to identify them as Muslim) and the pig troughs. It is also interesting that the retribution was supposedly aimed not at the Ispah regime but at Pu Shougeng's treachery against the Song, surely a Ming formulation.

The Li genealogy provides a more measured description of this period: "In the late Yuan the [area by the] sea was a bubbling cauldron. Great families scattered from their homes, which were burned by the soldiers, and few genealogies survived."[124] The Li family itself was relatively fortunate, thanks to the actions of Li Lü (styled Muzhai).

[122] Wu Youxiong, *Quanzhou zongjiao wenhua*, pp. 222–223.
[123] *Qingyuan Jin shi*, p. 222.
[124] "Chuiqi lun," *Rongshan Lishi zupu*, in *Quanzhou Huizu pudie ziliao xuanbian*, p. 76.

At this time the Yuan knot was being loosened and foreigners 夷人 controlled Quanzhou. Amidst the disturbances of warfare, litigation flourished. Every year the starving appeared, and Muzhai used his stores to aid them, so that many survived. Although many of the foreigners were cruel, none dared oppose them. But many marveled at Muzhai's virtue.[125]

The Lis' good fortune in this period did not translate into an easy transition to the post-Yuan order. As we will see in Chapter 5, their Muslim identity was a contentious issue for the first Li generations in the Ming, with different individuals responding in different ways.

For the Dings of Jinjiang, flight from Quanzhou city was the answer to disturbances, and so they moved to Jinjiang (or Chendai) on the coast southeast of the prefectural city.[126] Even the family of the Chinese Muslim Su Tangshe was sundered, perhaps because of its close ties to the Pus. Apart from his eldest son, who remained in Quanzhou and cared for his kinsmen, "in the late Yuan, the five sons fled the disturbances [going to] the four quarters, and no one knows what became of them."[127]

The Ispah regime and its dramatic demise marked an end to the privileged Muslim community of Quanzhou. The privileged status of Muslims in the semi-colonial political structure of Yuan China gave them unprecedented visibility and power but also made them easy targets when the Yuan order collapsed, resulting in their dispersion, as Wu Youxiong describes. When the Ming founder enacted his prohibition on overseas trade, the conditions for a Muslim trade diaspora anchored in China disappeared. In Chapter 5 we will explore the Muslim dispersion and the accompanying economic and cultural transition of those families that were able to maintain themselves in Fujian as well as new diasporic configurations that emerged in the fourteenth- and fifteenth-century world of maritime Asia.

---

[125] "Li shi shixi tu" 李氏世系圖, in *Quanzhou Huizu pudie ziliao xuanbian*, p. 78b.

[126] Ding Kunjian, "Yuan Ming shidai Jinjiang diqu," p. 286.

[127] *Yanzhi Su shi zupu*, p. 87a.

5 Endings and Continuities

The coming of the Ming dynasty (1368–1644) marked the end of the Chinese Muslim communities that had flourished for centuries on China's southeastern coast and that had been a key part of the Muslim trade diaspora of maritime Asia. This was the result not of the violence marking the end of the Yuan discussed in Chapter 4, but rather of anti-trade policies established by the emperor Taizu 太祖 (Zhu Yuanzhang 朱元璋, the Ming founder) and maintained for the following two centuries. An ex-peasant whose rebel movement grew and matured in the Yangzi Valley, Taizu had little experience with the ocean or maritime trade, though he initially seems to have welcomed it. In 1367, after the defeat of rivals in the Yangzi Delta region where they had encouraged foreign trade, he opened a maritime trade office in Taicang 太倉 (Zhejiang), which had been an important port in the Yuan. When Zhu Daoshan 朱道山, a merchant from Quanzhou who had emerged as a leader of maritime merchants in the Zhejiang region, led a group of merchants to an audience with Zhu Yuanzhang, they were well received, thus encouraging other merchants to come to the court in Nanjing. At the beginning of 1369, envoys were sent abroad to Japan, Champa, Java and the western ocean (Xiyang 西洋), announcing the establishment of the new dynasty and inviting tribute missions.[1]

Such positive beginnings were short lived. Piracy had long been a problem, but a 200-ship attack on Mingzhou by pirates in 1368 made clear to the new dynasty the threat that they posed, and poor treatment of the envoys to Japan seems to have soured the new emperor on overseas ventures. In Quanzhou, where Ming forces had arrived by sea to take control in 1369, the maritime trade office from Yuan times was closed the following year, as was the Taicang office. Then, in 1371, bans were enacted on travel by sea to foreign countries and also on private individuals going to sea. Maritime offices were subsequently reestablished in

---

[1] *Ming shilu* 明實錄 38, p. 11a, translated by Geoff Wade, *Southeast Asia and in the Ming Shi-lu* (http://epress.nus.edu.sg/msl/).

Quanzhou, Guangzhou and Mingzhou, but their exclusive purpose was to handle the tribute missions arriving from overseas, with all trade from the Nanhai being routed through Guangzhou, from Japan to Mingzhou, and from the Ryukyus to Quanzhou. Then, in 1422, the Quanzhou and Mingzhou offices were abolished, leaving only the Guangzhou office, a situation that continued until the late sixteenth century.[2]

The Ming prohibition on overseas trade, coming as it did on the heels of the anti-Muslim riots in Quanzhou, brought an abrupt end to the activities of the maritime merchants, particularly the Muslims. As we noted in Chapter 4, flight was the dominant reaction, but it took different forms. Many fled China altogether, and we will be considering them at length. But first, we will examine those who remained in Quanzhou – though often fleeing the city itself – and redefined themselves.

Diasporic Transformations

The situation faced by the Quanzhou Muslim families in the early Ming was complicated. Although the Ming movement had xenophobic elements and maritime trade was banned, Ming Taizu himself seems to have been quite tolerant of Muslims, having received significant support from Muslim generals during his unification campaign.[3] Then, in 1407, the Yongle 永樂 emperor (r. 1403–1424) had imperial stelae placed in mosques throughout the empire (including Quanzhou) that decreed protection for Muslims against mistreatment by officials or private individuals.[4] In the early Ming, there was sometimes conflicting legislation concerning Muslims: a requirement that they intermarry with non-Muslim families, but also another that they not take Chinese surnames.

The Quanzhou Muslim genealogies that we encountered in Chapter 4 are our primary sources of information about the Muslim families that remained. This is of course a select group, representing families that had the resources to reestablish themselves, survive through the centuries and maintain genealogies, which then made their way into the hands of scholars. Nevertheless, their accounts are instructive, particularly

---

[2] Billy So, *Prosperity, Region, and Institutions*, pp. 125–126; Chen Gaohua 陳高華 and Chen Shangsheng 陳尚勝, *Zhongguo haiwai jiaotong shi* 中國海外交通史, pp. 167–170. The account of Zhu Daoshan is from the latter work (p. 168), citing Wang Hui 王彙, *Wang Changzong ji* 王常宗集.

[3] It has even been argued by Yusuf Haji Chang, "The Ming Empire: Patron of Islam in China and Southeast-West Asia," *Journal of the Malaysian Brance of the Royal Asiatic Society* 61.2 (1988), pp. 1–44, that Zhu Yuanzhang (Taizu) was Muslim. Although this argument has not been generally accepted, Chang makes a compelling case for close ties between Zhu and the Muslims.

[4] Chen Dasheng, *Quanzhou Yisilan jiao shike*, pp. 11–12.

because, as Fan Ke has noted, their descendants are unique among the Hui communities in contemporary China in tracing their origins to Muslim maritime merchants of the Yuan period.[5] As we saw in Chapter 4, these families relocated elsewhere in Quanzhou, where they were able to establish themselves. But the ways in which that occurred varied greatly among them.

According to their genealogy, when the Dings moved to Chenjiang 陳江 in Jinjiang 晉江 (the county just south of Quanzhou city), their adjustment to local society proved difficult. Despite the very large size of their newly acquired landholdings (in the thousands of *qing* 頃), their social intercourse with reputable families (*mendi* 門第) was limited to only a few that were close neighbors. There followed a traumatic incident in which Ding Shan 丁善, a fourth-generation descendant of the lineage founder Ding Jin (Shansi Ding 苫思丁), and his son were accused of involvement with a White Lotus Sect (*Bailian hui* 白蓮會) in Chenjiang and were saved from execution only by an imperial pardon. According to the lineage historian Kunjian Ding, the Dings became very reticent about discussing their Muslim, *semu* origins.[6] Over the course of time, the Dings made a concerted effort to adapt themselves to gentry culture, establishing a family school (*jiashu* 家塾) and producing their first *jinshi* examination graduate in 1505.[7]

The post-Yuan Muslim lineages were not of one mind in their treatment of their Muslim heritage. Although the Dings were reticent about advertising their origins and religion, their genealogical writings were clear on these matters. In an essay on the "teachings of the ancestors" (*zujiao shuo* 祖教說), there is a detailed and unapologetic description of Islamic practices.[8] The genealogy of the Sus of Yanzhi, which traced the family's beginnings to Su Tangshe, and who, as we saw in Chapter 4, converted to Islam, gives no indication of their continuing to practice Islam during the Ming and Qing. However, the genealogy also exhibits considerable pride in their Muslim origins. Writing in 1670, Su Zuanche 蘇纘轍 recounts how he inquired of an imam (*jiaoshi* 教師) the meaning of Ahemo 阿合抹, the Muslim name taken by Su Tangshe; the answer was that it meant "elder" (*zhanglao* 長老).[9]

---

[5] Fan Ke, "Maritime Muslims and Hui Identity: A South Fujian Case," *Journal of Muslim Minority Affairs* 21.2 (2001), pp. 309–332.

[6] Ding Kunjian, "Yuan Ming shidai Jinjiang diqu Huiyi Chenjiang Ding," pp. 286–287.

[7] Ding Kunjian, "Yuan Ming shidai Jinjiang diqu Huiyi Chenjiang Ding," p. 290. The Dings currently maintain an active mosque in their hometown south of Quanzhou city.

[8] Ding Kunjian, "Yuan Ming shidai Jinjiang diqu Huiyi Chenjiang Ding," p. 281.

[9] "Yanzhi Su shi zupu," in *Quanzhou Huizu pudie ziliao xuanbian*, p. 90b.

In marked contrast to the Dings and Sus, for the Lis of Rongshan their Muslim heritage was a source of discomfort and dissension. As we saw in Chapter 4, the family's founder Li Lü (Muzhai), who was involved in maritime commerce, was praised for his virtue and especially his generosity during the Ispah period, which helped the family survive that difficult time. However, his Muslim faith was regarded with some puzzlement: "Muzhai followed foreign teachings (*yijiao* 夷教) which seem to have been his fundamental [principles]. Some followed these Yuan customs, [but] no one could understand them in detail."[10] Religious differences then led to a parting of the ways between Muzhai's two sons, Nu 駑 and Duan 端. Nu is not graced with a biography in the Li genealogy, but Duan's is revealing. He is described as intelligent and philanthropic, generous to the needy, a lover of ancient music who enjoyed planting trees and a quiet life, and a father who instructed his sons in the study of the *Classics of Poetry* and *Documents*. He also moved his home to the south of the Great Wall "because he could not change the strange practices of his elder brother."[11]

The Lis' ambivalence about their Muslim past is evident in a remarkable 1426 essay called "Instructing the Kinsmen" (*Chuiqi lun* 垂戚論), by Li Guangqi 李廣齊, the oldest son of Li Duan.[12] He begins by describing the dire situation at the end of the Yuan:

When the Yuan house lost control, among the *semu* who had come and taken control of Fujian, the blaze was greatest in our Quanzhou. Tribal groups spread, wantonly spreading destruction, and oppressing (lit. rubbing mud in) our spirits.

He then interrogates the nature of foreign (*semu*) identity:

Even today, although households have been registered, there are true (*zhen* 真) *semuren*, there are those who are false (*wei* 偽) *semuren*; there those who are *semuren* on account of their wives, and those who are *semuren* because their mothers were *semuren*, and they [all] practice strange customs (*yisu* 異俗). The fires have disordered our people (*zulei* 族類), [leading to] the devaluing of our common statutes and the damaging of our social relationships.

The central issue with which Guangqi is wrestling is how ethnic identity and its concomitant cultural and religious practices had become confused. In a clear indication of the considerable intermarriage between Muslim and Han families, he critiques the "false *semuren*" who resulted

---

[10] *Rongshan Lishi zupu*, in *Quanzhou Huizu pudie ziliao xuanbian*, p. 77b.

[11] *Rongshan Lishi zupu*, in *Quanzhou Huizu pudie ziliao xuanbian*, pp. 78a–b.

[12] *Rongshan Lishi zupu*, in *Quanzhou Huizu pudie ziliao xuanbian*, pp. 76a–77a. Guangqi's original name was Tianyu 天與; for reasons unexplained, in 1422 he moved to Nan'an and registered there using the name Guangqi. Subsequently, three of his cousins (sons of Nu) joined him there (pp. 77a–b).

from wives and mothers practicing "strange customs." He proceeds to critique those customs, which are clearly Muslim: their funerary and mourning practices and well as more general practices (including circumcision), contrasting them unfavorably with Chinese practices, and then turns his attention to his uncle (Li Nu):

> Although our Quanzhou is on the Fujian coast, people all know the way of the Former Kings... Now my uncle is a gentry member by birth (*yiguan jinshen zhi yi* 衣冠縉紳之裔), but he is deceived and blinded by *semu* customs. Grandfathers do not act as grandfathers, so his conduct as a grandfather is not proper conduct but rather that of the barbarians. This has caused his sons and grandsons all to be barbarians. Why is this? They are drowned in a love of the strange, alas!

Li Guangqi concludes by quoting Han Fei Zi 韓非子 – "When the barbarians enter China (the Central Kingdom), they act like Chinese; when Chinese enter the barbarian [lands], they act like barbarians" – and expressing his fear that later generations would continue in their errant ways despite his warnings.

There is one other intriguing element in the Li family's response to the Yuan-Ming transition. Faced in the late Yuan with the costs of provisioning troops, forced exactions of silver and, apparently, the wives of Nu and Duan, the family sent the orphaned children to live with their maternal grandmother's family (*waima zhi jia* 外媽之家), the Lins 林. Then, in 1422, Tianyu (Guangqi) moved from Quanzhou city to the thirtieth district of Nan'an county, where he registered his surname as Li and his surname as Guangqi. He was followed several years later by two of his cousins, who changed their surnames to Li, while his brother Xinyu (who had no children) and another cousin, Xiangbao, remained in the city and kept their Lin surname.[13] This surname change was not unique. It appears to have been used by a number of Muslim families as a survival strategy, and we will encounter more examples as we continue.

Since Guangqi was the spokesman for the family's Chinese cultural strategy (writing his *Chuiqi lun* four years after his move to Nan'an, it is possible that the Nan'an/Quanzhou separation paralleled the Chinese/Muslim divide, and that it was the Quanzhou Lins who then maintained their Muslim heritage, though because we have no further information about that group, we can only speculate.

The Lis were a family divided, not by disputes over land or inheritance (so far as we can tell), but rather by culture and religion. Even the Li/Lin (Nan'an/Quanzhou) division seems to have been driven by this issue, for Guangqi, the spokesman for the family's Chinese cultural strategy, also

---

[13] *Rongshan Lishi zupu*, in *Quanzhou Huizu pudie ziliao xuanbian*, pp. 77a–78a.

led the move to Nan'an. The question that he raised – Could one be Chinese and be accepted as a member of the elite while maintaining one's Islamic practices? – is one that the Muslim families that remained in Quanzhou must all have faced, even while they differed in their answers to it.

But what about the Pus, the target of much of the violence at the end of the Yuan? In the early Ming, the Pus were the target of special legislation by Taizu, who denied them the right to use the title of *shi* 士 (gentleman) and barred them from sitting for the examinations. This prohibition was presumably in response to Pu Shougeng's act of treachery against the Song, for the descendants of three other Song collaborators were also barred.[14]

In light of this, it is remarkable that Pu Benchu 蒲本初 passed the *jinshi* examination in 1385, and went on to hold the prestigious title of Hanlin Bachelor (*Hanlinyuan shujishi* 翰林院庶吉士).[15] He did so, however, as a Yang 楊, not a Pu. The Pu genealogy explains:

In the eighth year of Hongwu 8 (1375), the emperor angrily said: "During the preceding dynasty the Pus brought tyranny and chaos to Quanzhou, and many were killed under them." [He] commanded that none [be allowed to] remain. Fortunately, [the Pus] had a friend surnamed Wang, from Anping, who harbored the infant for several months. He was taken as an infant to the home of his mother in Dongshi, Lady Yang, where he was nurtured and raised. He studied poetry and history, and became an official reaching the position of Hanlin Bachelor. He subsequently changed his surname, taking Pu as his surname and Benchu as his name.[16]

As in the case of the Rongshan Lis, this change of surname was driven by a concern for survival. However, it also enabled Benchu to avoid the prohibition on Pus in the examinations and thus made possible his later success. When it was that he changed his surname back to Pu, as asserted

---

[14] Kuwabara, "P'u Shou-keng," Pt. 2, p. 99, citing Chen Mouren's *Quannan zazhi* concerning the *shi* prohibition and *Minshu* 52 concerning the examinations; and Luo, *Pu Shougeng yanjiu*, p. 75. The other three were Liu Mengyan 留孟炎, Sun Shengfu 孫勝甫 and Huang Wanshi 黃萬石.

[15] Benchu was purportedly the second son of Pu Chongmo, who, as we saw in Chapter 4, had a very successful official career. The problem with this is that Chongmo died in 1334, which would have put Benchu in his mid-30s at the youngest, when he was adopted by the Wangs. In Luo Xianglin's detailed treatment of the Pu genealogy, Benchu is described as the "second oldest great-grandson" of Shougeng, but no mention is made of his father. By contrast Pu Taichu (about whom more below) is described as the "oldest great-grandson" and a son of Chongmo (Luo, *Pu Shougeng yanjiu*, pp. 74–75.) Given the shared generational name between Taichu and Benchu, people have assumed that they were brothers. I would suggest that Benchu was actually the son of one of Chongmo's younger brothers.

[16] Cited in Luo, *Pu Shougeng yanjiu*, p. 75. The 1385 date for his *jinshi* degree comes from a Quanzhou gazetteer and the *Min shu*.

by the genealogy, is unclear. He is identified in a biography of Yang Yiweng 楊頤翁, a minor official from Jinjiang, as Yiweng's son and heir, but also as having died before Yiweng, who lived to the age of 95.[17] Benchu, however, was not the only Pu to change surnames. A report from the 1930s on the discovery of the Dehua Pu genealogy described how, as the Pu lineage scattered in the early Ming, many took the surname of Wu, since that sounded much like Pu. It cites tombstones on the front sides of which the name is given as Wu so-and-so, while on the back it says Pu so-and-so.[18]

Pu Taichu 蒲太初, identified as the eldest son of Chongmo, provides another example of Pu success in the early Ming. In 1375, he served in a Quanzhou guard unit where his technical expertise (*jiyi* 技藝) allowed him to advance, and in 1392 he was appointed as an officer to a guard position in Shandong.[19] On the face of it, this record is more puzzling than that of Benchu, since Taichu's service began less than a decade after the founding of the Ming and he served as a Pu. Oded Abt plausibly suggests that his service may have been the result of his family being registered as a soldier-household with an obligation to provide a soldier and supply provisions to that soldier's unit.[20] Thus, even though Taichu flourished in the military, this was not a sign of Pu membership in the Quanzhou elite.

This is as far as the extant sources take us concerning the Muslim families that remained in Quanzhou. There remains the tantalizing question of what role, if any, the former Muslim merchants had in the seven naval expeditions under Zheng He 鄭和 (1371–1433) in the early fifteenth century. Zheng was a eunuch from a Muslim family in Yunnan, originally named Ma He 馬和. His military prowess gained him the attention and favor of Zhu Di, later the Yongle emperor, and when Zhu decided to launch the first of his massive expeditions he chose Zheng to lead it. Whether Zheng was a practicing Muslim is debatable, for he was active in the support of Buddhist and Daoist establishments, but the Muslim connections to the expeditions were numerous.[21] It is said that a number of the officers as well as sailors accompanying the expeditions were Muslim, as was Ma Huan 馬歡 (1380–1460), the principal

---

[17] Luo, *Pu Shougeng yanjiu*, p. 76, citing the Tongzhi (1862–1874) *Quanzhou fu zhi*, zh. 55. Some scholars also believe that Benchu was an ancestor of the early Qing writer Pu Songling 蒲松齡 (1640–1715), whose family was said to have migrated from Fujian to Shandong and to have temporarily changed its surname from Pu to Yang. Abt, "Locking and Unlocking the City Gates," pp. 11–12.

[18] Luo, *Pu Shougeng yanjiu*, pp. 77–78.   [19] Luo, *Pu Shougeng yanjiu*, p. 74.

[20] Abt, "Locking and Unlocking the City Gates," pp. 10–11.

[21] See Edward L. Dreyer, *Zheng He: China and the Oceans in the Early Ming Dynasty, 1405–1433* (New York, NY: Pearson Longman, 2007), pp. 148–149, 166.

chronicler of the expeditions, though he was a convert to Islam from Kuaiji 會稽, Zhejiang.

Did the expeditions draw upon the Muslims of Quanzhou or other port cities? This seems likely, since the Muslims harbored a wealth of knowledge and experience relating to long-distance maritime voyages and trade, but the evidence is sparse. The Pu genealogy has an entry for one Pu Rihe 蒲日和, who reportedly accompanied Zheng He to the Western Sea;[22] and Geoff Wade has argued plausibly that the Yongle emperor's 1407 proclamation protecting Muslims was part of "an effort to soothe the remaining Muslims of Fujian, to aid the conscription of interpreters and pilots for the eunuch-led armadas and to facilitate links with those who fled southwards."[23] If this was indeed the case, it was the last act of the coastal Muslims as participants in the maritime Asian world. Such, however, was not the case for those who did flee China at the end of the Yuan, and it is to them that we will now turn.

Sino-Muslims in Southeast Asia

Throughout this study we have observed the presence of Muslim merchants across maritime Asia involved with the China trade and going to China themselves, as in the case of Shi Nuowei from Srivijaya, who, as we saw in Chapter 3, established a cemetery in twelfth-century Quanzhou for his coreligionists. But at what point did Sino-Muslims, that is, Muslims from China, become a visible presence in maritime trade? There is some evidence that it predated even the Yuan. As we noted in Chapter 3, there is in Brunei a Muslim tomb for a "supervisor" (*panyuan* 判院) surnamed Pu, dated 1264. Regardless of whether this was a kinsman of Pu Shougeng, as has been suggested, it certainly demonstrates a Sino-Muslim presence in Brunei. In Chapter 4, we also noted the increasing visibility of Chinese merchants across maritime Asia and the emergence of Chinese merchant communities in southeastern Asia during the Yuan. Given the importance of the *ortoy*, and of the Pu family in particular, it is likely that many of these merchants were Muslim. However, the primary impetus for the development of a Sino-Muslim trade diaspora in southeastern Asia was the flight of Muslim merchants from China at the end of the Yuan.

---

[22] Luo, *Pu Shougeng yanjiu*, pp. 63, 69. The Dehua genealogy incorrectly equates him with Pu Shoucheng's second son with the same name who was associated with the renovation of the Qingjing Mosque in 1349 that was described in Chapter 4.
[23] Geoff Philip Wade, "Southeast Asian Islam and Southern China in the Second Half of the Fourteenth Century," in Geoff Wade and Li Tana, eds., *Anthony Reid and the Study of the Southeast Asian Past* (Singapore: Institute for Southeast Asian Studies, 2012), p. 136.

Chang Pin-tsun has assembled a considerable body of evidence from the fifteenth and early sixteenth centuries of sizeable and thriving Chinese Muslim communities throughout both continental and maritime southeastern Asia, particularly in Java, Sumatra, Borneo, Malacca and the Philippines.[24] That relating to Java is the best documented and most important.

One of the most valuable and intriguing sources on Chinese Muslims in fifteenth-century southeastern Asia is the *The Malay Annals of Sĕmarang and Cĕrbon*, a chronicle in Sino-Malay of the Javanese states of Sĕmarang and Cĕrbon in the fifteenth and sixteenth centuries. Despite a cloudy history and evidence that the text contains a number of later interpolations, both the translator-editor M. C. Ricklefs and his colleagues, H. J. de Graaf and Th. G. Th. Pigeaud, were convinced of its essential authenticity, in all likelihood based upon early Chinese records in Java.[25]

The *Malay Annals* begin in the year 1407 at the time of the first visit of the Ming admiral Zheng He's fleet to southeast Asia, and specifically with Zheng's capture of the "pirate" Chen Zuyi, described as a non-Muslim Hokkien (i.e., southern Fujianese, which includes Quanzhou). The work goes on to provide the following accounts of Chinese Muslims:

1407 – In Kukang (i.e., Palembang) the first Hanafite Muslim Chinese community in the Indonesian Archipelago was established.[26] In the same year another was settled in Sambas, Kalimantan.

1411–1416 – Hanafite Muslim Chinese communities were also established in the Malay Peninsula, in Java and the Philippines. In Java mosques were built in Ancol/Jakarta, Sĕmbung/Cĕrbon, Lasĕm, Tuban, Tse Tsun/Grĕsik, Jiaotung/Joratan, Cangki/Majakĕrta and in other places.

1413 – The fleet of the emperor of China put in for a month at Sĕmarang for ship repairs. Admiral Sam Po Bo (i.e., Zheng He), Haji Mah Hwang and Haji Feh Tsin came very often to the Hanafite Chinese mosque in Sĕmarang for divine service.[27]

The *Malay Annals* subsequently describe, among other things, the appointment by Zheng He of an individual to "control the flourishing

---

[24] Chang Pin-tsun, "The First Chinese Diaspora in Southeast Asia in the Fifteenth Century," in *Emporia, Commodities and Entrepreneurs in Asian Maritime Trade, c. 1400–1750*, eds., Roderich Ptak and Dietmar Rothermund (Stuttgart: Franz Steiner Verlag, 1991), pp. 13–28.

[25] H. J. de Graaf and Th. G. Th. Pigeaud, *Chinese Muslims in Java in the 15th and 16th Centuries: The Malay Annals of Sĕmarang and Cĕrbon*, M. C. Ricklefs, ed., Monash Papers on Southeast Asia No. 12 (North Melbourne: Ruskin Press, 1984), pp. 1–4, 48.

[26] Hanafite Islam constitutes one of four schools in the Sunni tradition, and was founded by Abu Hanifa (d. 767). de Graaf and Pigeaud, *Chinese Muslims in Java*, p. 50.

[27] de Graaf and Pigeaud, *Chinese Muslims in Java*, pp. 13–14.

Hanafite Muslim Chinese communities" spreading throughout the South Sea countries and specifically the Philippines; the degeneration of the Chinese Muslim communities after the cessation of the Chinese expeditions; ethnic tensions between Muslim and Hindu-Javanese communities; and rivalry between the Chinese Muslims and Hokkienese in Sĕbung.

The *Malay Annals*' account of these and other historical events raise a number of issues, especially when compared with Chinese accounts of the Zheng He voyages, such as Ma Huan's *Yingyai shenglan* 瀛涯耘覽. These are treated in some detail by de Graaf and Pigeaud (see pp. 55–62, especially), some with greater success than others, but concerning the general appearance and activities of these Chinese Muslims there seems little doubt. This brings us to the critical question: Where were they from and why did they flourish in fifteenth-century southeast Asia?

Answers to this question have varied. The *Malay Annals* themselves point only to the impact of the Zheng He voyages. (Of course Zheng He – "Sam Po Bo" in the *Malay Annals* – was a Muslim by birth, a fact that undoubtedly contributed to the development of a cult-like following in Java.) But this leaves unanswered the matter of where the people who apparently coalesced into Hanafite communities in the years following 1407 had come from. Yusuf Chang has suggested that those in Java, at least, were the descendants of Muslim soldiers who were part of Khubilai 1292–1293 expedition against Java and remained there to live with local Javanese Muslims.[28] But while it is plausible that some may have traced their origins back to that expedition – which had been launched with a force of 20,000 from Quanzhou – it seems unlikely that deserting soldiers would have been able to carve out an enduring social/ethnic identity for themselves, especially since, less than 20 years after the Yuan occupation of Quanzhou, those troops who were Muslim were unlikely to have been very Chinese and those who were Chinese were probably not Muslim.[29]

De Graaf and Pigeaud have their own answer to the question of origins, namely that the Chinese Muslims came from Yunnan. A *Malay Annals* entry from 1452 mentions the isolation of the Chinese Muslim community in Sĕbung, which had been cut off from contact with Islam in Yunnan for four generations. More generally, the editors cite a considerable literature arguing for the connection to Muslim Yunnan, especially insofar as the spread of the Hanafite school is concerned.[30]

---

[28] Yusuf Chang, "The Ming Empire," p. 23.   [29] Rossabi, *Khubilai Khan*, pp. 219–220.
[30] de Graaf and Pigeaud, *Chinese Muslims in Java*, pp. 50–51.

This theory has its attractions. Yunnan had emerged during the Yuan as a major center of Islam in China, and as Roderich Ptak has noted, "Chinese Muslims came under pressure ... when Ming troops advanced into Yunnan" so that "small groups may have left for Southeast Asia."[31]

As a mono-causal explanation for the Chinese Muslims, however, the Yunnan theory has problems. The Muslim refugees who came out of that province were probably a varied group, including ex-officials, soldiers, merchants and possibly farmers, and they undoubtedly arrived with some wealth, but they were not seafarers – most had probably come to China from the Middle East by land – and they had no previous connection with maritime southeast Asia. Thus, the challenge of, first, getting themselves to Sumatra, Java and other islands and, second, establishing themselves there economically would have been considerable. There is the further problem of the Philippines, where the *Malay Annals* describe Muslim Chinese communities thriving from the early fifteenth century on. That Yunnanese Muslims would have pushed on to that distant corner of maritime Asia and established themselves there is, frankly, incredible.

The hypothesis that the Chinese Muslims came first and foremost from Quanzhou, by contrast, addresses these problems neatly. As noted earlier, there is evidence from as early as the late thirteenth century of Sino-Muslim traders from Quanzhou in southeast Asia, and evidence of a more generalized nature of the development and articulation of increasingly complex commercial networks in southeast Asia through the activities of Chinese merchants. Those merchants certainly included many non-Muslims – thus the Hokkien communities referred to in the *Malay Annals* – but Sino-Muslim merchants must have played an active role as well, especially in light of their privileged position in Quanzhou's maritime trade (i.e., the *ortoy*). Thus, at the time of their exodus in 1368 they would naturally have gone to those places where they had already been doing business, and of course they were traveling with their means of livelihood: their ships.

There is also the intriguing evidence from a Muslim cemetery in Tralaya (near Majapahit in northern Java) in which the tombstones have Javanese script on one side and Arabic Islamic inscriptions on the other, the earliest of which dates to 1376 (Saka 1298).[32] Are these the

---

[31] Roderich Ptak, "Ming Maritime Trade to Southeast Asia, 1368–1567," in Claude Guillot, Denys Lombard and Roderich Ptak, eds., *From the Mediterranean to the China Sea: Miscellaneous Notes* (Wiesbaden: Harrassowitz Verlag, 1998), pp. 160–161.

[32] Louis-Charles Damais, "Études Javanaises: Les tombes Musulmans dates de Tralaya," *Bulletin de l'École Française d'Etrême Orient* 48 (1967), pp. 353–415. The ten datable tombstones range in date from 1376 to 1611, with the second earliest dated to 1380 and

graves of Sino-Muslims who fled the disturbances in Quanzhou, as Geoff Wade has speculated?[33] The dates are suggestive and certainly indicate the increasing presence of Muslims in Java at the very time that the Sino-Muslims would have been arriving.

The Quanzhou hypothesis is even more compelling with regard to the Philippines. Historically, the two primary sea routes from southeast Asia to China were coast-hugging up the coast of Champa, Vietnam and southeastern China, or going north from eastern Java through the Sulu Sea and the Philippines, and then north to Quanzhou; the shallow South China Sea was infamous for its shoals and was generally avoided. There was, therefore, a long-standing link between Quanzhou and the Philippines. To quote Kenneth Hall,

The Chinese presence was not new – Chinese traders had established these bases in the Philippines during the eleventh and twelfth centuries. By the fourteenth century an intensive and extensive network of native trade had evolved to dis-tribute imports and to gather the forest products desired by Chinese traders... Archaeological research has revealed urban settlements of over five hundred households in the Manila area dating to the pre-Spanish period, as well as other urban sites on the Mindoro, Mindanao, and Cebu coasts. Each of these commu-nities' trade links with China are demonstrated by their association with signifi-cant deposits of Sung and Ming porcelain dating to the thirteenth and fourteenth centuries.[34]

In light of this connection, the Quanzhou origins of the Filipino Muslim communities referred to in the *Malay Annals* make eminent sense.

Yet more evidence to support the Quanzhou hypothesis comes from early sixteenth-century Melaka. According to Portuguese accounts, Melaka under the Sultan (who ruled until the Portuguese conquest in 1511) was divided into four ethnic communities, each with its own chief: Gujaratis, Kelings (Tamils), Javanese and Chinese. Under the Javanese there was a subgroup of Filipino Luzonese, which Luis Filipe Thomaz has described as follows:

These Luzonese were mostly Muslims, though Islam had not yet even reached the north of what was to become the Philippines archipelago. We presume that these Luzonese merchants had come and settled in Melaka in order to eliminate the Brunei middlemen, who had previously controlled exchanges between Melaka and Luzon and that, once settled in the city, they had adopted the religion of the majority. It is not impossible, furthermore, that the Muslim Luzonese of Melaka

---

the remaining seven from the fifteenth century. See the detailed descriptions and textual transcriptions of the tombstones on pp. 392–411 and the table on p. 411.
[33] Wade, "Southeast Asian Islam and Southern China," 132–133.
[34] Hall, *Maritime Trade and State Development*, pp. 226–227.

had originally belonged to the small Muslim community of Manila, that the Spanish came across later.[35]

Although Thomaz may be correct about the conversion of the Luzonese after settling in Melaka, it seems more likely that their Islamic origins were in the Philippines.

The composition of Melaka's Chinese community is also suggestive, for according to Kenneth Hall both Chinese and Western sources distinguished between "the *Chincheu* (Quanzhou and/or Hokkiens who were frequently Muslims) and *Chinas* (Cantonese)."[36] Thomaz's gloss for *Chincheu* is that it referred to the Hokkienese linguistically and Muslims religiously.[37] This provides the most explicit evidence of the Quanzhou Muslims maintaining a discrete ethnic identity, and doing so over a century after their flight from Quanzhou.

If many or most of the southeast Asian Chinese Muslims had their origin in Quanzhou, and therefore could claim descent from the Muslim trade diaspora of Song and Yuan times, how did they differ from the earlier group? I would suggest two important points of differentiation. First, they were doubly cut off from their historical roots: from Quanzhou and China by the circumstances of their flight and by early Ming trade policies, and from their west Asian origins by centuries of life in east Asia. This, incidentally, would also have held true for the Chinese Muslims who had come from Yunnan. Second, in the competitive world of fifteenth- and early sixteenth-century southeast Asia, the Chinese Muslims fragmented into several groups: Chincheu and Luzonese, as we saw in the description of Melaka, and the Javanese Chinese Muslims, who, according to the *Malay Annals*, played a significant role in the politics of that island through the sixteenth century.[38] We can presume that, without a continuing anchor to a Chinese or Middle Eastern homeland, local identifies took hold and predominated, and with the subsequent Islamicization of large portions of maritime southeast Asia under the

---

[35] Luis Filipe F. R. Thomaz, "Melaka and Its Merchant Communities at the Turn of the Sixteenth Century," in Denys Lombard and Jean Aubin, eds., *Asian Merchants and Businessmen in the Indian Ocean and the China Sea* (New Delhi: Oxford University Press, 2000), p. 31.

[36] Kenneth Hall, "Multi-Dimensional Networking: Fifteenth-Century Indian Ocean Maritime Diaspora in Southeast Asian Perspective," *Journal of the Economic and Social History of the Orient* 49.4 (2006), p. 469; see also Thomaz, "Melaka and Its Merchant Communities," p. 31. Hall proceeds to describe the *Cinas* and *Chincheu*: "In both cases the Melaka communities included permanent and sojourning residents, who maintained houses, centers of worship, and warehouses. The most elite among the merchants, who owned or fitted out their own ships or were financiers, also had rural estates on the edges of the city (*dusun*), which doubled as valued recreational space" (p. 469).

[37] Thomaz, "Melaka and Its Merchant Communities," p. 31.

[38] de Graaf and Pigeaud, *Chinese Muslims in Java*, pp. 31–45.

influence of Arab and Indian (especially Bengali and Gujarati) traders and missionaries and of Muslim rulers in southeast Asian states, the Chinese Muslims were gradually absorbed by the larger body of the faithful.

The Muslim Trade Diaspora through History

This study has attempted to uncover the history of the community of foreign merchants who were predominantly west Asian in origin and Muslim in religion and flourished in the ports of China for a period of over 600 years. Its history included disruptions, namely the late-ninth-century break following the Huang Chao massacre of 879 and the movement of the center of activity and settlement from Guangzhou to Quanzhou during the Song. But we can also discern long-term continuities, stemming from the fact that the community in China provided the Muslim trade diaspora, which spanned maritime Asia, with an anchor in the wealthiest country in the medieval world. As such, it played a critical role in the world system that flourished for most of that period.

Considered as a whole, the six-century history of the Muslim maritime community in China can be seen as consisting of two semi-colonial periods at the beginning and end, sandwiching a period of relative integration. In the eighth and ninth centuries, a large west Asian merchant population was located primarily in Guangzhou, which was itself an outpost of the Tang empire, where the Han residents – officials, soldiers, the children of disgraced officials and merchants – lived amidst a largely non-Han population. This was an entrepôt through which coursed a luxury trade with goods destined for the court and capital, where foreign merchants were known for their great wealth, and where the local officials were notorious for their corruption, in particular the eunuch commissioners of maritime trade. These factors help explain the episodes of violence that punctuated its history, though the greatest of these – the massacre of 879 – came at the hands of rebels from the north.

The semi-colonialism of Yuan dynasty Quanzhou was very different in nature. Far from being a frontier city like Tang Guangzhou, it had developed during the Song into a metropolis in which commercial activity was accompanied by cultural production in the form of literati learning and examination accomplishment. Over this successful society was placed a ruling group consisting first and foremost of Mongols, as well as other foreigners, many of them Muslim, and Chinese (with northerners favored). The new political order of the late thirteenth century benefited the Muslim merchant families that had established themselves in Song society and fundamentally changed them, for the influx of Muslims, most of whom arrived via government service and the military, and the establishment of close ties with the west Asian Islamic world – as illustrated by Ibn Battuta – served to emphasize the foreignness of all Muslims. And the key role played by the *ortoy* in maritime trade meant that the Quanzhou merchants needed to participate in it in order to thrive. As in the Tang, violence was also prominent, from the massacre of Song imperial clan members by Pu Shougeng in 1276 to the Ispah Rebellion pitting Muslim against Muslim in the late Yuan and culminating in the massacre of Muslims at the dynasty's end.

Between these two periods was a period beginning with the southern kingdoms of Southern Han and Min in the tenth century and continuing with the Song when the pro-trade policies of the governments involved, combined with the development and maturation of the Asian world system, resulted in a west Asian – increasingly Muslim – merchant community that was remarkably integrated into its host society. In size, it was smaller than its Tang or Yuan counterparts, in large part because of the rise of segmented long-distance trading, which resulted in a decrease in direct west-Asia-to-China shipping. Described as "hybrid Sino-Muslims" by Mukai Masaki, this group was more geographically diverse than the Tang predecessors, for Muslims from Champa, Srivijaya and southeast Asian polities – and quite possibly from south Asia, though this is harder to document – were visible in the Chinese port cities.[39] Apart from the Muslims, embassies and merchants from across the Indian Ocean, the waters of southeast Asia as well as Korea and Japan all actively participated in the activities of the Asian world trading system. Again, by way of contrast to the Tang and Yuan, it is noteworthy that records of violence directed by or against maritime merchants – Muslims or others – are singularly absent throughout this period.

As we have seen, the maritime trade prohibitions of the Ming, coming as they did in the wake of the anti-Muslim events in Quanzhou, effectively dissolved the Muslim merchant communities in China, and this fact calls into question their historical significance. Here we must distinguish between the Muslim merchant communities in China and the Muslim trade diaspora. Although the Muslim trade diaspora had its competitors – Indian, southeast Asian and others – its vast geographical scope and its ability to connect co-religionists from varied countries and regions gave it a vital role in the maintenance of the world trading system. And the role of the Chinese Muslim communities was critical, given the great importance of China as both producer and consumer of that trade.

[39] Mukai Masaki, "Transforming Dashi Shippers," pp. 9–11.

Arguably the most lasting legacy of the Muslim trade diaspora can be found in the large Muslim populations of Indonesia, Malaysia, Bangladesh and Gujarat, places where Muslim merchants – including Sino-Muslim merchants in fourteenth-century Java – were agents of the propagation of Islam. Ironically, that legacy does not extend to China, for the longevity of the Muslim maritime merchant communities and their economic importance did not result in any significant Islamic penetration of the Chinese coastal populations. Such was not the case elsewhere in China – notably the southwest, northwest and far west – but in those places the groups and dynamics were very different, and certainly did not involve maritime merchants.

So what accounted for the relative lack of conversions in coastal China, especially when compared with southeast Asia? I would suggest that the main reason lay in the political and cultural contexts in which the merchants operated. The story we encountered in Chapter 2 of an elderly Muslim ship owner who, in his audience with the King of Zabaj, was permitted to sit, thus establishing a custom that Muslims could henceforth "sit in front of the king as they like," is indicative of the kind of political entrée that Muslim merchants had in southeast Asia. More generally, Kenneth Hall's depiction of southeast Asian societies as territorially amorphous, "relatively open, people-centered realms" – also treated in Chapter 2 – can help explain that region's relative openness to Islam.

In Guangzhou, Quanzhou and other port cities, by contrast, the Muslim merchants confronted an elaborate state system with lines of authority stretching to the capital in the distance, and a social and cultural order that was intertwined with that system. Muslim merchants had no entrée to the emperor except in the formal setting of tribute missions, and in the port cities they had little to offer the local officials and elites that might have lured them away from their Confucian focus. To be sure, popular religions flourished among the populations of Guangdong and Fujian, and Buddhism was omnipresent there and elsewhere. But from the late Tang if not before, Buddhism had secured a place in the socio-cultural order, patronized by the state, practiced by elites and non-elites alike, but was not a threat to Confucian culture or the Confucian state. There was, in short, no cultural space into which Islam might have made headway.

There are some indications of a change during the Yuan. The empire was ruled by foreigners, many of them Muslim; merchants had unprecedented status and privileges; and Confucian learning no longer offered a significant path to office through the examinations. The case of the Su family – treated in Chapter 4 – suggests a willingness among elite families to convert to Islam that would have been rare if not unthinkable in the

Song. And the report of six to seven mosques in Quanzhou indicates a very sizeable Muslim population, possibly including Chinese converts. The evidence to support this speculation is exceedingly thin, but even if there had been significant conversion to Islam during the Yuan, the changes wrought by the Ming would have put an end to it. The issues facing the Muslim families whose genealogies we examined earlier in this chapter were how best to deal with their own beliefs and practices in the revived Confucian order, and certainly not how to make converts. Muslims continued worshiping within Quanzhou city through the Ming and Qing, but in small numbers, and in fact in the nineteenth century there were reports of Muslims living in the ruins of the Ashab Mosque, which by then had lost its roof.[40]

This evidence of decline tells only part of the story when we consider the historical significance of the maritime Muslim communities in China, for they were an essential part of what Dru Gladney has called the first of three "tides of Islam" in China, which he characterizes as having been descended "from the Arab, Persian, Central Asian, and Mongolian Muslim merchants, militia, and officials who settled along China's southeast coast and in the northwest in large and small numbers from the seventh to the fourteenth centuries."[41] Over the course of the Ming and Qing dynasties, Islam grew and developed, not only in the northwest and southwest, where large populations took root, but in the central regions of China as well. Of special note was the emergence of the Han Kitab, a school of Islamic-Confucian studies that flourished in the seventeenth and eighteenth centuries, which crafted a version of Islam that was profoundly shaped by the cultural landscape of Confucian discourse.[42] Although there is no direct connection of the Han Kitab to the southeastern Muslims, the struggle that we earlier observed within the Li family of Rongshan between their Muslim and Confucian cultures can be seen as a prefiguring of the synthesis that was later achieved. Moreover, memories of their maritime origins, including the legendary visits of the seventh-century Sahaba Saad Wakkas that were discussed in Chapter 1, constituted one of the "cultural bits" that, Zvi Benite argues,

---

[40] Steinhardt, *China's Early Mosques*, p. 44. For an account of Quanzhou's Muslims in the Ming and Qing, see Wu Youxiong 吳幼雄, *Quanzhou zongjiao wenhua*, pp. 190–195.

[41] Dru C. Gladney, *Muslim Chinese: Ethnic Nationalism in the People's Republic* (Cambridge, MA: Council on East Asian Studies, Harvard University, 1991), p. 37. The second tide he identifies as the entry of Sufism in the seventeenth century and the third as the modernist reforms of the early twentieth century (pp. 41–62).

[42] This has been brilliantly treated by Zvi Ben-Dor Benite, *The Dao of Muhammad: A Cultural History of Muslims in Late Imperial China* (Cambridge, MA: Harvard University Asia Center, 2005). See too, Sachiko Murata, William C. Chittick and Tu Weiming, *The Sage Learning of Liu Zhi: Islamic Thought in Confucian Terms* (Cambridge, MA: Harvard University Asia Center for the Harvard-Yenching Institute, 2009).

Figure 5.1 Su ancestral temple, Quanzhou

were brought together by the Han Kitab thinkers "to create one distinct and flexible form of Chinese Muslim identity, an identity in which 'Chineseness' was as central as 'Muslimness.'"[43]

In recent decades there has been a resurgence of interest in China's maritime Muslim communities. Both the Chinese government and Muslim countries have, each for their own reasons, supported the efforts of local scholars to recover much of the heritage of those communities. This support has also taken the form of public art, to wit, a huge sculpture that I saw on display in downtown Quanzhou in 2006 featuring Arabs leading camels standing on board a ship. More importantly, the Huaisheng Mosque in Guangzhou, the well-preserved ruins of the Ashab Mosque in Quanzhou, the Quanzhou Muslim cemetery, and, most especially, the Quanzhou Maritime Museum with its large collections of stone inscriptions and an active research program all serve to preserve the historical memory of those communities. The Su family, noteworthy for its conversion to Islam during the Yuan, maintains an ancestral temple in downtown Quanzhou advertising their Muslim

---

[43] Benite, *The Dao of Muhammad*, p. 11.

heritage (see Figure 5.1). And as I learned during a visit to the ancestral shrine and mosque of the Ding family of Chendai on the southwestern suburbs of Quanzhou in 2006, the contemporary Dings have not only participated in this historical preservation through a small museum in their complex illustrating their Yuan origins; they have also connected to the broader population of Muslims across China, for their imam was appointed by a national Muslim organization.

As the Ding example suggests, historical closure is never complete, and the maritime Muslims of middle-period China may yet have a further, albeit very different, existence. Nevertheless, the six-century history that we have examined can be taken as a discrete historical chapter, and an illuminating one. Through it we have seen how the Chinese – primarily their governments and elites – treated and interacted with these foreigners who were a virtually permanent feature of Guangzhou and Quanzhou. It has also provided a picture – however incomplete – of the central role played by the Muslim trade diaspora over the long course of the Asian world order.

Bibliography

Chinese Primary Sources

Cai Tao 蔡絛, *Tieweishan congtan* 鐵圍山叢談 (Beijing: Zhonghua shuju, 1998).

Chen Dazhen 陳大震, *Dade Nanhai zhi canben* 大德南海志殘本 (Guangzhou: Guangzhou shi difang zhi yanjiusuo, 1986).

Du You 杜佑, *Tong dian* 通典 (Hangzhou: Zhejiang guji chubanshe, 2000).

Fang Xinru 方信孺, *Nanhai bai yong* 南海白詠 (Shanghai: Jiangsu guji chubanshe, 1988).

Gong Mingzhi 龔明之, *Zhongwu jiwen* 中吳纪闻 (Shanghai: Shanghai guji chubanshe, 1986).

Gu Yanwu 顧炎武, *Tianxia junguo libing shu* 天下郡國利病書 (Siku quanshu zhenben ed.).

Haishang sichou zhi lu – Guangzhou wenhua yichan: Dishang shiji juan 海上丝绸之路–广州文化 遗产：地上史迹卷 (*Maritime Silk Road – Cultural Heritage in Guangzhou: Historical Sites*) (Guangzhou: Wenwu chubanshe, 2008).

He Qiaoyuan 何喬袁, *Min shu* 閩書, 5 vols. (Fuzhou: Fujian renmin chubanshe, 1995).

Hong Mai 洪邁, *Yijian zhi* 夷堅志 (Taipei: Mingwen shuju, 1982).

Li Fang 李昉, *Taiping guangji* 太平廣記 (Taipei: Xinxing shuju, 1962).

Li Tao 李燾, *Xu zizhi tongjian changbian* 續資治通鑑長編 (Beijing: Zhonghua shuju, 1979).

Li Zhao 李肇 (active 806–825), *Tang guoshi bu* 唐國史補, Sheng Zhongjian et al., eds., abridged edition (Hangzhou: Zhejiang Guji Chubanshe, 1986).
　Tang guoshi bu 唐國史補. (Shanghai: Gudian wexue chuban, 1957).

Lin Zhiqi 林之奇, *Zhuozhai wenji* 拙齋文集 (Siku quanshu edn.).

Liu Xu 劉煦, *Jiu Tangshu* 舊唐書 (Beijing: Zhonghua shuju, 1987).

Lou Yue 樓鑰, *Gongkui ji* 攻媿集 (Song; Sibu congkan chubian edn.).

Ma Duanlin 馬端臨, *Wenxian tongkao* 文獻統考 (Taipei: Xinxing shuju, 1964).

Ouyang Xiu 歐陽修, *Xin Tangshu* 新唐書 (Beijing: Zhonghua shuju, 1975).

Qingyuan Jin shi zupu 清源李氏族谱, in Quanzhoushi Quanzhou lishi yanjiuhui 泉州市泉州历史研究会, ed., *Quanzhou Huizu pudie ziliao xuanbian* 泉州回族谱牒资料选编, (Quanzhou, 1980).

Rongshan Lishi zupu 榮山李氏族谱, in Quanzhou shi Quanzhou lishi yanjiuhui 泉州市泉州历史研究会, ed., *Quanzhou Huizu pudie ziliao xuanbian* 泉州回族谱牒资料选编, (Quanzhou, 1980).

181

Sima Guang 司馬光, *Zizhi tongjian* 資治通鑒 (Song; Beijing: Zhonghua shuju, 1956).

Song huiyao jigao 宋會要輯稿 (Taipei: Shijie shuju, 1964).

Song huiyao jigao bubian 宋會要輯稿補編 (Beijing: Quanguo tushuguan wenxian shuwei fuhi zhongxin chuban, 1988).

Song Lian 宋濂, *Yuan shi* 元史 (Beijing: Zhonghua shuju, 1976).

Su Che 蘇轍, *Longchuan lüe zhi* 龍川略志 (Beijing: Zhonghua shuju, 1982).

Tang huiyao 唐會要 (Taipei: Shijie shuju, 1968)

Tuo Tuo 脫脫, *Song shi* 宋史 (Beijing: Zhonghua shuju, 1977).

Wang Dayuan 王大源 (1311–1350), *Daoyi zhilüe xiaoshi* 島夷誌略校釋 (Yuan; Beijing: Zhonghua shuju, 1981).

Wang Pu 王溥, *Wudai huiyao* 五代會要 (Beijing: Zhonghua shuju, 1998).

Wu Cheng 吳澄, *Wu Wenzheng ji* 吳文正集 (1484 ed.; rpt Yuanren wenji zhenben congkan 元人文集珍本叢刊), vol. 3, 16/10b–11a.

Wu Jian 吳鑒. *Daoyi zhi lue xiao shi* 島夷誌畧校釋 (Beijing: Zhonghua shuju, 2000).

Xue Juzheng 薛居正, *Jiu Wudai shi* 舊五代歷史 (Beijing: Zhonghua shuju, 1976).

Yanzhi Sushi zupu 燕支蘇氏族譜, in Quanzhoushi Quanzhou lishi yanjiuhui 泉州市泉州历史研究会, ed., *Quanzhou Huizu pudie ziliao xuanbian* 泉州回族谱牒资料选编 (Quanzhou, 1980).

Yu Ji 虞集, Daoyuan lei gao 道園類稿, in *Yuanren wenji zhenben congkan* 元人文集珍本叢刊 (Taipei: Xinwenfeng chuban, 1985).

Yuan dianzhang 元典章 (Beijing: Zhongguo shudian, 1990).

Yue Ke 岳珂, *Tingshi* 桯史 (Beijing: Zhonghua shuju, 1981).

Zhen Dexiu 真德秀, *Zhen wenzhong gong wenji* 真文忠公文集 (Sibu conkan edn.).

Zheng Xia 鄭俠, *Xitang ji* 西塘集 (Siku quanshu edn.).

Zhou Mi 周密, *Guixin zashi* 癸辛雜識, 2, 26 (Beijing: Zhonghua shuju, 1988).

Zhou Qufei 周去非, *Lingwai daida jiaozhu* 嶺外代答校注. Yang Wuquan 楊武泉, ed. (Beijing: Zhonghua shuju, 1999).

Zhu Mu 祝穆, *Fangyu shenglan* 方輿生覽 (Taipei: Wenhai chubanshe, 1981).

Zhu Xi 朱熹, *Zhu Wengong wenji* 朱文公文集 (Siku quanshu zhenben ed.).

Zhu Yu 朱彧, *Pingzhou ketan* 萍洲可談 (Shanghai: Shanghai guji chubanshe, 1989).

Arab and Other Western Primary Sources in Translation

Abu Zayd al-Sirafi, Accounts of China and India, edited and translated by Tim Mackintosh-Smith, in Two Arabic Travel Books, Philip F. Kennedy and Shawkat M. Toorawa, eds. (New York, NY: New York University Press, 2014)

Ahmad, S. Maqbul, *Arabic Classical Accounts of India and China* (Calcutta: Indian Institute of Advanced Study, 1989). Buzurg ibn Shahriyār (c. 900–953), *The Book of the Wonders of India, Mainland, Sea, and Islands (Kitab 'Aja'ib al-Hind)*, G. S. P. Freeman-Grenville, trans. (London: East-West Publications, 1981). English extracts in Hourani, *Arab Seafaring* (Princeton, NJ: Princeton University Press, 1951).

al-Mas'udi, Abu al-Ḥasan 'Ali ben al-Ḥusain, Murūj al-dhahab wa-ma'ādin al-jawāhir (Meadows of Gold and Mines of Gems), in Barbier de Meynard and Pavet de Courteille, *Les Prairies d'Or. Texte et Traduction* (Paris: Imprimé par authorisation de l'Empereur à l'Imprimerie Impériale, 1861), tome I, 303. (Collection d'Ouvrage Orientaux Publiée par la Société Asiatique). Online version, cf. www.archive.org/stream/lesprairiesdor01masduoft#page/n5/mo de/2up.

Ibn Battuta, *The Travels of Ibn Battuta, A.D. 1325–1354*, trans. with revisions and notes from the Arabic text ed. by C. Defrémery and B. R. Sanguinetti, ed. by H. A. R. Gibb and annotated by C. F. Beckingham, 5 vols. (London: The Hakluyt Society, 1994).

Ferrand, Gabriel, *Relations de voyages et textes géographiques arabes, persans et turks relatifs de l'Extrème-Orient du VIIIe au XVIIIe siecles*, 2 vols. (Paris: Ernest Leroux, 1913–1914).

Polo, Marco, *The Travels of Marco Polo*, trans. and with an introduction by Ronald Latham (London: Penguin Books, 1958).

Sirafi, Abu Zayd Hasan ibn Yazid, Ahbar al-Sin wa'l-Hind, *Relation de la Chine et de l'Inde, rédigée en 851*. Arabic text, French trans. and notes by Jean Sauvaget (Paris: Belles Lettres, 1948).

Tibbetts, G. R., *A Study of the Arabic Texts Containing Material on South-East Asia* (Leiden and London: E. J. Brill, 1979).

Secondary Sources

Abramson, Marc S., *Ethnic Identity in Tang China* (Philadelphia, PA: University of Pennsylvania Press, 2008).

Abt, Oded, "Locking and Unlocking the City Gates: Muslim Memories of Song-Yuan-Ming Transition in Southeast China," Harvard Middle Period Conference, June 2014.

Abu-Lughod, Janet L., *Before European Hegemony: The World System A.D. 1250–1350* (Oxford: Oxford University Press, 1989).

Allsen, Thomas T., *Culture and Conquest in Mongol Eurasia* (Cambridge: Cambridge University Press, 2001).

"Mongolian Princes and Their Merchant Partners, 1200–1260," *Asia Major*, 3rd Ser. 2–2 (1989), pp. 83–126.

Aslanian, Sebouh David, *From the Indian Ocean to the Mediterranean: The Global Trade Networks of Armenian Merchants from New Julfa* (Berkeley, CA: University of California Press, 2011).

Blake, Robert P., "The Circulation of Silver in the Moslem East Down to the Mongol Epoch," *Harvard Journal of Asiatic Studies* 2.3/4 (1937), pp. 291–328.

Bulliet, Richard W., *Conversion to Islam in the Medieval Period: An Essay in Quantitative History* (Cambridge, MA, and London: Harvard University Press, 1979).

Cahill, Suzanne Elizabeth, "Taoism at the Sung Court: The Heavenly Text Affair of 1008," *Bulletin of Sung Yuan Studies* 16 (1980), pp. 23–44.

Chaffee, John W., "At the Intersection of Empire and World Trade: The Chinese Port City of Quanzhou (Zaitun), Eleventh-Fifteenth Centuries," in Kenneth

R. Hall, ed., *Secondary Cities and Urban Networking in the Indian Ocean Realm, c. 1400–1800* (Lanham, MD: Rowman and Littlefield Publishers, 2008), pp. 99–122.

Branches of Heaven: A History of the Imperial Clan of Sung China (Cambridge: Harvard University Asia Center, 1999).

"Cultural Transmission by Sea: Maritime Trade Routes in Yuan China," *Eurasian Influences on Yuan China: Cross-Cultural Transmissions in the 13th and 14th Centuries*, Morris Rossabi, ed. (Singapore: Nalanda Srivijaya Centre, 2013), pp. 41–59.

"Diasporic Identities in the Historical Development of the Maritime Muslim Communities of Song-Yuan China," *Journal of the Economic and Social History of the Orient* 49.4 (2006), pp. 395–420.

"The Impact of the Song Imperial Clan on the Overseas Trade of Quanzhou," in Angela Schottenhammer, ed., *The Emporium of the World: Maritime Quanzhou, 1000–1400* (Leiden: Brill, 2001), pp. 13–46.

"Muslim Merchants and Quanzhou in the Late Yuan-Early Ming: Conjectures on the Ending of the Medieval Muslim Trade Diaspora," in Angela Schottenhammer, ed., *The East Asian "Mediterranean": Maritime Crossroads of Culture, Commerce and Human Migration* (Wiesbaden: Harrasowitz Verlag, 2008), pp. 115–132.

"Pu Shougeng Reconsidered: Pu, His Family, and Their Role in the Maritime Trade of Quanzhou," in Robert J. Antony and Angela Schottenhammer, eds., Beyond the Silk Road: New Discoursses on China's Role in East Asian Maritime History (Wiesbaden: Harrassowitz Verlag, 2018), pp. 63–76.

"Song China and the multi-state and commercial world of East Asia," *Crossroads: Studies on the History of Exchange Relations in the East Asian World* 1 (2010), pp. 33–54.

"Songdai yu Dong Ya de duoguo xiti ji maoyi shijie 宋代与东亚的多国係提及贸易世界" (Song China and the multi-state and commercial world of East Asia), *Beida xuebao* 北大学报 46.2 (2009), pp. 99–108.

The Thorny Gates of Learning in Sung China: a Social History of Examinations, new edition (Albany: State University of New York Press, 1995).

Chang Bide 昌彼得, Wang Deyi 王德毅, Cheng Yuanmin 程元敏 and Hou Junde 侯俊德, eds., *Songren zhuanji ziliao suoyin* 宋人傳記資料索引, 6 vols. (Taipei: Dingwen shuzhu, 1974–1975).

Chang Hsing-lang (Zhang Xinglang), "The Rebellion of the Persian Garrison in Ch'üan-chou (1357–1366)," *Monumenta Serica* 3 (1938), pp. 611–627.

Chang Pin-tsun, "The First Chinese Diaspora in Southeast Asia in the Fifteenth Century," in *Emporia, Commodities and Entrepreneurs in Asian Maritime Trade, c. 1400–1750*, Roderich Ptak and Dietmar Rothermund, eds. (Stuttgart: Franz Steiner Verlag, 1991), pp. 13–28.

Chang, Yusuf Haji, "The Ming Empire: Patron of Islam in China and Southeast-West Asia," *Journal of the Malaysian Brance of the Royal Asiatic Society* 61.2 (1988), pp. 1–44.

Chaudhuri, K. N., *Trade and Civilization in the Indian Ocean. An Economic History from the Rise of Islam to 1750* (Cambridge: Cambridge University Press, 1985).

Chen Dasheng 陳達生, "A Brunei Sultan of the Early Fourteenth Century," in Vadime Elisseeff, ed., *The Silk Roads: Highways of Culture and Commerce* (New York, NY, and Oxford: UNESCO Publishing, Berghahn Books, 1999), pp. 145–157.

"Chinese Islamic Influence on Archaeological Finds in South Asia," in *South East Asia & China: Art, Interaction and Commerce*, Rosemary Scott and John Guy, eds., *Colloquies on Art and Archaeology in Asia*, No. 17 (London: University of London Percival David Foundation of Chinese Art, 1995), pp. 55–63.

"Jin Ali yu Qingjingsi 金阿里与清净寺," in *Quanzhou Yisilanjiao yanjiu lunwenxuan* 泉州伊斯兰教研究论文选 (Fuzhou: Renmin chubanshe, 1983), 126–130.

"Persian Settlements in Southeastern China during the Tang, Sung, and Yuan Dynasties," in *Encyclopedia Iranica*, Eshan Yarshater, ed. (Costa Mesa, CA: Mazda Publishers, 1992), vol. 5, p. 445.

"Quanzhou Yisilan jiaopai yu Yuanmo Yisibaxi zhanluan xingdun shitan 泉州伊斯蘭教派与元末亦思巴奚战乱性质试探," in *Quanzhou Yisilanjiao yanjiu lunwenxuan* 泉州伊斯兰教研究论文选(Fuzhou: Renmin chubanshe, 1983), pp. 53–64.

Quanzhou Yisilan jiao shike 泉州伊斯蘭教石刻 (Fu-chou: Ningxia renmin chubanshe, Fujian renmin chubanshe, 1984).

"Synthetical Study Program on the Islamic Inscriptions on the Southeast Coastland of China," in *Zhongguo yu haishang sichou zhi lu* 中国与海上丝绸之路 (*China and the Maritime Silk Route*), edited by Lianheguo jiaokewen zuzhi haishang sichou zhilu zonghe kaocha Quanzhou guoji xueshu taolunhui zuzhi weiyuanhui 联合国教科文组织海上丝绸上之路综合考察泉州国际学术讨论会组织委员会 (Fuzhou: Fujian renmin chubanshe, 1991), pp. 159–182.

Chen Dasheng 陳達生 and Ludvik Kalus, *Corpus d'Inscriptions Arabes et Persanes en Chine, Vol. 1, Province de Fu-jian* (Paris: Librairie Orientaliste Paul Geuthner, 1991).

Chen Dasheng 陳達生 and Claudine Salmon, "Rapport préliminaire sur la découverte de tombes musulmanes dans l'ile de Hainan," *Archipel*, 1989, No. 38, pp. 75–106.

Chen Dasheng 陳達生 and Chen Shangsheng 陳尚勝, *Zhongguo haiwai jiaotong shi* 中國海外交通史 (Taipei : Wenjin chubanshe, 1998).

Chen Gaohua 陳高華, and Chen Shangsheng 陳尚耘, *Zhongguo haiwai jiaotong shi* 中國海外交通史 (Taipei: Wenjin chubanshe, 1998).

Christie, Jan Wisseman, "Javanese Markets and the Asian Sea Trade Boom of the Tenth to the Thirteenth Centuries A.D.," *Journal of the Economic and Social History of the Orient* 41.3 (1998): 341–381.

"The Medieval Tamil-language Inscriptions in Southeast Asia and China," *Journal of Southeast Asian Studies* 29.2 (1998), pp. 239–268.

Clark, Hugh, *Community, Trade, and Networks: Southern Fujian Province from the Third to the Thirteenth Centuries*. (Cambridge, MA: Cambridge University Press, 1991).

"Moslems and Hindus in the Economy and Culture of Song Quanzhou," *Abstracts of the 1993 Annual Meeting*, 4 (Ann Arbor, MI: Association for Asian Studies, 1993).

"The Politics of Trade and the Establishment of the Quanzhou Trade Superintendency," in *Zhongguo yu haishang sichou zhi lu* 中国与海上丝绸之路 (*China and the Maritime Silk Route*), edited by Lianheguo jiaokewen zuzhi haishang sichou zhilu zonghe kaocha Quanzhou guoji xueshu taolunhui zuzhi weiyuanhui 联合国教科文组织海上丝绸上之路综合考察泉州国际学术讨论会组织委员会, vol. 2. (Fuzhou: Fujian renmin chubanshe, 1991), pp. 375–393.

"The Southern Kingdoms between the T'ang and the Sung," in *The Cambridge History of China, Vol. 5 Part One: The Sung Dynasty and Its Precursors*, Denis Twitchett and Paul Smith, eds., pp. 133–205.

Cohen, Abner, *The Development of Indigenous Trade and Markets in West Africa: Studies Presented and Discussed at the Tenth International African Seminar at Fourah Bay College, Freetown, December 1969* (London: Oxford University Press, 1971), pp. 266–281.

Curtin, Philip D., *Cross-Cultural Trade in World History* (Cambridge: Cambridge University Press, 1984).

Damais, Louis-Charles, "Études Javanaises: Les tombes Musulmans dates de Tralaya," *Bulletin de l'École Française d'Etrême Orient* 48 (1967): 353–415.

Davis, Richard, "The Reign of Tu-tsung (1264–1274) and His Successors to 1279," in The Cambridge History of China. *Vol. 5, Part 1:* The Sung Dynasties and Its Precursors, 907–1279, Denis Twitchett and Paul Jakov Smith, eds. (Cambridge: Cambridge University Press, 2009), pp. 913–961.

de Graaf, H. J. and Th. G. Th. Pigeaud, *Chinese Muslims in Java in the 15th and 16th Centuries: The Malay Annals of Sĕmarang and Cĕrbon*, M. C. Ricklefs, ed., Monash Papers on Southeast Asia No. 12 (North Melbourne: Ruskin Press, 1984).

de la Vaissière, Étienne, *Sogdian Traders: A History*, translated by James Ward (Leiden: Brill, 2005).

Deng Gang, *Maritime Sector, Institutions and Sea Power of Premodern China* (Westport, CT: Greenwood Press, 1999).

Di Meglio, Rita Rose, "Arab Trade with Indonesia and the Malay Peninsula from the 8th to the 16th Century," in in D. S. Richards, ed., *Islam and the Trade of Asia: A Colloquium* Papers on Islamic History: II (Oxford: Bruno Cassirer, 1970), 105–135.

Ding Kunjian 丁崑健, "Yuan Ming shidai Jinjiang diqu Huiyi Chenjiang Ding xing zuren de Hanhua" 元明時代晉江地區回族陳江丁氏族人的漢化, in Ding Shouzhen, ed., *Ding Xieyuan jiapu* 丁協源家譜 (Taipei: Chongsi zhiye youxian gongsi, 1997), 277–294.

Ding Shouzhen 丁壽真, ed., *Ding Xieyuan jiapu* 丁協源家谱 (Taipei: Chongsi zhiye youxian gongsi, 1997).

Drake, F. S., "Mohammedanism in the T'ang Dynasty," *Monumenta Serica* 7 (1943): 1–40.

Dunn, Ross E., *The Adventures of Ibn Battuta: A Muslim Traveler of the 14th Century*, Revised edition with a new preface (Berkeley, CA: University of California Press, 2005).

Endicott-West, Elizabeth, "Merchant Associations in Yüan China: The Ortoy," *Asia Major*, 3rd Ser., 2–2 (1989): 127–154.

Ennin, *Diary: The Record of a Pilgrimage to China in Search of the Law*, Edwin O. Reischauer, trans. (New York, NY: Ronald Press Co., 1955).

Fan Ke, "Maritime Muslims and Hui Identity: A South Fujian Case," Journal of Muslim Minority Affairs 21.2 (2001), pp. 309–332.

Flecker, Michael, "A Ninth-Century Arab or Indian Shipwreck in Indonesian Waters," *International Journal of Nautical Archaeology* 29.2 (2000), pp. 199–217.

"A Ninth Century Arab or Indian Shipwreck in Indonesia: First Evidence for Direct Trade with China," *World Archaeology* 32.3 (February 2001), pp. 335–354.

Franke, Wolfgang, "China's Overseas Communications with Southeast Asia as Reflected in Chinese Epigraphic Materials, 1264–1800," in *Zhongguo yu haishang sichou zhi lu* 海上丝绸之路–广州文化遗产：地上史迹卷 *(China and the Maritime Silk Route)*, edited by Lianheguo jiaokewen zuzhi haishang sichou zhilu zonghe kaocha Quanzhou guoji xueshu taolunhui zuzhi weiyuanhui 联合国教科文组织海上丝绸上之路综合考察泉州国际学术讨论会组织委员会, vol. 2. (Fuzhou: Fujian renmin chubanshe, 1991), 309–322.

Franke, Wolfgang and Chen Tieh Fan, "A Chinese Tomb Inscription of A.D. 1264, discovered recently in Brunei," *Brunei Museum Journal*, 3 (1973), pp. 91–99.

Fu Zongwen 傅宗文, "Houzhu guchuan: Song ji nanwai zongshi haiwai jingshang di wuzheng" 后渚古船：宋季南外宗室海外经商的物证, *Haiwai jiaotong yanjiu* 海外交通研究 2 (1989), pp. 77–83.

Gedalecia, David. "Wu Ch'eng and the Perpetuation of the Classical Heritage in the Yuan," in John D. Langlois, Jr., ed., *China under Mongol Rule* (Princeton, NJ: Princeton University Press, 1981), pp. 186–211.

Goitein, S. D., *A Mediterranean Society: The Jewish Communities of the Arab World as Portrayed in the Documents of the Cairo Geniza, Vol. 1* (Berkeley, CA: University of California Press, 1967). *Vol. 2 The Community* (Berkeley, CA: University of California Press, 1971).

"Portrait of a Medieval Indian Trader: Three Letters from the Cairo Geniza," *Bulletin of the School of Oriental and African Studies* 50.3 (1987): 449–464.

Goitein, S. D. and Mordechai Akiva Friedman, *India Traders of the Middle Ages: Documents from the Cairo Geniza ("India Book")* (Leiden: Brill, 2008).

Green, Jeremy, "The Song Dynasty Shipwreck at Quanzhou, Fujian Province, People's Republic of China," *International Journal of Nautical Archaeology and Underwater Exploration* 12.3 (1983), pp. 253–261.

Guy, John, "Early Ninth-Century Chinese Export Ceramics and the Persian Gulf Connection: The Belitung Shipwreck Evidence," *China-Mediterranean Sea Routes and Exchange of Ceramics Prior to 16th century/Chine-Méditerranée Routes et échanges de la céramique avant le XVIe siècle* (Suilly-la-Tour: Éditions Findakly, 2006), pp. 9–20.

"Tamil Merchant Guilds and the Quanzhou Trade," in Angela Schottenhammer, ed., *The Emporium of the World: Maritime Quanzhou, 1000–1400* (Leiden: Brill, 2001), pp. 283–309.

"The Phanom Surin Shipwreck, a Phalavi Inscription, and Their Significance for the History of Early Lower Central Thailand," *Journal of the Siam Society,* 105 (2017), pp. 179–196.

Haishang sichou zhi lu – Guangzhou wenhua yichan: Dishang shiji juan 海上丝绸之路–广州文化遗产：地上史迹卷 *(Maritime Silk Road – Cultural Heritage in Guangzhou: Historical Sites)* (Guangzhou: Wenwu chubanshe, 2008).

Hall, Kenneth R., "Coastal Cities in an Age of Transition: Upstream-Downstream Networking and Societal Development in Fifteenth- and Sixteenth-Century Maritime Southeast Asia," in Kenneth Hall, ed., *Secondary Cities and Urban Networking in the Indian Ocean Region, c. 1400–1800* (Lanham, MD: Rowman and Littlefield, 2008), pp. 177–204.

"Indonesia's Evolving International Relationships in the Ninth to Early Eleventh Centuries: Evidence from Contemporary Shipwrecks and Epigraphy," *Indonesia* 90 (Fall 2010), pp. 15–45.

"Local and International Trade and Traders in the Straits of Melaka Region: 600–1500," *Journal of the Economic and Social History of the Orient* 47.2 (2004): 213–260.

Maritime Trade and State Development in Early Southeast Asia (Honolulu, HI: University of Hawaii Press, 1985).

"Multi-Dimensional Networking: Fifteenth-Century Indian Ocean Maritime Diaspora in Southeast Asian Perspective," *Journal of the Economic and Social History of the Orient* 49.4 (2006), pp. 454–481.

Hartwell, Robert M., *Tribute Missions to China, 960–1126* (Philadelphia, PA, 1983).

Hasan, Hadi, *A History of Persian Navigation* (London: Methuen & Co., 1928).

Heng, Derek T. S., Economic Interaction between China and the Malacca Straits Region, Tenth to Fourteenth Centuries A.D. (Ph.D. dissertation, University of Hull, 2005).

"Economic Networks between the Malay Region and the Hinterlands of Quanzhou and Guangzhou: Temasek and the Chinese Ceramics and Foodstuffs Trade," in Ann Low, ed., *Early Singapore, 1300s–1819; Evidence in Maps, Text and Artifacts* (Singapore: Sikngapore History Museum, 2004), 73–85.

Malay Trade and Diplomacy from the Tenth through the Fourteenth Century, Ohio University Research in International Diplomacy, Southeast Asia Series No. 121 (Athens, OH: Ohio University Press, 2009).

Hirth, Frederick and W. W. Rockhill, trans., *Chau Ju-kua: His Work on the Chinese and Arab Trade in the Twelfth and Thirteenth Centuries, Entitled* Chu-fan-chi (St. Petersburg: Imperial Academy of Sciences, 1911; reprinted: Taipei: Ch'eng-wen Publishing Company, 1971).

Hourani, G. F., *Arab Seafaring in the Indian Ocean in Ancient and Early Medieval Times.* (Princeton, NJ: Princeton University Press, 1951).

Hsiao Ch'i-ch'ing, "Mid-Yüan Politics," in Herbert Franke and Denis Twitchett, eds., *The Cambridge History of China. Vol. 6. Alien Regimes and Border States* (Cambridge: Cambridge University Press, 1994), 490–560.

Huang Chunyan 黃純艳, *Songdai haiwai maoyi* 宋代海外贸易 (Beijing: Shehui kexue wenxian chubanshe, 2003).

Hucker, Charles, *A Dictionary of Official Titles in Imperial China* (Stanford, CA: Stanford University Press, 1985).

Israeli, Raphael, "Medieval Muslim Travelers to China," *Journal of Muslim Minority Affairs*, 20.2 (2000): 313–321.

Jacq-Hergoualc'h, Michel, *The Malay Peninsula: Crossroad of the Maritime Silk Road*, Victoria Hobson, trans. (Leiden: Brill, 2002).

Karashima Noboru, "South Indian Merchant Guilds in the Indian Ocean and Southeast Asia," in Hermann Kulke, K. Kesavapany, and Vijay Sakhuja, eds., *Nagapattinam to Suvarnadwipa: Reflections on the Chola Naval Expeditions to Southeast Asia* (Singapore: Institute of Southeast Asian Studies, 2010), pp. 135–157.

Kauz, Ralph, "The Maritime Trade of Kish during the Mongol Period," in Linda Komaroff, ed., *Beyond the Legacy of Genghis Khan, Islamic History and Civilization, Studies and Texts 64* (Leiden, Boston: Brill, 2006), pp. 51–67.

Kervran, M., "Famous Merchants of the Arabian Gulf in the Middle Ages," *Dilmun, Journal of the Bahrain Historical and Archaeological Society*, No. 11 (1983), pp. 21–24.

Komoot, Abhirada Pook, "Recent Discovery of a Sewn Ship in Thailand: Challenges," Proceedings of the Underwater Archaeology in Vietnam Southeast Asia: Cooperation for Development, Quang Ngai, Vietnam, 2014.

Kracke, Edward A., "Early Visions of Justice for the Humble in East and West," *Journal of the American Oriental Society* 96.4 (1976), pp. 492–498.

Krishna, Brajesh, *Foreign Trade in Early Medieval India* (New Delhi: Harman Publishing House, 2000).

Kuhn, Dieter, *The Age of Confucian Rule: The Song Transformation of China* (Cambridge, MA: Belnap Press of Harvard University Press, 2009).

Kulke, Hermann, "The Naval Expeditions of the Cholas in the Context of Asian History," in Hermann Kulke, K. Kesavapany, and Vijay Sakhuja, eds., *Nagapattinam to Suvarnadwipa: Reflections on the Chola Naval Expeditions to Southeast Asia* (Singapore: Institute of Southeast Asian Studies, 2010), pp. 1–19.

Kuwabara, Jitsuzō 桑原隲藏, *Ho Jukō no jiseki* 蒲壽庚の事蹟 (Tokyo: Kazama shobō, 1935).

"On P'u Shou-keng, a Man of the Western Regions, Who Was the Superintendent of the Trading Ships' Office in Ch'üan-chou towards the End of the Sung Dynasty, Together with a General Sketch of Trade of the Arabs in China during the T'ang and Sung Eras, Part 1" *Memoirs of the Research Department of the Tōyō Bunko* 2 (1928), pp. 1–79.

"On P'u Shou-keng, Part 2," *Memoirs of the Research Department of the Tōyō Bunko* 7 (1935), pp. 1–104.

Pu Shougeng 蒲壽庚, trans., Chen Yujing 陳裕菁 (Beijing: Zhonghua shuju, 1954).

Lambourn, Elizabeth, "Carving and Communities: Marble Carving for Muslim Communities at Khambhat and around the Indian Ocean Rim (late 13th to

Mid-15thCenturies CE)," *Ars Orientalis. 50th Anniversary Volume on Communities and Commodities: Western Indian and the Indian Ocean, Eleventh to Fifteenth Centuries*, vol. 34 (2004), pp. 99–133.

"India from Aden: *Khutba* and Muslim Urban Networks in Late Thirteenth-Century India," in Kenneth R. Hall, ed., *Secondary Cities and Urban Networking in the Indian Ocean Realm, c. 1400–1800* (Lanham, MD: Rowman & Littlefield Publishers, 2008), pp. 55–98.

Lee, Hee-Soo, *The Advent of Islam in Korea: A Historical Account* (Istanbul: Research Centre for Islamic History, Art and Culture, 1997).

Lee, Risha, "Rethinking Community: The Indic Carvings of Quanzhou," in Hermann Kulke, K. Kesavapany and Vijay Sakhuja, eds., *Nagapattinam to Suvarnadwipa: Reflections on the Chola Naval Expeditions to Southeast Asia* (Singapore: Institute of Southeast Asian Studies, 2010), pp. 240–270.

Leslie, Donald Daniel, *Islam in Traditional China: A Short History* (Canberra: Canberra College of Advanced Education, 1986).

Lewicki, Tadeusz, "Les premiers commerçants Arabes en Chine," *Rocznik orientalistyczny*, 11 (1935): 173–186.

Levy, Howard, *Biography of Huang Ch'ao*, Chinese Dynastic History Translations, no. 5 (Berkeley CA: University of California Press, 1961).

Li Tana, "A View from the Sea: Perspectives on the Northern and Central Vietnamese Coast," *Journal of Southeast Asian Studies*, 37.1 (2006), pp. 83–102.

Li Yukun 李玉昆, *Quanzhou haiwai jiaotong shilue* 泉州海外交通史略, A brief history of Quanzhou's overseas communications (Xiamen: Xiamen University Press, 1995).

Liebner, Horst, "Cargoes for Java: Interpreting Two 10th Century Shipwrecks," Southeast Asian Ceramic Society, West Malaysia Chapter, Lecture Series (Kuala Lumpur, 2009), pp. 1–50.

The Siren of Cirebon: A Tenth-Century Trading Vessel Lost in the Java Sea (Ph.D. dissertation, University of Leeds, 2014).

Liu Yingsheng 刘迎耗, "An Inscription in Memory of Sayyid Bin Abu Ali: A Study of Relations between China and Oman from the Eleventh to the Fifteenth Century," in Vadime Elisseeff, ed., *The Silk Roads: Highways of Culture and Commerce* (New York, NY, and Oxford: UNESCO Publishing, Berghahn Books, 1999), pp. 122–126.

"Muslim Merchants in Mongol Yuan China," in Angela Schottenhammer, ed., *The East Asian "Mediterranean": Maritime Crossroads of Culture, Commerce and Human Migration* (Wiesbaden: Harrasowitz Verlag, 2008), pp. 133–144.

Lo Hsiang-lin [Luo Xianglin 羅香林], "A Preliminary Discussion on the Building Year of Quanzhou Moslem Holy Tomb and the Authenticity of Its Legend," in Committee for the Preservation of Quanzhou Islamic Sites and the Chinese Cultural Historical Sites Research Center, ed., *The Islamic Historic Relics in Quanzhou* (Fuzhou: Fujian People's Publishing House, 1985).

"Islam in Canton in the Sung Period: Some Fragmentary Records," in F. S. Drake, ed., *Symposium on Historical Archaeological and Linguistic*

Studies in Southeast Asia (Hong Kong: Hong Kong University Press, 1967), pp. 176–179.

Pu Shougeng yanjiu 蒲壽庚研究 (Hong Kong: Zhongguo xueshe, 1959).

Lo Jung-pang, *China as a Sea Power, 1127–1368: A Preliminary Survey of the Maritime Expansion and Naval Exploits of the Chinese People during the Southern Sung and Yuan Periods* (1957; Hong Kong: Hong Kong University Press, 2012), Bruce A. Elleman, ed., 2007.

"Chinese Shipping and East-West Trade from the Xth to the XIVth Century," in Michel Mollat, ed., *Sociétés et companies de commerce en Orient et dans l'Océan Indien. Actes du Huitième Colloque International d'Histoire Maritime* (Paris: S.E.V.P.E.N., 1970), pp. 167–178.

Lombard, Denys, "Introduction," in Denys Lombard and Jean Aubin, eds., *Asian Merchants and Businessmen in the Indian Ocean and the China Sea* (New Delhi: Oxford University Press, 2000), pp. 1–9.

Ma Juan 馬娟, "Tang Song shiqi Yisilan fanfang kao 唐宋時期伊斯兰蕃坊考," *Huizu yanjiu* 回族研究, 1998, No. 3, pp. 31–36.

Ma, Laurence J. C., *Commercial Development and Urban Change in Sung China (960–1279)* (Ann Arbor, MI: Department of Geography, University of Michigan, 1971).

Maejima Shinji, "The Muslims in Ch'üan-chou at the End of the Yuan Dynasty." 2 pts. *Memoirs of the Research Department of the Tōyō Bunko* 31 (1973), pp. 29–51; 32 (1974), pp. 47–71.

Manguin, Pierre-Yves, "The Introduction of Islam into Champa," in Alijah Gordon, ed., *The Propagation of Islam in the Indonesian-Malay Archipelago* (Kuala Lumpur: Malaysian Sociological Research Institute, 2001), pp. 287–328.

"Trading Ships of the South China Sea," *Journal of the Economic and Social History of the Orient* 36.3 (Aug. 1993): 253–280.

Momoki Shiro 桃木至朗, "Dai Viet and the South China Sea Trade: From the Tenth to the Fifteenth Century," *Crossroads: An Interdisciplinary Journal of Southeast Asian Studies* 12.1 (1999): 1–34.

Momoki Shiro 桃木至朗 and Hasuda Takashi 蓮田隆志, "A Review of the Periodization of Southeast Asian Medieval/Early Modern History, in Comparison with That of Northeast Asia," in Fujiko Kayoko, Makino Naoko and Matsumoto Mayumi, eds., *Dynamic Rimlands and Open Heartlands: Maritime Asia as a Site of Interactions.* Proceedings of the Second COE-ARI Joint Workshop. (Osaka: Research Cluster on Global History and Maritime Asia, Osaka University, 2007), 1–26.

Mukai Masaki 向正樹, "Regenerating Trade Diaspora: Supra-Regional Contacts and the Role of "Hybrid Muslims" in the South China Sea since the late 10th to mid-13th Century," in *Exploring Global Linkages between Asian Maritime World and Trans-Atlantic World*, Global History and Maritime Asia Working and Discussion Paper Series, No. 19 (Osaka: Osaka University, 2010), 66–80.

"The Interests of the Rulers, Agents and Merchants behind the Southward Expansion of the Yuan Dynasty," *Journal of the Turfan Studies: Essays on The Third International Conference on Turfan Studies, the Origins and*

Migrations of Eurasian Nomadic Peoples (Shanghai: Shanghai Guji, 2010), pp. 428–445.

"Transforming Dashi Shippers: The Tributary System and the Trans-national Network during the Song Period," Harvard Conference on Middle Period China, 2014.

Nakamura Kushirō, "Tō-jidai no Kanton" *Shigaku Zasshi*, 28 (1917): 242–258, 348–368, 487–495, 552–576.

Nakamura Tsubasa, "The Maritime East Asian Network in the Song-Yuan Period," paper presented at the Conference on Middle Period China, 800–1400, Harvard University, June 5–7, 2014.

Park, Hyunhee, *Mapping the Chinese and Islamic Worlds: Cross-Cultural Exchange in Pre-Modern Asia* (Cambridge: Cambridge University Press, 2012).

Peterson, Charles A., "Court and Province in Mid- and Late T'ang," in Denis Twitchett, ed., *The Cambridge History of China, Vol. 3: Sui and T'ang China, 589–906, Part 1* (Cambridge: Cambridge University Press, 1979), pp. 464–550.

Pryor, John H., "The Origins of the Commenda Contract," *Speculum* 52.1 (1977), pp. 5–37.

Ptak, Roderich, "Ming Maritime Trade to Southeast Asia, 1368–1567," in Claude Guillot, Denys Lombard and Roderich Ptak, *From the Mediterranean to the China Sea: Miscellaneous Notes* (Wiesbaden: Harrassowitz Verlag, 1998), pp. 157–191.

Quanzhou Huizu pudie ziliao xuanbian 泉州回族谱牒资料选编, Quanzhoushi Quanzhou lishi yanjiuhui 泉州市泉州历史研究会, ed. (Quanzhou, 1980).

Ravaisse, Paul, "Deux inscriptions coufiques du Campa," *Journal Asiatique* (Paris), Série II, 20.2 (1922): 247–289.

Richards, D. S., ed., *Islam and the Trade of Asia. A Colloqium* (Oxford: Bruno Cassirer and University of Pennsylvania Press, 1970).

Risso, Patricia, *Merchants and Faith: Muslim Commerce and Culture in the Indian Ocean* (Boulder, CO: Westview Press, Inc., 1995).

Rossabi, Morris, *China among Equals: The Middle Kingdom and Its Neighbors, 10th–14th Centuries* (Berkeley, CA: University of California Press, 1983).

Khubilai Khan: His Life and Times (Berkeley, CA: University of California Press, 1988).

"The Mongols and Their Legacy," in Linda Komaroff and Stefano Carboni, eds., *The Legacy of Genghis Khan: Courtly Art and Culture in Western Asia, 1256–1353* (New York, NY, New Haven, CT, and London: The Metropolitan Museum of Art and Yale University Press, 2002), pp. 12–35.

"Muslim and Central Asian Revolts," in Jonathan Spence and John Wills, Jr., eds., *From Ming to Ch'ing: Conquest, Region, and Continuity in Seventeenth Century China* (New Haven, CT: Yale University Press, 1979), pp. 167–200.

"The Muslims in Early Yüan Dynasty," in *China under Mongol Rule*, John D. Langlois, Jr., ed. (Princeton, NJ: Princeton University Press, 1981), pp. 257–295.

Saunders, Graham, *A History of Brunei* (Kualah Lumpur: Oxford University Press, 1994).

Schafer, Edward H., *The Golden Peaches of Samarkand: A Study of T'ang Exotics* (Berkeley, CA: University of California Press, 1963).

"Iranian Merchants in T'ang Dynasty Tales," in *Semitic and Oriental Studies: A Volume Presented to William Popper* (Berkeley, CA: University of California Publications in Semitic Philology, vol. XI, 1951), 403–422.

The Vermilion Bird: T'ang Images of the South (Berkeley, CA: University of California Press, 1967).

Schottenhammer, Angela, "China's Emergence as a Maritime Power," in John Chaffee and Denis Twitchett, eds., The Cambridge History of China, *Volume 5, Part 2:* The Five Dynasties and Sung China, 960–1279 (Cambridge: Cambridge University Press, 2015), pp. 437–525.

"China's Increasing Integration into the Indian Ocean World up to Song Times: Sea Routes, Connections, Trade," in Angela Schottenhammer, ed., *Transfer, Exchange, and Human Movement across the Indian Ocean World*, Palgrave Series in Indian Ocean World Studies, 2 vols. (London: Palgrave Macmillan, forthcoming).

"Guangzhou as China's Gate to the Indian Ocean: The Importance of Iranian and Arab Merchant Networks for Long-Distance Maritime Trade during the Tang-Song Transition (c. 750–1050), Part 1: (750–c. 900)," *Harvard Journal of Asiatic Studies* 76 (2016): 135–179.

"The Role of Metals and the Impact of the Introduction of Huizi Paper Notes in Quanzhou on the Development of Maritime Trade in the Song Period," in Angela Schottenhammer, ed., *The Emporium of the World: Maritime Quanzhou, 1000–1400* (Leiden: Brill, 2001), pp. 95–176.

Schurmann, Franz, *Economic Structure of the Yuan Dynasty* (Cambridge, MA: Harvard-Yenching Institute, 1956).

Sen, Tansen, "Buddhism and the Maritime Crossings," in Dorothy Wong and Gustav Heldt, eds., *China and Beyond in the Mediaeval Period: Cultural Crossings and Inter-Regional Connections* (Amherst, MA, and Delhi: Cambria Press and Manohar Publishers, 2014), pp. 39–61.

Buddhism, Diplomacy, and Trade: The Realignment of Sino-Indian Relations, 600–1400 (Honolulu, HI: University of Hawaii Press, 2003).

"South Asia and the Mongol Empire," in Michal Biran and Kim Hodong, eds., *The Cambridge History of the Mongol Empire*, vol. 1 (Cambridge: Cambridge University Press, forthcoming).

Seshadri, Gokul, "New Perspectives on Nagapattinam: The Medieval Port City in the Context of Political, Religious, and Commercial Exchanges between South India, Southeast Asia and China," in Herman Kulke, K. Kesavapany, and Vijay Sakhuja, eds., *Nagapattinam to Suvarnadwipa: Reflections on the Chola Naval Expeditions to Southeast Asia* (Singapore: Institute of Southeast Asian Studies, 2010), pp. 102–134.

Shiba Yoshinobu, *Commerce and Society in Sung China*, Mark Elvin, trans. (Ann Arbor, MI: Center for Chinese Studies, University of Michigan, 1970).

"Sung Foreign Trade: Its Scope and Organization," in Morris Rossabi, ed., *China among Equals: The Middle Kingdom and Its Neighbors, 10th–14th Centuries* (Berkeley, CA: University of California Press, 1983), pp. 89–115.

Shokoohy, Mehrdad, *Muslim Architecture of South India: The Sultanate of Ma'bar and the Traditions of the Maritime Settlers on the Malabar and Coromandel Coasts (Tamil Nadu, Kerala and Goa)* (London: Routledge Curzon, 2003).

So, Billy Kee Long [Su Jilang 蘇基朗], "Financial Crisis and Local Economy: Ch'üan-chou in the Thirteenth Century," *T'oung Pao* 77 (1991): 119–137.

"Lingshan sheng mu niandai kaobian" 靈山聖墓年代考辨, in Su Jilang, *Tang Song Minnan Quanzhou shidi lungao* 唐宋時代閩南泉州史地論稿 (Taipei: Taiwan Shangwu yinshuguan, 1992), 62–94.

Prosperity, Region, and Institutions in Maritime China. The South Fukien Pattern, 946–1368 (Cambridge, MA: Harvard University Asia Center, 2000).

Tang Song shidai Minnan Quanzhou shidi lungao 唐宋時代閩南泉州駛抵論稿 (Taipei: Shangwu yinshuguan, 1991).

Somers, Robert M., "The End of the T'ang," in Denis Twitchett, ed., *The Cambridge History of China, Vol. 3: Sui and T'ang China, 589–906, Part 1* (Cambridge: Cambridge University Press, 1979).

Standen, Naomi, "The Five Dynasties," in Denis Twitchett and Paul Smith, eds., *The Cambridge History of China, Vol. 5, Part 1: The Sung Dynasty and Its Precursors* (Cambridge: Cambridge University Press, 2009), pp. 38–132.

Steinhardt, Nancy Shatzman, "China's Earliest Mosques," *Journal of the Society of Architectural Historians* 67.3 (September 2008), pp. 330–361.

China's Early Mosques. Edinburgh Studies in Islamic Art (Edinburgh: Edinburgh University Press, 2016).

Stern, S. M., "Rāmisht of Sīrāf, a Merchant Millionaire of the Twelfth Century," *The Journal of the Royal Asiatic Society of Great Britain and Ireland* No. 1/2 (Apr., 1967), pp. 10–14.

Takakusu, J., "Aomi-no Mabito Genkai (779), *Le voyage de Kanshin en Orient* (742–754)," *Bulletin de l'Ecole Française d'Extrême Orient*, 28 (1928), pp. 1–41, 441–472; 29 (1929), pp. 47–62.

Tampoe, Moira, Maritime Trade between China and the West: An Archaeological Study of the Ceramics from Siraf (Persian Gulf), 8th to 15th centuries A.D. (BAR International Series 555, 1989).

Thomaz, Luis Filipe F.R., "Melaka and Its Merchant Communities at the Turn of the Sixteenth Century," in Denys Lombard ane Jean Aubin, eds., *Asian Merchants and Businessmen in the Indian Ocean and the China Sea* (New Delhi: Oxford University Press, 2000), pp. 24–39.

Twitchett, Denis, "Hsüan-tsung," in Denis Twitchett, ed., *The Cambridge History of China, Vol. 3, Sui and T'ang China, 589–906, Part 1* (Cambridge: Cambridge University Press, 1979), pp. 333–463.

Twitchett, Denis and Janice Stargardt, "Chinese Silver Bullion in a Tenth-Century Indonesian Wreck," *Asia Major*, 3rd Series, 15.1 (2002): 23–72.

Udovitch, Abraham L., "Commercial Techniques in Early Medieval Islamic Trade," in D. S. Richards, ed., *Islam and the Trade of Asia: A Colloquium*, Papers on Islamic History: II (Oxford: Bruno Cassirer, 1970), pp. 37–62.

Wade, Geoff Philip, "The 'Account of Champa' in the *Song Huiyao Jigao*," in Tran Ky Phuong and Bruce M. Lockhart, eds., *The Cham of Vietnam: History, Society and Art* (Singapore: NUS Press, 2011), pp. 138–167.

"Beyond the Southern Borders: Southeast Asia in Chinese Texts to the Ninth Century", in John Guy, ed., *Lost Kingdoms. Hindu-Buddhist Sculpture of Early Southeast Asia* (New York, NY: The Metropolitan Museum of Art; New Haven CT, London: Yale University Press, 2014).

"An Earlier Age of Commerce in Southeast Asia: 900–1300 C.E.?" in Fujiko Kayoko, Makino Naoko and Matsumoto Mayumi, eds., *Dynamic Rimlands and Open Heartlands: Maritime Asia as a Site of Interactions*. Proceedings of the Second COE-ARI Joint Workshop (Osaka: Research Cluster on Global History and Maritime Asia, Osaka University, 2007), pp. 27–82.

"Southeast Asian Islam and Southern China in the Second Half of the Fourteenth Century," in Geoff Wade and Li Tana, eds., *Anthony Reid and the Study of the Southeast Asian Past* (Singapore: Institute for Southeast Asian Studies, 2012), pp. 125–145.

Wang Gungwu, "The Nan-hai Trade. A Study of the Early History of Chinese Trade in the South China Sea," *Journal of the Malayan Branch of the Royal Asiatic Society*, 31:2 (1958), pp. 1–135.

Wang Zengyu 王曾瑜, "Tan Songdai zaochuanye" 宋代造船业, *Wenwu* 文物, no. 10 (1975), pp. 24–27.

Wang Zhenping, "T'ang Maritime Trade Administration," *Asia Major* 4.1 (1991), pp. 7–38.

Wheatley, Paul, "Geographical Notes on Some Commodities Involved in the Sung Maritime Trade," *Journal of the Malaysian Branch of the Royal Asiatic Society* 32.2, no. 186 (1959), pp. 1–140.

Whitehouse, David, "Chinese Stoneware from Siraf: The Earliest Finds," in Norman Hammond, ed., *South Asian Anthropology: Papers from the First International Conference of South Asian Archaeologists held in the University of Cambridge* (Park Ridge, NJ: Noyes Press, 1973), pp. 241–256.

Wink, André, *Al-Hind. The Making of the Indo-Islamic World. Vol. I. Early Medieval India and the Expansion of Islam 7th to 11th Centuries*, 3rd edition (Leiden, New York, NY, Köln: E. J. Brill, 1996).

Wyatt, Don J., *The Blacks of Premodern China* (Philadelphia, PA: University of Pennsylvania Press, 2009).

Wu Renchen 吳任臣, *Shiguo chunqiu* 十國春秋 (Beijing: Zhonghua shuju, 1983).

Wu Youxiong 吳幼雄, *Quanzhou zongjiao wenhua* 泉州宗教文化 (Xiamen: Lujiang chubanshe, 1993).

"Yuandai Quanzhou ba ci she sheng yu Pu Shougeng Ren Quanzhou xing-sheng pingzhang zhengshi kao" 元代泉州八次设省與蒲壽庚任泉州行省平章政事考, *Fujian difangshi yanjiu* 福建地方史研究 No. 2 (1988), pp. 43–46.

Yamauchi Shinji, "The Japanese Archipelago and Maritime Asia from the 9th to the 13th Centuries," in Fujiko Kayoko, Makino Naoko, and Matsumoto Mayumi, eds., *Dynamic Rimlands and Open Heartlands: Maritime Asia as a Site of Interactions*. Proceedings of the Second COE-ARI Joint Workshop

(Osaka: Research Cluster on Global History and Maritime Asia, Osaka University, 2007), pp. 82–99.

Yokkaichi Yasuhiro 四日市康博, "Chinese and Muslim Diasporas and the Indian Ocean Trade Network under Mongol Hegemony," in Angela Schottenhammer, ed., *The East Asian "Mediterranean": Maritime Crossroads of Culture, Commerce and Human Migration* (Wiesbaden: Harrasowitz Verlag, 2008), pp. 73–102.

"The Eurasian Empire or Chinese Empire? The Mongol Impact and the Chinese Centripetal System," in *Asian Empires and Maritime Contracts before the Age of Commerce II*, Empires, Systems, and Maritime Networks: Reconstructing Supre-regional Histories in Pre-19th Century Asia, Working Paper Series 03 (Osaka: KSI, Inc., 2011), pp. 23–34.

"Gencho kyūtei ni okeru kōeki to teishin shūdan' 元朝宮廷における交易と廷臣集団, *Bulletin of the Graduate Division of Literature of Waseda University* 早稲田大學大學院文學研究科紀要 45.4 (2000), pp. 3–15.

"The Structure of Political Power and the *Nanhai* Trade: from the Perspective of Local Elites in Zhejiang in the Yuan Period," paper presented to the annual meetings of the Association for Asian Studies, San Francisco, March 2006.

Zhang Yingsheng 張迎勝, *Yuandai huizu wenxuejia* 元代回族文学家 (Beijing: Renmin chubanshe, 2004).

Zhuang Weiji 庄為璣, "Quanzhou Qingjingsi de lishi wenti 泉州清净寺的历史问题," in *Quanzhou Yisilanjiao yanjiu lunwenxuan* 泉州伊斯兰教研究论文选 (Fuzhou: Renmin chubanshe, 1983), pp. 65–82.

Index